◌ WATCH IT ◌

❧ WATCH IT ❧

The Risks and Promises of Information Technologies for Education

NICHOLAS C. BURBULES
*University of Illinois,
Urbana-Champaign*

THOMAS A. CALLISTER, JR.
Whitman College

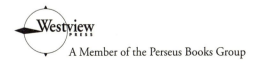

Westview
PRESS

A Member of the Perseus Books Group

Copyright © 2000 by Westview Press, A Member of the Perseus Books Group.

Published in 2000 in the United States of America by Westview Press, 5500 Central Avenue, Boulder, Colorado 80301-2877, and in the United Kingdom by Westview Press, 12 Hid's Copse Road, Cumnor Hill, Oxford OX2 9JJ

Find us on the World Wide Web at www.westviewpress.com

Library of Congress Cataloging-in-Publication Data
Burbules, Nicholas C.
    Watch IT: the risks and promises of new information technologies for education / Nicholas C. Burbules, Thomas A. Callister, Jr.
        p.   cm.
    Includes bibliographical references and index.
    ISBN 0–8133–9083-4 (hc.)—ISBN 0–8133–9082-6 (pbk.)
        1. Educational technology—United States. 2. Education—Technological innovations—United States. 3. Educational anthropology—United States. 4. Information technology—United States. I. Callister, Thomas A. II. Title.

LB1028.43.B87 2000
371.33—dc21
                                                                                    99–049176

The paper used in this publication meets the requirements of the American National Standard for Permanence of Paper for Printed Library Materials Z39.48-1984.

10   9   8   7   6   5   4   3   2   1

"The web of our life is of a mingled yarn,
good and ill together . . ."

—William Shakespeare, *All's Well That Ends Well*, Act 4, Scene 3

❧ CONTENTS ❧

ᖳ ACKNOWLEDGMENTS ᖲ

The authors would like to thank Cathy Murphy of Westview Press for her encouragement and support at every stage of the writing of this manuscript. We also appreciate the excellent assistance of Lesley Rock of PageMasters & Company and Steve Haenel of Westview Press in the preparation of this manuscript for publication.

Some of this material has appeared in different forms in previous publications over the past few years, although it has been entirely reworked for the present book. We would like to acknowledge these earlier versions:

>Nicholas C. Burbules, "Does the Internet constitute a global educational community?" *Globalization and Education: Critical Perspectives,* Nicholas C. Burbules and Carlos Torres, eds. (New York: Routledge, 1999). An abbreviated version was published as "Education and global communities." *Globalisierung: Perspektiven, Paradoxien, Verwerfungen. Jahrbuch für Bildungs- und Erziehungsphilosophie Bd. 2.* Walter Bauer, Wilfried Lippitz, Winfried Marotzki, Jörg Ruhloff, Alfred Schäfer, Christoph Wulf, eds. (Schneider Verlag: Hohengehren, 1999): 125–141.

>Nicholas C. Burbules and Thomas A. Callister, Jr., "The risky promises and promising risks of new information technologies for education." *Bulletin of Science, Technology and Society,* Vol. 19 No. 2 (1999): 105–112.

>Nicholas C. Burbules and Thomas A. Callister, Jr., "A post-technocratic policy perspective on new information and communication technologies for education." *Educational Policy,* James Marshall and Michael Peters, eds. (Gloucester, UK: Edward Elgar, 1999, 788–797).

>Nicholas C. Burbules, "Questions of content and questions of access to the Internet." *Access,* Vol. 17 No. 1 (1998): 79–89.

>Thomas A. Callister, Jr., and Nicholas C. Burbules, "Paying the piper: The educational cost of the commercialization of the Internet." *Electronic Journal of Sociology,* Vol. 3 No. 3 (1998). An online, refereed journal: www.sociology.org/content/vol003.003/callister. html.

>Nicholas C. Burbules and Thomas A. Callister, Jr., "Access to new educational technologies: Democratic challenges." *Critical Forum,* Vol. 5 No. 1/2 (1997): 32–41.

>Nicholas C. Burbules, "Privacy, surveillance, and classroom communication on the Internet." *Access,* Vol. 16 No. 1 (1997): 42–50.

>Nicholas C. Burbules, "Misinformation, malinformation, messed-up information, and mostly useless information: How to avoid getting tangled up in the 'Net. *Digital Rhetorics: Literacies and Technologies in Education—*

Current Practices and New Directions, Chris Bigum, et al., eds. (Canberra, Department of Employment, Education, Training, and Youth Affairs/Brisbane, Queensland University of Technology, 1997), 109–120. Republished as "Struggling with the Internet," *Campus Review* (Aug. 13–19, 1997): 19–22.

Nicholas C. Burbules and Thomas A. Callister, Jr., "Who lives here? Access to and credibility within cyberspace." *Digital Rhetorics: Literacies and Technologies in Education—Current Practices and New Directions,* Chris Bigum, et al., eds. (Canberra, Department of Employment, Education, Training, and Youth Affairs/Brisbane, Queensland University of Technology, 1997), 95–108.

Nicholas C. Burbules, "Rhetorics of the Web: Hyperreading and critical literacy." *Page to Screen: Taking Literacy into the Electronic Era,* Ilana Snyder, ed. (New South Wales: Allen and Unwin, 1997), 102–122.

Nicholas C. Burbules and Thomas A. Callister, Jr., "Issues of access and equity for new educational technologies." *Insights,* Vol. 32 No. 1 (June 1996): 9–11.

Thomas A. Callister, Jr., and Nicholas C. Burbules, "Public spaces and cyberspace: Issues of credibility in educational technologies." *Insights,* Vol. 32 No. 1 (June 1996): 11–14.

Nicholas C. Burbules and Thomas A. Callister, Jr., "Knowledge at the crossroads: Alternative futures of hypertext environments for learning." *Educational Theory,* Vol. 46 No. 1 (1996): 23–50.

Papers based on this material were presented at the following universities or conferences: University of California (Berkeley), University of Illinois (Urbana/Champaign), and Pennsylvania State University, all in the U.S.; Central Queensland University, Cowan University, Deakin University (Geelong and Burwood campuses), Griffith University, Macquarie University, Queensland University of Technology, and University of Queensland, all in Australia; University of Canterbury and University of Waikato, in New Zealand; the American Educational Research Association; and the American Educational Studies Association. We appreciate the feedback, criticism, and advice given by audience members on all of these occasions.

Finally, we wish to thank personally those who have read and commented upon portions of this manuscript in one form or another and have helped us to improve it: Joyce Atkinson, Chris Bigum, Nicole Bishop, Geof Bowker, Chip Bruce, Barbara Duncan, Noel Gough, Zelia Gregoriou, Bill Green, Carolyn Haythornthwaite, Alaina Kanfer, Jane Kenway, Michele

Knobel, Colin Lankshear, James Levin, Allan Luke, Carmen Luke, James Marshall, Ralph Page, Michael Peters, and Ilana Snyder.

This book is dedicated to our children, who are growing up in a different world from the one we have known.

℘ chapter one ℘

THE RISKY PROMISES
AND PROMISING RISKS OF NEW
INFORMATION TECHNOLOGIES
FOR EDUCATION

This book is about a different way of thinking about technology issues in education. We are not primarily interested here in addressing questions such as, "Are computers good for teaching? Does the Internet help children learn?" and so on. In fact, we think that such questions are fundamentally misframed, and represent a way of thinking about technology that needs to be reconsidered. No one would think today to pose questions such as, "Are blackboards good or bad for teaching? Do textbooks help children learn? Does television promote or inhibit educational opportunities?" We do not ask such questions because we take it for granted that these familiar elements of classroom and social life can be used well or badly, that they have advantages and limitations, and that the key issues concern *how* they are used, by whom, and for what purposes. One of the main ideas of this book is that the familiarity of certain objects, materials, and practices makes them relatively invisible to us as "technologies." Most people no longer view their use as involving conscious choices, choices that could have been made differently, choices that reflected deeper values and assumptions that might be questioned. They are simply part of the way things are.[1] Newer technologies, such as computers, software, or the Internet, are more apparent to us. They are strange, mysterious, and sometimes even threatening. So they are problematized in ways, and for reasons, that do not get applied to other choices that are every bit as much debatable (even if society regards them as no longer subject to debate).

But the word "choice" here obscures a deeper issue as well: in many instances, the introduction of new technologies into complex social practices and institutions is not a matter of specific choices, but a constellation of changes, some active, some passive, some intentional, some only evident

1

in hindsight. There may be a brief moment when a key decision or choice is made, but it is rarely, if ever, made in full awareness of alternatives to and implications of that choice; and it is often quickly enveloped by ancillary changes that swamp the significance of that first "choice." New technologies in education have *become* an educational issue, a challenge, an opportunity, a risk, a necessity—all of these—for reasons that have little to do with willful choices made by educators. Once computers and the Internet became widely available and affordable in this country, for example, it was *no longer* a choice subject to educators' control whether they would become important to jobs, to entertainment, to social interaction, and to a host of learning opportunities outside of the control of schools at all levels. Now that this has happened, schools might try to avoid some of these issues, but, stated simply, they can no longer choose whether these technologies are educationally relevant or not. If they neglect them, that too becomes a decision with consequences that extend beyond what schools can control.

Our primary purpose here, then, is to explore what it means to think about new technologies in education in ways that we do not think simply in terms of selecting and "using" technologies for our purposes. The overall effects and relations of technologies cannot be understood simply in terms of our means/ends intentions. Nor do we believe that these effects can be easily separated from one another, or classified (in many cases) as straightforwardly "good" or "bad." Technological change is a constellation of what is chosen and what is not chosen; what is foreseen and what cannot possibly be foreseen; what is desired and what is not. Hence the title of this chapter: risky promises and promising risks. We believe that this way of approaching the question will better enable us to confront the difficult, conflicted alternatives that face our educational activities and policies today. New technologies will become, have already become, indispensable to the practices of schooling, for better or for worse (or, as we tend to say it, for better *and* for worse).

In this opening chapter, we want to develop the conceptual and value orientation that guides the remainder of our arguments. Briefly, this orientation is built around three challenges to conventional thinking about new technologies and education. First, questioning the phrase "information technologies" as a way of characterizing some of these technologies; second, proposing a relational (as opposed to instrumental) view of technology; and third, arguing for what we call a "post-technocratic" policy perspective, a different starting point for thinking about the ifs and whys of new technologies for teaching and learning. The other chapters in this book will explore a number of current controversies surrounding new technologies and education (access, credibility, hypertext, critical Web literacy, censorship, privacy, commercialization, and community). These are *meta-issues*, in the sense that they are overarching to particular issues of teaching and learning; they direct critical reflection to the assumptions and implications that guide particular teaching/learning practices and trace out some consequences of those practices that may not be immediately apparent. If the framework developed in this opening chapter is beneficial, it will allow these issues to be considered in a different light. It will make more apparent the inherently complex (and often contradictory) nature of our choices in this context, and by making those choices more obviously problematic, make it more difficult to take these technologies for granted or to see them merely as "tools" that we can "use" to make our teaching "better." We have the somewhat grandiose ambition to change the terms of debate in some of these areas, to question some unfruitful dichotomies or forced alternatives, and generally to go beyond the simplistic value positions of boosterism (new technologies will save the schools) or rejectionism (new technologies will destroy the schools).[2]

"INFORMATION" TECHNOLOGIES

In our title we invoke the common label "information technologies" (IT). But already this is inadequate. The *information* metaphor captures an important part of what some of these new technologies have to offer, and it is a far from trivial benefit. For students in schools (and outside them) to have access to a vast library of information sources, statistics, quotations, graphic images, sound files, video clips, and other sorts of data is a tremendous educational resource. If these technologies did nothing more than this they would be of tremendous potential value. But the information metaphor is sorely inadequate, for a number of reasons.

First, there is a givenness to the idea of "information." As with words like "fact" and "data," "information" seems to suggest something taken for granted, to be weighed for significance, to be put together with other pieces of information to suggest conclusions, and so on, but—as people say— "raw." This assumption obscures not only the crucial point that much of what poses as "information" is in fact partial, biased, or simply false. But even more profoundly than this, information is never "raw." Researchers use the phrase "cooked data" to suggest information that has been made up or altered to fit pre-existing conclusions.[3] But actually information is always cooked (as opposed to raw): it is always selected, filtered, interpreted, and extracted from a background set of assumptions that are implicit (rarely explicit) in the "information" itself. This does not make the information false, or worthless; but it is in no way "given," even for the most widely accepted and obvious of "facts."[4] Not long ago, students were routinely taught the "fact" that Columbus discovered America in 1492. Today we scrutinize words like "discover" with a different evaluative lens, and that "fact," that piece of information, is no longer assumed to be true as such.

Second, the new technologies we are most interested in here (computers, Web pages, the Internet) cannot be understood simply as information technologies. They are also *communication* technologies. While some models of communication characterize communicative relations simply as an exchange of information, this is a very superficial characterization. We do send and receive information, through all sorts of media, in communication. But as the philosopher Ludwig Wittgenstein points out, there are many "language games," each with different rules and purposes: joking, apologizing, praying, cajoling, singing, questioning, protesting, pleading, and so on.[5] None of these can be understood in anything like the full richness of human practice as simple exchanges of information.

Bertram Bruce and James Levin offer a very useful taxonomy for capturing the variety of so-called "information technologies" and their many uses by adapting four categories borrowed from John Dewey: inquiry, communication, construction, and expression.[6] For Dewey, these represented four basic interests of the learner, human inclinations that motivate the activities that make learning possible. Bruce and Levin ingeniously expand these categories to include a rich subset of technology-based activities in each of the four areas, and classify particular kinds of hardware and software according to each subtopic. The result is a multifaceted view of the kinds of teaching and learning activities that can be supported by various new technologies, very few of which can be captured by the idea of accessing, archiving, or disseminating "information."

Third, and even more fundamentally, these new technologies constitute, not only a set of tools, but an *environment*—a space, a *cyberspace*—in which human interactions happen. The Internet is increasingly becoming a context in which interactions that cut across and combine the activities of inquiry, communication, construction, and expression are occurring. More and more the Internet is described as a "public space," a place where people gather, discuss, and debate issues, like the ancient Greek *agora* or the community town hall. It is described as a collaborative environment, in which researchers or creative workers share ideas, co-construct new ideas and understandings, and design new products. The Internet is seen as one of the central engines to the growth of a "global" context, spanning particular locations of space and time, fostering human relations that inhere always and only within that environment, not as a substitute for "real, face-to-face interaction," but as the only environment in which such relations can exist at all—indeed, relations that have unique characteristics and distinct advantages (as well as disadvantages) compared to face-to-face relations.

Hence, even the term "medium" is insufficient, if it connotes a mere path or channel through which something (such as information) is transmitted. Here a space is an environment in which *things happen*, where people act and interact. This suggests that a richer way of conceiving of the role of technologies in education is not as a "delivery system" through which teachers "provide" information and learners "access" it. Rather, it is to think of these technologies themselves as a potential collaborative space, a place where teaching and learning activities can happen. These collaborations can bring together people who cannot possibly interact in face-to-face ways; or can bring together people in a *way* that cannot be accommodated in face-to-face encounters. As we will discuss, this does not make these technologies (or their effects) always benign or even neutral, and the spaces fostered by these technologies can be incomplete, distorting, or exclusionary. But in this they are no better or worse than any other social space.

Hence, as a first step, we want to question the centrality of "information" as a way of characterizing these new technologies for education. Apart from oversimplifying the range of purposes these technologies can serve, and the variety of teaching and learning interactions they can support, this characterization also tends to reify what these technologies supposedly give access to ("information") and to obscure the active social processes by which information is actually made humanly useful.

INFORMATION "TECHNOLOGIES"

Another set of reflections questions some of the conventional ways in which people talk about technology. Two types of rhetoric dominate current discussions. One is to view technologies as tools, things to use to accomplish specific purposes: a coffee-maker makes coffee, a down jacket keeps you warm, a word processor is an electronic typewriter, and so on. This *instrumental* view externalizes technologies, views them as fixed objects with a use and purpose. One decides whether to adopt them by considering their use and purpose, considering their cost, and weighing costs and benefits.

There are a number of problems with the instrumental view.[7] Tools do not only help us accomplish (given) purposes; they may create new purposes, new ends, that were never considered before the tools made them possible. In these and other ways tools change the user: sometimes quite concretely, as when the shape of stone tools became a factor in the evolution of the human hand; or sometimes as an influence on human culture and values. Tools may have certain intended uses and purposes, but they frequently acquire new, unexpected uses and have new, unexpected effects. What this suggests is that we never simply use tools, without the tools also "using" us. We never use technologies to change our surroundings without being changed ourselves (sometimes in recognized, sometimes in entirely unrecognized and unexpected ways). The relationship with technology is not just one-way and instrumental, but two-way. Here we will call this a "relational" view of technology.[8]

This relational view helps to highlight two important points. One is the way in which the very distinction between human and technology is never clear-cut. As just noted, there are the fairly specific ways in which we are changed, culturally and psychologically, by the technologies we use—this point, we think is fairly clear. But there is also a quite concrete, material interrelation. Our bodies, our health, the physical environment in which we try to survive, are altered as well. Physical maladies that were once rare now become commonplace (carpal tunnel syndrome, for example). Our posture, our capacities for strength, dexterity, and coordination, the way our eyes move and process information, and on and on, all change with new technologies. New technologies affect the ways that we think about our physical selves as well. New imaging techniques and new biochemical tests change the way that we understand the conditions of health and sickness. Categories of "disability" get redefined, and new ones emerge, as we rethink our abilities relative to the new tasks we expect to be able to perform (or others that seem no longer so important to perform). Finally, technologies enter our bodies and change them in very specific ways: prostheses and artificial joints, pins and staples to hold together broken parts, pacemakers and chemical substitutes to help regulate the body's own metabolism and processes. The Human Genome Project, a massive effort to map our DNA code, with the express purpose of allowing genetic modification of human characteristics, would be impossible without the power of supercomputers. It is no exaggeration or metaphor to accept Donna Haraway's once-shocking claim that we are all cyborgs now.[9] In a relational framework, this means rethinking not only the nature of "technology," but the nature of ourselves.

The other way in which a relational view of technology is important is to recognize the way in which choices about technology use (to the extent that these are consciously and collectively decided) always stand in relation to a whole host of other changing practices and social processes.[10] An ethnographic team, studying a tribal culture, finished their field work and, as a gesture of appreciation to the tribe, left behind a few metal pots and pans to replace the breakable clay pots that the tribe had been using. It was (they thought) a simple gesture, with no transformative intent. When they returned later to revisit the tribe, they found enormous shifts in cultural practices, changed social relationships, more conflict, and so on. There are many interesting ethical issues raised by this case: should they have "interfered" with the culture they were studying (imagine if they had provided medical supplies or better advice on treating certain local illnesses)? But in this context, the lesson of the story is that changes in technology are always accompanied by a host of other changes in social processes and patterns of activity and it may be these latter changes that have the greatest overall impact in changing the society, not the "technologies" themselves. The technology, then, is not just the *thing* but the thing and the patterns of use to which it is put, the ways people think about and talk about the thing, and the changing expectations and problems the thing introduces. And if this is true for something as plain as a metal cooking pot, how much more so is it for something as powerful and pervasive in its effects as the computer, or the Internet? Therefore, when discussing "new" technologies, it must be made clear that what is most "new" may not be the technology, the thing itself, but a whole host of other changes that accompany it. By the same token, changing technologies themselves may play only a small part in educational reform (and more and newer technologies may not be any better), unless other educational practices and relations are changed as well. The capacity for transformation is not intrinsic to the technology itself. Imagining that it is, is part of what we call the "technocratic dream."

A POST-TECHNOCRATIC PERSPECTIVE ON TECHNOLOGY

Deliberations over the potential benefits and limitations of new technologies for education highlight the ways in which policy choices often require a *reframing* of the issues at stake, and not simply a "balancing" or "tradeoff" between assumed givens. In our view, the implications of new information and communication technologies for education offer a mixture of transformative possibilities and deeply disturbing prospects, not as "benefits and costs" to be weighed against each other, but as inseparable dimensions of the type of changes these technologies represent. Here we want to trace out some of the ways in which choices about new technologies in education are typically framed, explain why we think they are unhelpful, and propose a different way of thinking about such policy choices.

The first way in which technology issues are often framed can be called the "computer as panacea" perspective: new technologies carry inherent possibilities that can revolutionize education as we know it. If we simply unleash this potential many educational problems will be solved. Computers can help alleviate overcrowded classrooms; computers can ease the burden of overworked teachers; or computers can make teachers unnecessary at all. Such views are promoted enthusiastically by those who have a commercial stake in encouraging the sale and use of their hardware or software. The education market is so large that if even a few states or districts can be persuaded that a particular new technology will take care of their difficulties, millions of dollars can be made on the deal. But because so many problems of education are the result of inadequate resources or the misallocation of resources, funneling more of the finite amount of funding available into one area of spending might actually exacerbate these problems, not remedy them.

Furthermore, the proclamation of panaceas is not simply a marketing ploy; it is a mantra long familiar to the educational scene. The history of education in the United States can be traced from technical innovation to innovation, from gimmick to gimmick, from reform to reform. All in an effort to find the One Best Way of Teaching, for the next New Thing that will help educators cope with the fundamentally imperfect and indeterminate nature of the teaching process itself.[11] Rather than acknowledge the inherent difficulty of the teaching-learning endeavor, rather than accept a sloppy pluralism that admits that different approaches work in different situations, many educational theorists and policymakers seize upon one fashion after another and then try to find new arguments that will promote widespread acceptance and conformity under the latest Revolution. The Information Technology Revolution is just the latest in this long line of utopian dreams, and there will always be a ready audience in education for such overpromising.

To be fair, many computer producers and advocates have actually been among the forefront in trying to limit exaggerated claims for new technologies; those most familiar with these machines know best what they are and are not capable of. Ironically, it is often educational leaders who have raised the fevered sense of urgency that everything has to change, right now, before schools fall behind some perceived "wave" of technological innovation.

One consequence of the search for panaceas is that when the Revolution does not come to pass, when the imperfections of each New Thing become all too apparent, there is typically an equally exaggerated rejection of the reform, not because it is of no use but because it falls short of the hyperbole marshaled in its favor. As a result, educational change lurches from one New Thing to another, with the shortest of memories about similar reforms tried in the past. There is a failure to learn from experience and to integrate the partial benefits of multiple approaches and technologies, into a pragmatic orientation that seeks workable approaches to different problems as they arise.

We are already seeing some of this backlash toward computers and related technologies. Schools that spent millions of dollars to purchase equipment and software in the first heady rush to be sure that they did not fall behind in some perceived race with what other schools were doing, find that much of this equipment is unused and already obsolete. Schools that are rushing now to obtain fast connections to the Internet are finding that this raises unexpected new difficulties, when students actually take advantage of the access provided but for purposes that authorities find troubling or inappropriate. The panacea approach reinforces a certain naiveté in educators, and in the public that evaluates education, by suggesting to them that spending money to acquire new technical resources solves more problems than it creates. In reality, the potential of new technologies *increases* the need for imagination, careful planning, and coping on the fly with unexpected new challenges.

The second type of technocratic dream, much more subtle and seductive than the first, is the "computer as tool" perspective. Advocates of this view rightly excoriate the "panacea" perspective, and argue that it expects far too much of new technologies which are, as they say, merely tools that can be used for good or bad purposes. Tools carry within them neither the guarantees of success or failure, or of benefit or harm—it is all a matter of how wisely people use them.

Unfortunately, as our discussion has already shown, this technocratic dream simply errs in the opposite direction from the first. Where the panacea perspective places too much faith in the technology itself, the tool perspective places too much faith in people's abilities to exercise foresight and restraint in how new technologies are put to use. It ignores the possibilities of unintended consequences or the ways in which technologies bring with them inherent *limits* to how and for what purposes they can be used. A computer is not just an electronic typewriter; the World Wide Web is not just an online encyclopedia. Any tool changes the user, especially, in this instance, in the way in which tools shape the conception of the purposes to which they can be put. As the old joke goes, if you give a kid a hammer they'll see everything as needing hammering.

A slightly more sophisticated variant on this perspective is the "computer as non-neutral tool" perspective. Yes, advocates say, every technology carries within it certain tendencies of how it is likely to be used and shapes the conception of purposes to which it can be put. Users should be reflective and critical, therefore, about the unexpected consequences of using these technologies, and should be prepared for the possibility that the benefits gained from the technology's usefulness may be tempered by unforeseen problems and difficulties created by its use (pollution caused by automobiles, for example).

This third version of the technocratic dream is probably where most thoughtful observers are today in regard to new information and communication technologies. It is a sensible, level-headed approach. It understands balancing costs and benefits, tradeoffs, the mix of good and bad that comes from attempts at major reform. It understands the language of unintended consequences and accepts the imperfections of human rationality. It does not see technology as a panacea, nor does it imagine that technology is just a tool. Yet, we want to argue, it is still a variant of the technocratic dream. We will provide three arguments for why this is so.

(1) The technocratic mindset maintains a clear distinction between the conception of a tool and the aims it serves. The "computer as non-neutral tool" perspective represents a transitional step away from this, stressing that people do not simply use new tools to pursue old purposes more efficiently or effectively. New tools cause people to imagine new purposes that they had not even considered before. But, as we have seen, the problem goes even further than this. It is not simply a matter of an unproblematic relation of means to ends (even new ends). People's conception of what constitutes "success" is changed in light of the means used to pursue it. The technocratic mindset takes the *relation of means and ends* itself as given. A crude version simply defines problems as matters of relative efficiency or effectiveness in this relation. A less crude version sees changing purposes, even multiple or conflicting purposes, but still sees the relation of means to ends as given. Thinking beyond technocracy means seeing the means/ends relation itself as an artifact of a particular cultural and historical formation. The more relational perspective we have proposed would regard the blending of people's conceptions of means and ends, each continually redefined in light of the other. It would regard new technologies not simply as a means for doing what people used to do, better and faster, and not even simply as innovations that now allow people to do things they had never imagined before. The relational perspective explores how technologies reshape people's perceptions of themselves as agents, their relations to one

another, their perceptions of time and speed, their expectations of predictability, and so forth—all dimensions of *changing* people's ways of thinking about means and ends, purposes and efficacy. The point here is to see
the relation of means to ends not as a given, but as itself a particular way of
thinking, one subject to criticism and change like any other. The pursuit of
"success," defined as the effective and efficient attainment of specific goals,
needs to be situated in the context of a less linear conception of actions and
outcomes, intentions and effects.

(2) A second aspect of moving beyond the technocratic mindset is to
rethink the calculus of costs and benefits as a way of evaluating change.
Once again, there are relatively crude and relatively subtle versions of
cost/benefit analysis. Crude versions regard such decisions as basically a matter of drawing two columns and listing considerations pro and con; perhaps
these individual factors need to be given different weightings as to their
importance in relation to one another. But then you add up each column
and determine the result. A more subtle formulation of this mode of thinking would acknowledge that there are unintended consequences, to which
values cannot be ascribed because they cannot be anticipated. It would
acknowledge multiple consequences that may be difficult to isolate from one
another or evaluate separately. Hence it might acknowledge that cost/benefit
assessments are a matter of imperfect approximations, not a formal calculus.

But it is, again, a significant step beyond this mode of thinking to regard
the "cost/benefit" framework as itself artificial and simplistic. It is a matter
of seeing decisions as more than an issue of tradeoffs or pros and cons. It
stresses the value-laden character of even the most rudimentary identification of pros and cons. Pros and cons for whom, within what time frame,
relative to what *other* goals or values? In addition, it would stress the hubris
that often underlies attempts to foresee the discrete effects of complex social
decisions. It is not only the problem of unintended consequences, multiple,
conflicting consequences, and short-term versus long-term consequences. It
is the problem of a web of contingencies, caught up in complex relations of
interdeterminacy. It is the obstinacy of circumstance, refusing to give people
what they want without also giving them what they do not want.
Sometimes, as Edward Tenner points out, these unintended consequences
are not only unfortunate ancillary affects that accompany the changes we
are trying to achieve; he adds that sometimes changes have "revenge
effects," changes that actually worsen the problem that the technology was
supposed to help "solve."[12]

We want to emphasize that nowhere is this clearer than in the case of major
and complex new technologies, such as computers, which are continually

confronting us with the inseparability of consequences, the desirable and the undesirable. But the final step beyond technocratic thinking and the cost/benefit mindset is the most challenging of all.

(3) The assessment of means and ends, the weighing of costs and benefits, also assumes that people can distinguish and evaluate the "good" and "bad" aspects of different aims and consequences. The inseparability and interdependence of many consequences should begin to shake the faith that such determinations can be so readily made. But, again, the problem is more than this: the *very same* effects can be regarded as "good" or "bad," depending on other considerations, or when evaluated by different people, or when judged within alternative time frames. For example, the widespread use of antibiotics to eliminate infectious bacteria has, clearly, saved many millions of lives. This is a good thing. But it is also hastening the development of more and more virulent strains of bacteria, some of which now are resistant to all antibiotics. That is a very bad thing. Note that this is not a simple matter of intended and unintended consequences: the very same decisions that give rise to one set of effects give rise to the others. Nor is this a simple matter of weighing competing "short-term" benefits against potential "long-term" costs—for one thing, the "long-term" costs of such policies might be of incalculable harm. The post-technocratic mode of thinking we are proposing here would stress the limits to human foresight and planning; the interdependency of multiple consequences; and the problematic attempt to sort out "good" from "bad" outcomes. Instead we want to stress the inseparability of good and bad in all complex human circumstances and the error of imagining that we can readily evaluate such matters individually and discretely. Anything powerful enough to do good on a broad scale is always also dangerous. We must always keep in mind that new technologies are inherently dangerous, and not fool ourselves in imagining that we are their masters.

THE GOOD, THE BAD, AND THE UNKNOWN

We mean these observations as comments on technological innovation and reform generally; but they apply to the field of new information and communication technologies especially. Why? Because they have shown themselves to be particularly susceptible to overpromising and hyperbole, especially but not only in their purported impact upon educational change. If our arguments about multiple effects, the indeterminacy and inseparability of consequences, and the difficulty of isolating "good" and "bad" outcomes hold any weight generally, they apply with special force to these technologies.

First, the field of information and communication technologies is changing at an extremely rapid pace, one that appears to be accelerating even faster. These areas of innovation feed back on themselves in some unique ways. The increasing capacities of machines, programming languages, and other software hasten the development of still further innovations. The very horizon of capabilities is continually re-invented, as new possibilities that were not imagined previously suddenly become within the reach of development, then soon within the scope of the taken-for-granted. This field of development is also socially, technologically, and commercially self-generating. For example, as operating systems and software become easier to use, and as more people then use them, this creates both a broader talent base and a widened scope of incentive to imagine and create new products. The problem field of these new technologies is, in a way, fundamentally about itself. In other words, it is self-reflexive in the way in which new developments make possible more and more developments. This is one reason why companies like Apple, Linux, and Netscape have given away the code for proprietary products, encouraging developers to use it to write compatible programs and extensions. Yet this self-reflexive character makes it especially susceptible to defining its problems and goals hermetically, as technical objectives of value in and of themselves, apart from clear consequences for human society generally.

Second, and related to this point, because a primary object of these new technologies is information, and the production, organization, and dissemination of information, there is a sense in which it is also continually re-inventing the perceptions of its use and purpose. All new technologies, as we discussed earlier, change people's understandings of what they can do, what they want to do, what they think they need to do. And when those technologies refer to the material with which people imagine, plan, and evaluate change—that is, information—there arises a strong likelihood that what falls outside of the readily available raw material will fall outside the decision itself. So, as argued previously, a particular relation of means to ends needs to be situated in a larger constellation of what is known and what is not known; multiplied in this instance by a critical reflection on what the medium of information *about* what is known and not known can and cannot tell us.

Third, the various considerations about information and communication technologies, which we have been discussing here, press an even more radical conclusion about the indeterminacy of effects. In this instance, we would argue, the future lines of development are *literally* inconceivable—not only because of the rapidity and complexity of change in this field, and not only because of the self-reflexive nature of innovation, but because new developments in information and communication technologies are uniquely also new developments in our imaginings of capabilities and goals. Conventional descriptions of the enormity of these changes (the computer as the new Gutenberg printing press, and so on) are merely analogies. What made the printing press a momentous innovation was not only that it created a mechanism for a new kind of textual delivery. It was that by doing so it fundamentally changed the conditions for its own accessibility and uses (for one thing, it made it possible—and necessary—for more people to learn to read). It created a mechanism for a new kind of production, organization, and dissemination of information, a new medium of communication, and as such it created possibilities that were not, and could not have been, imagined previously. That is the scale of change represented by new information and communication technologies. It should buttress our sense of humility to realize that we *cannot* know all of the changes they portend, and that what we might consider today "good" or "bad" prospects will certainly appear to others who have passed through those changes in a very different light. But we are not those others; or, at least, not yet.

For all of these reasons, reflections upon new information and communication technologies must proceed with a profound modesty and caution. They are, literally, dangerous. Yet they are dangerous precisely because they hold such tremendous potential—a potential that goes beyond our capacities to imagine it fully. Hence we need to go beyond the simplistic categories in which much current assessment of information and communication technologies has proceeded (especially, but not only, in the field of education). Douglas Kellner refers to the polarities of "technophobic" and "technophilic" perspectives.[13] Jane Kenway, similarly, describes "utopian" and "dystopian" alternatives.[14] Along with these commentators, and others, we want to press the need to go beyond such easy dichotomies, dichotomies that rely fundamentally on the illusion that we can easily separate and imagine "good" and "bad" effects in this field.

A great deal of rhetorical ink has been spilled excoriating the "fraudulent" promises of new information technologies in education. Books with titles like *Technopoly* or *Silicon Snake Oil*[15] or articles with titles like "The Regime of Technology in Education" or "The Computer Delusion,"[16] have attracted a wide readership and have fundamentally shaped the perception of new educational technologies among many groups, especially those with relatively little direct experience with these new technologies themselves. The fact that such accounts serve a popular taste for reports of scandal and fraud partly explain their appeal. They suggest something insidious, something to be exposed. Part of the explanation also must be attributed to people's anxieties about changes they do not entirely understand. And, we have argued, a certain healthy skepticism and caution is more than justified in this context, especially given the commercial interests at stake in promoting the sales of expensive equipment, software, and networking resources to schools across the country.

But we believe that a more modulated position is necessary. For one thing, these changes are upon us and have a particular momentum of their own. One way or another, these are issues society will need to struggle with. Furthermore, we persist in believing that there are multiple potentials in these technologies, and it is yet to be determined what forms they will take and the purposes to which they will be put. Adopting a rejectionist position and yielding these decisions to others merely guarantees that the skeptics will be ignored and the enthusiasts given free rein. We want to push the policy debate beyond the false choices of rejectionism or boosterism. We want to interject a critical perspective *within* discussions about new information and communication technologies, not in simple, wholesale opposition to them. We want to suggest a distinctive tone or feel to what the post-technocratic stance might mean: not just weighing "risks" and "promises" against each other, but of seeing their fundamental *inseparability*. The dangers and possibilities of information and communication technologies are not opposed to one another—they are aspects of one and the same capacities. We cannot simplistically choose one over the other. The post-technocratic perspective we are proposing calls for thinking more carefully about the complex relations of cause and effect, about the anticipated and unintended outcomes of change, and about the difficulty of defining (or separating) the "good" and "bad" effects of technological change.

Conclusions

These considerations leave us with two overarching impressions about the debate over new technologies in education up until now. First, there is the tendency to want to frame these matters *as* a debate.[17] This makes for an engaging rhetorical structure, but the idea of a "debate" frames issues in a particular, troublesome way. It tends to polarize and dichotomize the "good" and "bad" dimensions of change, with each side making the most of their case and minimizing the other's. It tends to entrench the views of the already-committed to one side or the other, and rarely goes beneath that complacency to force each perspective to engage the substance of the other. Most of all, it reinforces the policy perspective of cost/benefit analysis, where the "responsible" third perspective is to respect and balance off the respective pluses and minuses, and not, as we have argued, to see their more complex and disturbing interdependencies. In numerous panels and presentations that have addressed these issues of new technologies in education, the authors of this book have been framed (when speaking to skeptics) as enthusiasts and (when speaking to enthusiasts) as critics. It takes tremendous care and effort to help people see that this very way of framing the issue is part of the problem. We will never make much progress on these issues if we think it can be a matter of balancing out the "good" and the "bad," or trying to retain the "good" while minimizing the "bad." The discussions of each of the major issues explored in this book (access, credibility, hypertext, critical web literacy, censorship, privacy, commercialization, and community) is a lesson or case study in trying to avoid the either/or "debate" framework.

The second concluding point we draw from these reflections is to try to question the idea that simply doing "more research" will tell us which way to go in this area.[18] We are hardly opposed to the value of more research per se, and certainly most of the decision-making that currently goes on in this area is (like much of educational decision-making) primarily based on anecdotal evidence, interest-group pressure, or pre-existing prejudices and wish fulfillment. Decisions about new technologies and education have been, we believe, especially susceptible to hype and perceived immediacy based upon a sense of what others are already doing. Research on new technologies for teaching and learning should tell us more about their multiple effects (intended and not); their specific benefits for particular kinds of learners; their impact on access and equity issues for learners who do not benefit from them; and so on. But such research alone will not solve the conundrums we have tried to introduce here. Standard experimental designs like control-group comparisons, or altering single variables while attempting to hold all others "constant," are not sensitive to the sorts of complex, interrelated changes we see at work in this area. "Hawthorne effects"[19] will be rampant in such an area of dramatic change from classroom business as usual. Perhaps new kinds of research design, or combinations of quantitative and qualitative research methods, will address these problems and help us derive useful information to help think through the complex decisions we face. While this book is not primarily about empirical research methods and evidence, it is not anti-empirical. But this research information will not provide wisdom. Nor will it provide the sensitivity to see that we are in the midst of a process of *rethinking* the meaning and ends of education, and not just trying to find ways to do what we used to do, better, faster, or more economically.

NOTES

1. See Bertram Bruce and Maureen Hogan, "The disappearance of technology: Toward an ecological model of literacy," in D. Reinking, M. McKenna, L. Labbo, and R. Kieffer, eds., *Handbook of Literacy and Technology: Transformations in a Post-typographic World* (Hillsdale, NJ: Earlbaum, forthcoming).

2. A resource we have found helpful on some of these issues, which we discovered after completing most of this work, is the Technorealism Group (www. technorealism.org). Their unromantic and pragmatic orientation to a range of technology problems, including education, is much in line with the sentiments and point of view we are developing here.

3. Of course, we are also echoing Claude Levi-Strauss here.

4. See James Marshall, "Education in the mode of information: Some philosophical issues," in Frank Margonis, ed., *Philosophy of Education 1996* (Urbana, Illinois: Philosophy of Education Society, forthcoming).

5. Ludwig Wittgenstein, *Philosophical Investigations*.

6. Bertram C. Bruce and James Levin, "Educational technology: Media for inquiry, communication, construction, and expression," *Journal of Educational Computing Research*, Vol. 17 No. 1 (1997): 79–102.

7. For a different, though similarly critical, analysis of this instrumental view, and other stances toward new technologies, see Bertram C. Bruce, "Literacy technologies: What stance should we take?" *Journal of Literacy Research*, Vol. 29 No. 2 (1997): 289–309.

8. Bruce describes this relation as "transactional" (Ibid.).

9. Donna Haraway, "A cyborg manifesto," in *Simians, Cyborgs, and Women* (New York: Routledge, 1991).

10. See Michele Knobel and Colin Lankshear, "What different people do with the same equipment," unpublished manuscript, Queensland University of Technology (1997).

11. See Nicholas C. Burbules and David T. Hansen, eds., *Teaching and Its Predicaments* (Boulder, CO: Westview Press, 1997).

12. Edward Tenner, *Why Things Bite Back: Technology and the Revenge of Unintended Consequences* (New York: Knopf, 1966).

13. Douglas Kellner, "Multiple literacies and critical pedagogy in a multicultural society," *Educational Theory*, Vol. 48 No. 1 (1998): 103–122.

14. Jane Kenway, "The Information Superhighway and Postmodernity: The Social Promise and the Social Price," *Comparative Education*, Vol. 32 No. 2 (1996): 217–231.

15. Neil Postman, *Technopoly: The Surrender of Culture to Technology* (New York: Vintage Books, 1992); and Clifford Stoll, *Silicon Snake Oil* (New York: Doubleday, 1995).

16. Douglas Noble, "The regime of technology in education," in Landon E. Beyer and Michael W. Apple, eds. *The Curriculum: Problems, Politics, and Possibilities* (Albany: State University of New York Press), 267–283; and Todd Oppenheimer, "The computer delusion," *The Atlantic Monthly* (July 1997): 45–62.

17. See, for example, the exchange between Roy Pea and Larry Cuban in a lively debate entitled "The Pros and Cons of Technology in the Classroom," sponsored by the online educational technology MUVE, "Tapped-In": www.tappedin.org/info/teachers/debate.html.

18. For a review of some of the relevant research in this area, see John Kosakowski, "The benefits of information technology," *Eric Digest* (online) www.ericir.syr.edu/ithome/digests/edoir9804.html (August 1998), and Mark Windschitl, "The WWW and classroom research: What path should we take?" *Educational Researcher* (January–February 1998): 28–32.

19. Hawthorne effects are effects that show up, often beneficial effects, not because of the particular benefits of the change being studied—but because often any change at all will produce some measurable benefits!

chapter two

DILEMMAS OF ACCESS AND CREDIBILITY: ACCESS FOR WHOM? ACCESS TO WHAT?

We begin with the issue of access because it is, for us, a matter of overarching importance. For one thing, we think it is the most pressing concern, because as new technologies become more important for educational opportunities and for participation in the social, economic, political, and cultural life of society, exclusion from this realm will mean severely limited life chances of many sorts. But we also think it is of first importance because issues of access, as we will describe them, affect and are affected by nearly every other major theme of this book. We will argue in this chapter that providing access cannot be seen merely as a matter of having a way to use computers and a connection to the Internet. "Access" needs to be rethought as a much more complex and multileveled social goal. We want to link two issues concerning the Internet that are often discussed separately, but that we believe are intimately related: issues of access and issues of credibility. Access issues include who can use the Internet, who can afford a computer, who can get an online connection, who knows how to operate the software, and so on. Issues of credibility include who can make sense of what they find on the Internet, who can judge what is and is not worthwhile, and who can gain credibility and visibility as an information provider. Users who cannot participate effectively across the full range of opportunities that the Internet represents cannot be said to have "access," even if they have a computer and online connection. Users who cannot gain a hearing for their ideas and point of view or who cannot discern what is and is not worthwhile, lack "credibility" and the means to evaluate the credibility of what they find.

The stakes of this problem have never been higher. Today we face the prospect that those who can work (and have fun) in cyberspace—those who have access to its resources and feel comfortable learning and interacting there—will benefit from a substantially different range of experiences and opportunities in life than those who do not. As providers of information, those who reside there will be visible and potentially influential within a global network of communication and information sharing. They will possess a cyber-identity in relation to others online that can supplement their face-to-face interactions and experiences. They can participate within broader communities constituted partly through the sharing of information and points of view. Moreover, these opportunities interact and reinforce one another: the more active and present people are in this environment, the more they stand to gain in terms of learning to use the network for their own purposes. Hence the cycles of information and further opportunities become self-perpetuating; someone not part of this network will fall further and further behind in even knowing what he or she is missing.

Here we discuss these dual aspects (access and credibility) in relation to one another. Being able to discern and gain credibility is an access issue: it could be termed a question of *quality* of access, as opposed of *quantity* of access. Yet, even the apparently more straightforward issue of access itself is not as straightforward as it appears.[1] What we will try to show throughout this discussion is how we are continually confronted with *dilemmas of access*: efforts to increase access for some, invariably raise problems of access for others.

ISSUES OF ACCESS

Access to the Internet and its vast resources are generally considered a technical problem. In the United States, for example, state and federal officials recently announced ambitious plans to put "every school on the Internet." Such pursuits, despite their merit, interpret issues of access in an overly narrow way. It is obvious enough that merely solving the technical problems of putting classrooms (or homes, for that matter) "online" will be insufficient if prospective users do not also have an opportunity to develop the skills and attitudes necessary to take advantage of those resources. Yet there are even deeper and less apparent criteria that determine actual access. Elsewhere Burbules et al. have suggested the terms "conditions of access" and "criteria of access" to draw attention to this general sort of problem. Conditions of access are the features of a situation that enable or restrict participation in it. Criteria of access are the personal characteristics that people require in order to actually gain access.[2] These two factors are interdependent, since the existence of certain conditions entail certain criteria;

just as the possession of certain criteria can compensate for or overcome certain conditions.

In the case of educational technologies, policy makers have focused too much on the conditions of access and too little on the criteria of access. Identifying criteria of access is difficult, because often the criteria entailed by a situation are implicit, not readily apparent; very often they are unintended. Left-handed people frequently discover that right-handedness is a criterion of access for all sorts of activities that no one planned to restrict their access to.

Earlier we talked about the futility of discussing the quantity of access without also discussing the quality of access. Here we want to put that point in a slightly different way. One can think of "thin" and "thick" conceptions of access. Thin conceptions put the focus of access on the metaphor of a gateway through which prospective users can enter, if they choose to. Thick conceptions of access look at all the factors that actually affect who does and does not make that choice, and why; who can take advantage of access in an effective way, and who cannot. Without the latter, the former is largely empty. In addition, thicker conceptions of access ask not only about "access for whom"; they also ask about "access to what, and for what purposes"? The avenues of access are not taken at face value—in large part because this broader conception recognizes that the question of what one is providing access to, and why, often directly affects the "who" question. Without addressing that problem, access for certain groups will be inadvertently limited, despite the best of intentions. In this section, therefore, we will discuss a few of the more subtle, tacit features of interacting with computer technologies that end up restricting access. These will carry us through four levels of providing access, of which technical access is only the first. Addressing these issues, if we are serious about providing access to a wide and diverse range of people, will require a much broader educational commitment than simply buying new equipment or teaching a few workshops to help people learn to use it. Certainly we need to do this. But certain implicit requirements for the effective and beneficial use of these technologies are just as indispensable as wires and equipment—and some of them might be much more difficult to change or compensate for.

Moreover, there are criteria of access that arise due to basic features of the digital environment itself. Such criteria cannot be "compensated for," because they are partly constitutive of what we are trying to provide access to. In such cases actual access will not have been achieved, and a significant number of people will have little or no opportunity to benefit from the resources and experiences that computer environments provide.

Technical Access

The challenge of providing technical access, we want to make clear, is hardly simple or straightforward itself. The idea that everyone will be able to plug into the Internet and surf World Wide Web sites is rather unrealistic. Many areas, especially when we are thinking internationally, lack even electricity or telephone service, and rates of adult illiteracy, even within the U.S., remain shockingly high. And given conditions of scarce resources, how exactly should poorer societies, or communities, weigh prospective high-tech benefits alongside roads, water and sewer systems, health care, and decent food supplies? The mania over getting "wired" is a luxury built on top of many other luxuries that a significant number of people, nationally and worldwide, cannot even dream about.

For poor schools, or schools in impoverished areas, these tradeoffs are especially vicious. In buildings that are dilapidated or substandard in other ways, it will (ironically) be even *more* expensive to provide them with adequate wiring and technical hookups, as well as computers; and these schools are already underfunded relative to their needs. So new funding, even where it is allocated, may be more seriously needed for other, more down-to-earth purposes (books, heating systems, decent toilets, metal detectors, and so forth). Or, more realistically, given fiscal constraints and priorities, technology purchases will come *de facto* out of funds that might have been allocated for those other purposes. How will such funding choices be made, given the "cost-benefit" thinking of most state agencies? How will impoverished schools manage the intolerable dilemmas of allocating such funds? Will a school that expends resources on new technologies be, ironically, worse off *overall* as a place to learn?

Considering disabled citizens raises a different aspect of technical access. Here is a clear instance where conditions of access, quite unintentionally, create significant barriers for many prospective users. The decision to base the computer interface on a moveable "mouse" is a problem for many with physical limitations. Screen technologies are not adequate for the needs of many with visual impairments, and so on. In this area, there has been an impressive amount of research and development, and there are many ingenious attempts to compensate for a wide range of disabilities. But the current costs of these devices and adaptations are very high.

Moreover, even when a large investment is made to lay in a basic technical system, soon after it is up and running new innovations surpass it. Upgrading to take advantage of new potentialities often means undoing or redoing what were expensive investments in the first place (such as the continually accelerating speeds of computers and network connections). Any large-scale system investment is sure to be superseded by the time it is put in place; so there will inevitably be a lag time between what most users have and can afford, and what a smaller, more privileged group will be able to take advantage of. It is an admirable social goal to try to bring all, or most, citizens up to some common minimal level of access. But the crucial paradox here is that the larger and more inclusive an attempt is to put all schools (or all homes) online, the more expensive it will be to have to upgrade it. For many schools, it will be left in place and accepted as second-rate, but good enough. Gains for some will always come at the expense of others.

Skills, Attitudes, and Dispositions of Access

It is not surprising to note that having machines does little good if people do not know how to use them. And workshops in effective use need to be a part of any full-fledged program devoted to access. But acquiring the skills of access remains only part of the problem, and not the most challenging part. For there are dispositions and attitudes that also determine effective use, and these may be much harder to develop in people through workshops. Contrasting dispositions and attitudes may be characteristic of certain types of people, or groups, and may be related to qualities that they do not *wish* to change or abandon. The gain of spending more time online may be regarded by some as a loss of other sorts of activities and values. But because a certain level of facility and confidence in using technologies is probably gained only through experience online itself, the cycle of inclusion and exclusion is to a degree self-perpetuating.

It is very illuminating to spend time teaching workshops or giving informal assistance to people who know very little about computers or the Internet and what they can do. Oversimplifying, one encounters two sorts of novices. Some, when they encounter an unfamiliar problem, when they are "stuck," feel quite comfortable just messing around, trying things out, guessing at what might work. In doing so, they not only have a chance of working their way out of the problem, but of possibly discovering new capabilities of the system they are using. It turns out that "just messing around" is an indispensable approach for users at all levels of sophistication. But others do not find this easy to do.

And this is not simply a matter of confidence and experience. At a deeper level, we are talking about an orientation to the world, and especially an orientation to machines, that allows the user to experiment with different options, to explore alternatives without always knowing what their effects will be. It may be easier to do this in contexts with which people are familiar and in which they feel generally comfortable. But even then some people simply do not have a very high tolerance for uncertainty, for frustration, for trial-and-error. Because the actual operation of computer programs is a rigorously logical procedure, educators often make the mistake of thinking that, developmentally, this is also how people should be brought along to effective computer use. But in fact such an approach can end up limiting access because it does not prepare novices very well for situations in which something is not working as expected and the manual is not available. For many computer users, this causes them to stay within the rigid bounds of what is familiar, continuing to do "what works" without running the risk of encountering the unexpected, even when that means that they are only exploring a very small portion of what is available to them. So we see, for example, people who prefer to use outdated machines or software rather than change over to something that might actually do more for them. Raising the ceiling of technological possibility only benefits certain groups or individuals; over time it may filter down to others, but by then something else will have come along to privilege those who have access to it and can use it.

Practical Access

Beyond these issues are the circumstances of social life that actually influence who has the time and opportunity to engage in work and play online, and who does not. These "pragmatics" of access are a source of concern because they systematically advantage certain groups, defined by social class, sex, and race or ethnicity, over others. Hence the overall pattern of their effects is not evenhanded across the board: they have consequences that are easily discernible in the patterns of Web-use statistics.

Having time is a criterion of access. Because so many new technologies have been marketed on the basis of increasing efficiency or productivity, there is a widespread belief that having these machines saves time. Any computer user knows that is simply not true. While it is often possible to do specific things more quickly, there is a significant amount of time first spent on setting things up, trouble-shooting, figuring out new shortcuts, and so forth—arrangements that we think will save us time on some future occasion. Well, maybe. Our point here is that not everyone has the amount of time, or the discretion in how they allocate their time, that others do. In schools, in the workplace, in the home, these divisions do not work out equitably.

When you start spending time online, if you have any enthusiasm for it at all, you find that, of course, it takes up much *more* of your time. But people still persist in thinking that with just a little investment of start-up time, those without much time on their hands will come to discover vast new quantities of time that will be freed up to spend online. Who has the time to sort through the chaff of material on the Internet to find the grains of enjoyable, worthwhile, information or personal interaction?

Related to this point are the nature of work, the locations of work, and the flexibility of work schedules. Someone working in a university or company with a computer on every desk, networked directly into the Internet, experiences access issues in a different way than someone working on an assembly line, or on a rural farm. Someone working at home, raising children and managing a household, experiences a different structure of time and scheduling, and may have less time that can be devoted to the Internet, even if a computer and modem are sitting in the corner of the room.

For many computer users, privacy issues and feeling safe from harassment are major concerns. Who chooses to participate in public forums and discussion groups? Who feels safe having their e-mail address made public? Who is willing to have their photo on their Web page? Who feels comfortable with the particular kinds of communication the Internet makes possible? Clearly these concerns will affect some persons and groups more than they do others. As this discussion makes clear, the question of access to technology, then, is mostly not about technology at all, but about the commitment of society to consider other far-reaching changes toward equity.

Issues of Form and Content as Issues of Access

As just discussed, what users find on the Internet is also itself a factor in who participates, how they participate, and how much they participate. These become tacit conditions of inclusion and exclusion as well.

In terms of form, for example, many access issues have to do with interface design.[3] Although new computer interfaces based on graphic icons, pull-down menus, and analogies with physical objects (such as the trash can) have become more intuitive and require less specific coded knowledge, effective use still involves a number of shortcuts, heuristics, and experience-based conventions that not everyone knows.[4] And the spread of tacit knowledge about such shortcuts, heuristics, and conventions generally travels within the communities of people who already have access to the Internet and have a context for making sense of them. At a very concrete level, this tacit knowledge is often exchanged within the online community itself. Changes in operating systems, new iterations of software programs, and other changes in technology occur so quickly that a person not actively engaged on a regular basis just barely manages to get a sense of what is going on at about the time that this information becomes superseded.

Furthermore, to the extent that there are distinct styles of human thought, the forms of thinking manifested in the workings of computer interfaces and software, the structure of the Web, and so forth may be more hospitable to the way certain people organize information or communicate. Computer programs, today, are highly customizable, but not infinitely so: they incorporate certain basic assumptions and decisions about problem-solving and the likely needs of users—and to this extent they inevitably privilege certain ways of thinking over others.

The basic architecture of the Web, as we will discuss in the next chapter, is built around the idea of "hypertext," a set of pages and information resources (numbering now in the millions of pages) all connected together by clickable links that carry us from one page to another. One "navigates" from information point to information point, often in a nonlinear, non-hierarchical manner.[5] Part of the exciting appeal of the Web is this continually evolving, "rhizomatic" structure. However, in the actual practice of exploring this labyrinth, users—especially novices—go through the experience of getting lost, of not being able to relocate information they had found, or of simply being overwhelmed by the volume of what is available online. The hyperlinked structure of the Web is experienced differently by different users: some can work through lateral as well as linear lines of association; others find them confusing or counterintuitive.

Inhabiting such a complex environment means living with a good deal of uncertainty; with the occasional feeling of being lost; with the need to make connections as one goes. These are not only matters of learning and experience, but also matters of confidence and attitude. Advocates of new technologies have not given enough thought to the ways in which environments that feel exciting and challenging to some users are experienced as chaotic and frustrating by others.

Add to this the other main feature of the Web, its multimedia capability, and you have the conditions for a real cacophony. For those with a fair amount of experience already in computer environments, dealing with graphics, video, and sound, these capabilities raise exciting possibilities. Experienced users scroll quite casually through long lists of options; they feel comfortable sampling what they find; and they have developed fairly sophisticated tacit strategies for screening and selecting what is worth their while. It may be hard for such experienced users to appreciate how overwhelming all of this can appear to new users. For those inclined to be intimidated by "high tech" anyway, this very richness and complexity often provides, not a sense of open possibilities, but another reminder of previous feelings of inadequacy.

In terms of content, there is a great deal on the Internet that ranges from the trivial, to the silly, to the bizarre, to the outrageous, to the offensive. It is easy enough to say that this comes with the decentralization and open, uncensored medium the Internet has evolved into; and we along with many others would say this openness is among its virtues. But a consequence of this openness is that particular experiences or encounters on the Internet may be profoundly disturbing, or worse, for some people—and there is no minimizing the harmful effects these can have. On the Net there is harassment, hate speech, unwanted solicitations, commercial and otherwise; there is pornography, graphic images and accounts of violence, and child exploitation. It is a microcosm of all that is bad and good about human societies generally. After encountering such materials, some people leave and never come back; others continue to live and work in cyberspace, but within much more cautious and narrowly drawn boundaries. On the surface these choices to withdraw from access may appear "voluntary" and self-imposed, but on another, deeper, level they are choices engendered by constraints that are not of people's choosing, which affect different groups of participants and individuals in different ways. In short, the content of the Internet will attract and fascinate some, frustrate and offend others.

It is also worthwhile to reflect on some of the implicit features of online communication itself. Once again, for those who spend a great deal of time using this technology, many of these features have become invisible, second nature—people may even think they are necessary or inevitable. They are not; and considering some of these features may remind us that what we have come to accept as easy or natural may appear otherwise to new users, and may constitute an active barrier or discouragement to their involvement.

We want to mention briefly five features of online communication that are not neutral in their nature and effects. We will present them as dyads, because we want to emphasize that within each pair there are clear advantages on either side of the choice; and that what will be seen as an advantage by one person will be seen as a disadvantage by another. Where computer systems have adopted one aspect over the other, it has created an environment that some will see as ideal, others as problematic or, worse, unwelcoming and alien. In other words, this is another dilemma of access: what might be done to encourage the participation of some may inhibit the participation of others.

(1) Computer networks allow both synchronous ("real time") and asynchronous communication. Chat groups work on the first principle; e-mail on the second (you do not need to worry if the recipient is there when you send an e-mail message; it is there and waiting whenever the person checks in). Each approach has advantages; each fosters a distinctive style of communication (length of messages, use of questions, and so forth). But not all computer setups allow both styles; asynchronous links make much lighter demands on limited equipment. What sorts of people will prefer each type? Who will feel the advantages of one approach as a disadvantage to them? For example, if I am not communicating in my native language, I may prefer a system that allows me a longer time to formulate and correct my response before sending it. For a different sort of person (or given certain subject matters), the lapse in time between sending a message and receiving a reply will feel like a risk they do not want to take, and they prefer to remain silent, or drop out of the exchange entirely.

(2) The conventions of online communication do not require one to disclose one's name or identity; one's return address can be a word or nickname or meaningless string of letters or numbers. In face-to-face communication, of course, we usually receive a good deal of information about the person with whom we are speaking. What are the advantages and disadvantages of online anonymity? On the one hand, does it enable those who are shy or intimidated to participate *more* by allowing them privacy? Does it mean that people must react to the content of what others say, and not to the color of their skin, their sex, and so forth, which are not visible in their digital persona? On the other hand, does it allow people to fraudulently hide their identity, misleading others as to who they are and where they might be positioned relative to a particular discussion? Does it allow people to make irresponsible statements that they do not need to be held accountable for, since their (real) name and identity are not attached to what they write? Or does this actually promote greater frankness by permitting socially unpopular views to be said openly, whereas before they were merely thought, but repressed from comment because of a fear of social retribution?

For example, at a recent conference one speaker was describing a university class discussing online the politics of requiring California teachers to report on "illegal" immigrant children in their classrooms (many of whom are Hispanic). Participants in the discussion were identified only by a letter code, not by name. One of the participants to the discussion was Hispanic, and clearly might have had a distinctive perspective on the issue. One might even say, she had a different authority to take a stand on it. But no one in the discussion knew that participant "D-4" (say) was speaking from that position. Is this a good thing for open dialogue, or a detriment? Should it be left up to that person to choose whether to identify herself, or should some of that information, while still protecting anonymity, have been made public? Would she have participated at all under those conditions? Our point here is that as these decisions are made in different contexts, decisions are also being (tacitly) made about who will have access, and how or whether they will participate.

(3) Another feature of online communication, as in the example just mentioned, is whether messages are sent to a collective, "public" group (as in a listserv or a chat room), or as specific person-to-person messages. In ordinary speaking situations, the same distinction arises, of course. What sorts of communications are fostered by each format and who will feel comfortable with each? When do public messages become communiquchés; and who will not wish to speak in such pronouncements? Who, in fact, will prefer face-to-face contact in all their communicative interactions, and find the impersonality of the online world fundamentally alienating? Are there cultural groups for whom the presence of facial expressions, bodily gestures, and so forth, are indispensable elements in conversation?

(4) Following on that point, for now online communication is still mostly in writing (although voice and video links are becoming better quality, easier to use, and less expensive to incorporate into networked systems). But written and spoken communications obviously have different forms, different conventions, and different effects. Issues of ability and disability arise again in this context. For some, spoken communication is not possible at all; for others it is the only alternative since they cannot use a keyboard or mouse. In some languages, and for certain cultures, tonal features of utterances are inseparable from meaning. Writing is *not* simply speech on paper (or on screen); what is gained and what is lost in each medium, and who will feel such gain or loss especially acutely?

(5) Finally, within the scope of writing itself new sub-forms are emerging. As the use of hypertext, discussed previously, becomes woven into the capabilities of all word processors and e-mail programs, a new distinction between predominantly linear writing online and branched, complex, interwoven "hypertextual" writing will create yet another feature of online communication that will be received by different people quite differently. Forms of thinking, features of syntax in different languages, and the intentions, problems, and purposes people bring to online communication will all influence whether this new hypertextual environment is experienced as a boon or a chaotic nightmare. Of course, our point here is that some will thrive in this context, and others will avoid it.

In all of these communicative settings decisions about access are implicit in choices about media and methods of interaction. They are often not considered as such, however. The result is that choices that are made and locked into place by system capabilities (choices sometimes made because of cost constraints) end up having subtle and not-so-subtle consequences for who can use them, or will want to use them, and who will not.

Now, as noted, all people do not possess these implicit criteria of access (and others that could be extended from this analysis) to the same degree, nor can they be developed with equal facility by different types of people. In many cases the "lack" of such characteristics will not be remedied easily. As noted this may not even be felt to *be* a lack by persons who are reluctant to give up or change what they consider to be important aspects of their identity and approach to the world. This makes the provision of access to technological environments a much deeper puzzle than simply the provision of hardware and software. We need to think about this problem in ways that do not assume that all users are the same; or that blame them when they are different.

What this discussion shows is that the question of "access" in a general way cannot be separated from an examination of what we are trying to give access *to*.[6] When the very experiences and opportunities that some find desirable are seen as much less attractive to others, what is the obligation of society to *change* aspects of the content—often at the cost of other values—when those aspects are seen to be barriers to access for certain citizens? Conversely, does society put certain people or groups in a no-win situation when it asks them to put up with experiences or content that for them might be uncomfortable, disturbing, or worse, for the sake of other purported benefits?

We see, then, four related levels of the issue of access and equity. First is the provision of technical access—an expensive and complicated proposition in itself. Second is the development of general skills, attitudes, and dispositions that are necessary for effective use of that equipment. Third is the complex interrelation of pragmatic conditions of access and criteria of access—examining the circumstances that differentiate, in practice, who can actually make productive use of new technologies and who cannot. Fourth are issues of access raised by the characteristics of the environment to which we are trying to provide access; characteristics that might not be changeable, or that grow out of the very benefits that (for some users) make that environment valuable. The challenge of the first two levels of access is itself a complex, costly undertaking—a price that we doubt society and educational institutions are truly prepared to pay. Some users will always lag significantly behind others in the quantity and quality of access they have to these technologies. The third and fourth levels raise even deeper conceptual and practical paradoxes that may not be "solvable" in any apparent way. Changes to the form and content of the Internet itself are not easily made or enforced. Even where they are changed to protect and encourage some prospective users, their access is obtained at the price of a limited access for them to other Internet resources, and at the price of restrictions that also might inhibit the access of others to what they want or need. Such considerations carry us deeper and deeper into reflections about the nature and benefits of the Internet itself rather than taking the benefits of new technologies as a given, and thinking solely about the problem of how to get everyone involved. "Everyone" is a meaningless concept in this context.

Like most followers of the Internet, we are interested to read reports that summarize demographic surveys of Internet use among various currently underrepresented groups in the U.S. (women, African-Americans). All trends show that while their early numbers were trailing, participation among these groups is rising sharply, sometimes at a greater rate than with other groups. This news is encouraging. But according to the analysis we have offered here, such statistical data do not tell us all we need to know to determine whether this society is making progress on the access issue or not. Clearly the discussion of quantity of access and quality of access (or thin and thick access) is relevant to this problem: there is a qualitative judgment in weighing access that cannot be read off of numbers of participants "online." The question of what one is obtaining access *to* needs to be evaluated. For example, even a simple technical matter such as the speed of one's Internet connection can practically limit access to a whole host of Web sites and material. But there is a further problem, a further dilemma, we think needs to be discussed also.

It might appear that a concern with access, and broadening access, derives from an egalitarian sentiment closely linked with the values of participatory democracy and an open society. And indeed often it is. But other motivations can lead to a concern with access also. A major factor, we believe, in current calls for increased access to the Internet are in the interest of online commerce. As advertising and sales online take on a greater market share, increasing the number of prospective customers has a cyclical influence on the growth of e-commerce. The more shoppers, the greater the volume and variety of goods available (including items sold *by* individuals through auction sites); the greater the opportunities for buying online (often at a discount), the greater the incentive for customers to shop there. At present, those benefiting most from the savings of shopping online are not those most needing to save money (we are reminded here of the frequent pattern that groceries in poorer neighborhoods often have higher prices for items than stores selling the same items in better-off neighborhoods).

Our point here is that access is often conceived on a *consumer* model: the aim of increasing access is linked with the purpose of broadening and diversifying prospective audiences for delivery-oriented sites, including commercial sites, *not* fundamentally with reshaping the Internet or increasing participation for democratic reasons. This issue pertains to educational concerns, as more and more commercially oriented education sites, especially at the levels of post-secondary and vocational education, seek potential students/customers. True, the educational goals may be linked with values of reaching and retraining new audiences (those in isolated rural areas, for example); but they are certainly motivated by financial interests as well. Do these sorts of interests conflict? We can only suggest that, just as quantity of access may not mean quality of access, trying to reach more consumers online may not mean involving them in the full range of opportunities that the Internet and related technologies make available.

On the Internet, when you have access to others, they have access to you. There is often a passivity to the consumer-oriented model of access that belies a commitment to promoting participation in a full sense. Promoting increased access to the Internet among underrepresented groups is not always motivated by a concern for their interests and opportunities. A focus on access does not necessarily imply a commitment to equity.

ISSUES OF CREDIBILITY

The relation between access issues and credibility issues is already implicit in the preceding discussion. One way of framing this question is, "What kind of access is *worth having?*" Because the form and content of the Internet affects different individuals and groups differently, it affects their access. Because wholesale changes to that form and content are not likely (or, if they happen, it will not be with access issues primarily in mind), the focus has to shift to the capacities of prospective users to select, evaluate, and question what they encounter there. The interrelation of issues of access and issues of content shows that a major barrier to effective access will be an inability or unwillingness to sort through and evaluate the enormous volume of material the Internet makes available. Another major barrier will be the inability to gain a voice and presence as a contributor of information, ideas, and points of view online. We are referring to these dual issues of credibility as *assessing* credibility, in the first instance, and *gaining* credibility, in the second. They are topics frequently raised in discussions about the Internet, but not, we would argue, in the context of access issues, which they are.

Assessing Credibility

As anyone who has used the Internet knows, the volume of information, voices, viewpoints, and opinions, some of them worthwhile and many not, can be overwhelming. A keyword search on the Web might pull up hundreds of thousands of references. An ordinary discussion group might generate dozens of messages per day. Unsolicited advertisements and solicitations come almost as soon as one's e-mail address is established. These experiences are not unlike those encountered through other media (ordinary mail, telephones, cable television, newspapers and magazines, and others), but the volume and speed of proliferating information points in the Internet is truly unprecedented. A user who cannot discern what is useful, what is believable, what is interesting, what is important, will literally be overwhelmed. Over time such users either will leave out of frustration, will squander a great deal of time sorting through trivia or junk, will attempt to truncate their exposure to the Internet, or (worst of all) will begin to lose the capability or patience to make such discriminations, regarding all online materials with a certain level of expectations—either too uniformly high or too uniformly low.

As a result, developing a critical capacity to read selectively, evaluate, and question information online is one of the central educational problems raised by these new information technologies. Later we will call this capability "hyperreading." Hyperreading is not only finding and reading what is on the Internet, but learning to make one's own connections in what one finds there, to question the connections (the "links") that others provide, and to interrogate the silences or absences of the Internet: what is not there (or who is not there).

Assessing the credibility of materials, or persons, has both an *internal* and an *external* dimension: part of this process involves evaluating elements of the material, or the person; part of it involves evaluating external elements, including associations with or references to others, which are evaluated at secondhand. Hence assessing credibility sometimes means having sufficient knowledge in an area to evaluate the information provided directly. If a person can independently judge that certain claims are valid, he or she is more likely to grant credence to other claims from the same source. Most often, however, people will not have this independent basis of judgment.

When users lack an independent expertise, assessing credibility will mean examining the sources of online information, and judging who they are (whether individuals, groups, or institutions): What experience or qualifications do they hold relative to the material they are providing? What interests do they have relative to promoting certain information and points of view over others? What space do they provide for users to interpret the information differently than they do? Have they been reliable in the information or viewpoints they have offered in the past? In the context of the Internet, as we will discuss in more detail in a later chapter, this means examining information from the address or URL, from Web pages that identify who made the page and when it was updated, and so on.

A special case of judging credibility is when others are entrusted to make the judgments on one's behalf: for example, editors or archivists who travel the Internet, find material, collect, filter, and organize it, and make it available in a useable form for others (via a newsletter, a journal, a Web site, and so on). Here the question of credibility is transferred to the person, group, or institution that is making the judgments on others' behalf; and there are just as many reasons to be skeptical about the qualifications, biases, and blind spots of these authorities. Yet their status is likely to become more and more important as the Internet grows. It will simply be impossible, from the standpoint of expertise or time, for individuals to perform these jobs entirely for themselves across the full range of interests that concern them. In certain areas, at least, they will need to rely on editors or archivists to make these selections and evaluations on their behalf. The sole protection against monolithic or exclusionary points of view, then, will be in maintaining a diverse number of people, groups, or institutions performing this service (in part so that their results can be compared). As the Internet stands now, the structure of access is relatively unregulated and decentralized, so that many different people and agencies are performing this function (for any significant topic, there are likely to be many Web pages of archived information, including links to other Web pages and resources). This becomes a major reason to be concerned about moves to centralize the Internet, to limit the number of information providers, to introduce prohibitive financial barriers to becoming an active provider or consumer of information, or to create a single gateway (or "portal") to the Internet.

A different dimension of credibility is in the links to and from a resource: when one person links to or cites another, there is a reciprocal transfer of credibility. Jones authorizes Smith by recommending Smith's statements, writings, Web page, and so forth, and transfers some of his or her credibility to Smith. Yet Jones also gains (or loses) credibility by citing

Smith's materials. The web of links that constitutes the Internet (especially the World Wide Web itself) is a vast network of relations of credibility. The people who establish active links to reliable information, and whose information or viewpoints are in turn identified and recommended by others, gain credibility both as users of information and as providers of it (another way in which these dynamics are linked). We call this network a system of *distributed credibility*. There is a degree to which our traditional criteria of credibility have been closely tied to the qualifications and characteristics of particular agents. But on the Internet users may not always be able to identify the particular agents who originally provided some piece of information. In such a case, judgments of credibility must rely wholly on the avenues through which that information was gained, the links others have made to that information, the frequency with which that information has been accessed, and so on. That these are indirect and imperfect measures of credibility must be emphasized, but they may be all that users have. They represent one more way in which this new information environment challenges some of our traditional ideas about how to gain and evaluate information.

Finally, there are dozens of Web pages devoted to the issue of evaluating credibility online, with checklists of criteria to enable users to make more informed judgments. Here, too, the Web is self-regulating, in that the means of evaluating information relies on other information provided on the Web. Predictably, then, one can also raise credibility issues about *those* criteria and checklists. As with other aspects of the Web, a certain cross-referencing of criteria that emerge on multiple pages, from multiple points of view, might make them more plausible as relatively objective and reliable standards. But the bootstrapping paradox persists.

Gaining Credibility

Many of the questions of how one gains credibility are the inverse of those mentioned under assessing credibility: How to gain an Internet presence; how to acquire the marks of institutional or personal authority; how to get others to link to or recommend one's information or viewpoints; and so on.

One important dimension of this process is acquiring the skills to become an information provider, such as learning to create a Web page or Web site so that people can publish their own writings. One can gather information from other sources and become an editor or archivist him/herself. One can collect links and make one's own site a resource that endorses and promotes the information sources that one wants to make more visible.

Yet there is another aspect of these skills: the more that one knows about creating Web resources, the better one's position to evaluate the resources of others. One can appreciate the qualities of good design. One can differentiate flash for the sake of flash from more imaginative and beneficial uses of graphics or multimedia. Most of all one can see through potentially superficial markers of importance (blinking items on a Web page, for example), to make more independent judgments of importance and quality for one's self.

What these discussions of assessing credibility and gaining credibility show is that there is a continuum of activity and passivity in matters of access. Some users simply "surf," looking through what is there, browsing or exploring with a certain degree of randomness. There can be real use in doing this sometimes, and pleasures as well. But as a single mode it is limited and runs the danger of superficiality and a consumer orientation to the information one finds. A critical reader of information, a "hyperreader," is more actively asking questions about what he or she finds and does not find; is continually making comparisons and judgments about credibility; is going beyond what browsing reveals to find what may be hidden or implicit behind what is apparent. An active provider of information, a writer, an archivist, or an editor, is using the networked relations of the Internet to gain credibility, to publish his or her own ideas and viewpoints, and to sponsor the ideas and viewpoints of others.

Yet these capabilities are not simply a consequence of the characteristics of individuals; they are not simply criteria of access or credibility that can be taught or provided to people. As we have stressed repeatedly, they are also related to conditions of access, outgrowths of the form and content of the Internet as an existing structure. Hence, issues of centralization or decentralization; issues of regulation; issues of censorship; issues of commercialization; issues of privacy and surveillance; and issues of global availability are all factors that will have specific consequences for who will and will not have access to this new information and communication environment. While there are important educational challenges raised by questions of access and credibility, they will be for naught if the structure and circumstances of the Internet itself are such that effective access for some individuals, groups, or regions of the world is not possible.

DILEMMAS OF ACCESS

The central dilemma that we have been exploring in this chapter is that it is neither realistic practically nor coherent conceptually to think about providing full access to the Internet to everyone. Resources are limited in this

area, in which equipment and services are not cheap, and in which continual upgrades are necessary. Changes made to increase access (for some) will
result in interfering with access (for others).[7] The more access that is provided, the more participants there are online, the more problems there will
be of congestion, garbage, and conflict (just as in urban areas). As with
other living spaces, some will prefer the equivalent of "gated communities,"
limiting their access (and limiting others' access to them) as a tradeoff for
the perception of security, exclusivity, and safety. Here again we see a recur-
ring theme of this book: that solving one problem always gives rise unexpectedly to another; and sometimes, as Edward Tenner points out, these
changes even exacerbate the problems they were meant to alleviate
("revenge effects").

These issues raise a number of challenges for societies committed to providing people with the means to a successful life. Some of these challenges
are educational in nature. They have implications not only for schooling,
but for learning opportunities before and beyond the school years; the
Internet makes the ideal of "lifelong learning" a feasible reality. There is an
important educational dimension to developing the knowledge, skills, and
dispositions of access; the critical capacities that will allow users to make
effective discriminations of credible and worthwhile information once it is
found; and the strategies of becoming an effective and visible information
provider and communicator as well. But the stakes here are not only educational. As noted before, they also concern employment opportunities,
access to cultural and entertainment resources, to social interactions, and,
increasingly, to political information and participation as well. Citizens
excluded, or alienated, from this new environment will find themselves cut
off from many other opportunities, because increasingly these networks
themselves become an avenue for new information and skills. Neglect of
these issues will, over time, create a two-tiered society, an "information caste
society," that, once in place, will be as intractable and self-perpetuating as
any that human society has yet witnessed. Like illiteracies of other sorts, a
lack of access to the Internet will mean a lack of opportunities to acquire
the skills and knowledge necessary to change that status.

Existing metaphors that have helped to conceive and organize society,
such as "public" and "private" spaces, and related notions of communication, community, political participation, credibility, personal identity, and
relations to others, are all being transformed by the increasing prevalence of
new information and communication technologies in our lives. As computers, telephones, televisions, and other media all begin to blend into new,
seamlessly integrated technologies, the ways in which we have thought

about how people communicate, how they send, receive, and interpret information, how they relate to one another, will have to change. This means that our ideas about "education" will have to change. Without a doubt, the physical locations we call schools and classrooms will need to change. They will become less exclusively the places where certain kinds of learning are possible. If they do not change, they may simply become holding tanks for those student populations with no other alternative. Each of these changes brings potential benefits, and dangers. What disturbs us is that the benefits, for some, inherently become the dangers, for others.

These sorts of access and credibility issues have, in our view, not yet received the attention they deserve. We who have the greatest stake in these technologies and who use them the most, who have generally free, unlimited access through our schools or universities, who often have upgraded equipment purchased for us, who have a fair amount of latitude in how we structure and allocate our time, are not always in the best position to anticipate the problems of those who see these technological changes from afar.

As educators, we are supposed to be more reflective than most people about the ways in which we can intentionally create learning experiences and opportunities that expand the scope of human possibility. We are also supposed to worry about those left out of these experiences and opportunities. Now is the time to begin to take these questions seriously: What forms are new educational technologies taking, and what forms are *we* taking along with them? Who is the "we" that is included here; and who is not being included? The answers, we hope to have suggested, are far from simple or obvious.

New technologies of communication and information sharing are drawing boundaries of inclusion and exclusion, influencing to a substantial degree the amount and kind of interactions that take place among people. The great trap of new technology is when it is simply defined as a means of convenience: Do what you used to do, faster, easier, cheaper! It never works out that way. Adopting new technologies changes what we want to do, what we try to do, what we see it to be possible to do. Success or satisfaction remains sometimes within reach, sometimes just out of reach, now as always. Technology does not solve any problem without creating a new one. So whatever we think we are trying to accomplish educationally with these new technologies, we will inevitably end up discovering that we have achieved something quite different instead.

Notes

1. It is important to add here that access to the Internet is not the only educational problem of access. There are advantages to be gained from other living and learning environments also, and we do not mean to contribute to the hype about "cyberspace" as the new learning frontier. Users can spend too much time in this space and too little outside it; and this becomes a disadvantage in learning also.

2. Nicholas C. Burbules, Brian Lord, and Ann Sherman, "Equity, equal opportunity, and education," *Educational Evaluation and Policy Analysis*, Vol. 4 No. 2 (1982): 169–187.

3. In our discussion here, we do not mean to imply any sharp form/content distinction. Indeed, as we will discuss in later chapters, the two are inseparable where the Internet is concerned.

4. Cynthia Selfe and Richard Selfe, Jr., "The politics of the interface: Power and its exercise in electronic contact zones," *College Composition and Communication*, Vol. 45 No. 4 (1994): 480–504.

5. See Michael Peters and Colin Lankshear, "Critical literacy and digital texts," *Educational Theory*, Vol. 46 No. 1 (1996): 51–70. See also Ilana Snyder, *Hypertext: The Electronic Labyrinth* (Melbourne: Melbourne University Press, 1996).

6. See, for example, Jane Kenway, "Backlash in cyberspace and why 'girls need modems,'" in Leslie Roman and Linda Eyre, eds. *Dangerous Territories: Struggles for Equality and Difference* (New York: Routledge, forthcoming).

7. A point made nicely by Bertram (Chip) Bruce in "Speaking the unspeakable about 21st century technologies," in Gail Hawisher and Cynthia Selfe, eds., *Passions, Pedagogies, and 21st Century Technologies* (Urbana, IL: University of Illinois Press, forthcoming).

chapter three

HYPERTEXT: KNOWLEDGE
AT THE CROSSROADS

As we noted in our opening chapter, when technologies become familiar, they tend to become invisible, taken as part of the natural order of things. The linear ways in which we write and read are examples of this. Some of the earliest forms of writing were on scrolls, continuous rolls of paper, pasted together. A later invention, the book, or the codex volume, was constructed of separate sheets of paper, bound together, designed to be read in sequence.[1] The page is written to be read in a particular order, left to right, top to bottom (in English, not in other languages—which have their own linear sequences). In fact, one could imagine an entire book written as a single line on a narrow, continuous, strip of paper (think of an unrolled typewriter ribbon).

Other aspects of the form of writing express this same sequential character. The classic form of an essay—introduction, body, and conclusion—implies an order in which these sections are meant to be read. Even individual paragraphs are often structured this way. The form of an outline, which many students are taught as the first stage of writing, is a hierarchical, sequential, organization of ideas, stressing superordinate and subordinate topics, ranked in importance and in relation to one another. The very form of syllogistic argument common to Western logic, premise one, premise two, conclusion, suggests a necessary sequence. The conclusion cannot precede the premises. In writing and in speech, even the forms of rhetoric follow this type of pattern, whether in actually enumerating points in sequence ("First . . . Second . . . Third . . .") or in similar words ("Furthermore . . . Finally . . . In conclusion . . .").

Now, from the fact that things are printed a certain way does not mean that they are necessarily either written this way or read this way. Writing, especially in the era of word processors, is often a process of cutting and pasting, moving pieces around, drafting later sections before earlier sections are finished, and so on. The illusion of continuity and sequential development often only emerges after many efforts to rewrite and smooth over the seams of material written at very different times. Similarly, the practice of reading is very often nonlinear and discontinuous. We skip sections, we pause, we read material out of sequence, we go back and reread sections before going on, and so forth.

Hypertext pushes these issues further. This way of making lateral as well as linear associations, of connecting ideas and text by links and juxtapositions, and not necessarily by a sequential logic, has taken on central importance as the underlying form of the World Wide Web (Hypertext Markup Language, or HTML). It is one of the structures that make the Web a web, a network.[2]

In this chapter we want to introduce readers to some of the possibilities and dangers that are entailed with hypertextual systems for learning.[3] New technical resources and systems for organizing information challenge traditional notions about what a "text" is, what it means to "read" different media or sources of information, and what the relation is between an "author" and a "reader." In this context, *quantitative* change—change in the amount of textual information that can be accessed, the speed with which it can be accessed, and the number of linkages that can be established between discrete textual components—can promote a *qualitative* change in the processes of reading and constructing knowledge. Such changes raise fundamental issues for educational theory and practice. In fact, we do not think it is an exaggeration to compare them in scale and significance with the invention of the printing press itself, a technical innovation that eventually had far-reaching effects on social, economic, political, religious, and educational practices.

We will discuss how hypertext is similar to, and how it differs from, other forms of information creation, organization, storage, and retrieval. We will examine the influence hypertext has on the information it organizes and the implications this has for both readers and authors of hypertext systems. Finally, we want to explore a number of problematic issues, focusing on the potential for bias and distortion within hypertexts and on the paradoxical demand that hypertext systems balance *flexibility* with *accessibility*. Educational uses of hypertext will be on the increase during the coming years, in CD-ROMs and on the World Wide Web. Yet the growth of hypertext has not always been accompanied by a critical reflection on its assumptions about cognition and learning, about its possible consequences for attaining certain educational benefits at the expense of other aims, or for issues of access and equity. We hope to initiate such a critical conversation here.

As a way of introducing readers to this new and conceptually complex learning environment, we will explore various analogies and literary parallels, seeking to develop different points of connection with the basic idea of hypertext. Because the first drafts of this chapter were written interactively, over electronic mail, we have also tried to maintain some of the flavor of two "voices" through the use of regular and italicized text in different sections of this chapter.[4] These sections can be read in a different order from that presented here. Readers who might consider these sections in an alternative sequence would no doubt see some new connections that we did not anticipate or highlight in our original organization. We sometimes return to the same topic or theme from different vantage points, suggesting a web-like connection between these ideas. In all of this, we are trying to incorporate some elements of the hypertext model in this chapter.[5]

What Is Hypertext?

Hypertext is not an unprecedented form. In written text, like this one, footnotes or inserted quotations from other sources have a hypertextual character, drawing the reader aside into other sources or points of view, woven into a linear narrative flow but allowing divergences from it. Rhetorical forms, including the use of phrases such as "Previously . . . In an upcoming chapter. . . In another published essay we argued . . . ," and so on, make points of connection to earlier or later pieces of text that may invite the reader to revert back or jump ahead to read the present text in conjunction with, or in contrast to, something written elsewhere. But in the standard rhetorical forms, these are seen as divergences, or supplements, to the "main" text, and most writers assume that the central argument of their case is presented in this central, structured, linear form. If readers choose not to follow the side paths, nothing essential is lost.

Hypertext, by contrast, describes a kind of informational environment in which textual material and ideas are linked to one another in multiple ways. Some familiar examples of hypertext systems that we use every day may help to illustrate further the ways in which hypertexts link information.[6] Hypertexts organize information, just as a library card catalogue or Rolodex file are systems for organizing information. But hypertext is more than just a new way of organizing existing information; it *influences* the kinds of information it organizes. As the organizing system of a hypertext grows and evolves, the structure of the information itself changes. Anyone who has designed a complex database knows how significant the decision can be to organize and represent certain content in relation to some as opposed to other possible points of connection. The process here is not only one of associating discrete givens, but of *changing* those elements by identifying and creating relations among them. This process might be seen in terms of how figurative language and tropes work: by juxtaposing certain terms or concepts in a simile or metaphor. Can anyone look at a rose and not think of romance? After watching *Forrest Gump*, can one ever see a box of chocolates as just a box of chocolates? In making such figurative connections, form and content become interdependent. The same is true of hypertext. This raises deeper questions about knowledge: because knowing depends upon the meaningful organization of information, new methods of organization imply changing forms of knowledge.[7] Furthermore, to the extent that hypertext systems incorporate the capacity both to impose patterns of organization on existing information and to facilitate the user's ability to imagine and create new patterns of organization, hypertext challenges sharp distinctions between *accessing* and *producing* new knowledge.

In hypertexts, as in texts generally, there is an interactive relation between the structure of a text and the strategies of reading it invites. The form of the text, or the author's intentions in organizing it in a particular way, do not determine the ways in which it can be read. The marginal comments, annotations, and highlighting or underlining added by readers to a text often represent their own ideas about the internal relations and orders of importance within a text, including links to other ideas based on associations they make as they are reading. In this process, the reader is actively modifying the text, customizing it, making it into his or her own hypertext. Hence, there is a sense in which *every* text is a rudimentary hypertext, implying choices—sometimes by the author, sometimes by the reader— about relevance, selectivity, and meaningful forms of linkage with other textual sources. Hypertexts produced with this potential explicitly in mind highlight an interlinked structure that is inherent to some extent in any text. The difference is that hypertexts actively invite and facilitate multiple, alternative readings of the same material. In this, the reader becomes not only a consumer of a text, but an active contributor to it: the distinction of author and reader, as Michel Foucault and many others have pointed out, begins to break down.[8]

We assume that the numbered pages and numbered chapters of a book are meant to be read in a particular order. But why must this necessarily be so? In the novel Hopscotch *by Julio Cortazar, the 155 short chapters can be read in different orders.*[9] *The order in which they were written, or the order in which they are printed on bound pages, need not determine how they can or should be read.*[10] Dictionary of the Khazars, *by Milorad Pavic (not just one book, in fact, but several different versions), takes a similar approach.*[11] *Novels and short stories by Jorge Luis Borges, Italo Calvino, Umberto Eco, and Milan Kundera all have hypertextual characteristics, or deal explicitly with hypertextual themes.*[12]

A hypertext, then, is a mode of composition or design as well as a process of writing. It may include a central narrative or discussion that one can read sequentially, but it also offers specific opportunities to branch off from that primary text into other textual materials. In fact, hypertext is sometimes described as "electronic footnotes." This description, however, is rather superficial. First, it ignores the way in which the relation of a primary text to subsidiary or ancillary materials, which exists in the idea of footnotes, is changed to a co-existence of multiple textual elements, possibly represented at the same level of importance, without any one of them being primary. Second, the idea of a "footnote" fails to capture the capacity of hypertext to incorporate richer and far more multidimensional linkages than any footnote can. We can imagine, further, that these many supplementary sources are themselves interlinked through a complex system of cross-referencing.

What is the "text" that I am reading? Should the "primary text" be the main focus of concern? Or is the primary text merely the top layer in one version, the entry point to an entire system of interlinked textual information in which, once I enter it, I might be led to points of discovery far afield from the primary text? Might I never return to that text, or feel the need to? For example, if I am drawn from a chance comment in the introduction of one text to a quotation, and from that to a biography of the speaker of the quote, and from that to an historical account of the era in which she spoke, I will be not only gaining new information, but relating these "nodes" together in ways that may be entirely independent from the purposes of the original essay. This type of environment provides much greater freedom in making determinations as a reader of a text about what relates to what, or what ideas should follow or precede others. The primary text is a gateway into a much larger, complex network of referential material to be explored. It is no longer useful to think strictly in terms of single texts. Of course, one can still talk in terms of "reading a book"—Simone de Beauvoir's The Second Sex, *for example. One starts on page one and continues through to the end. But in a new hypertext edition, this volume might be* *reproduced along with the original French (*Le Deuxième Sexe*), so that a reader can move effortlessly back and forth between the French text and the English translation. At key points, multiple translations of crucial or ambiguous phrases might be offered. Alternatively, de Beauvoir's book might be produced alongside Betty Friedan's* The Feminine Mystique *in an edition that cross-references passages from both books, emphasizing points of similarity and contrast between them. One might read such a hypertext, not linearly within each book, but in a criss-cross of moving back and forth between the original texts, forward and back within each text, and only indirectly getting a sense of the narrative line or argument within each book, separately.*[13] *What book are we reading: de Beauvoir? Friedan? or something new? This sort of reading implies a very different orientation to any given text or author, and raises a host of new questions about what it means to "read" effectively. A hypertext system develops an ambiguous relation to any primary texts that might be part of it—incorporating them, commenting upon them, but also altering them in the process.*

Gilles Deleuze and Félix Guattari suggest a powerful analogy for this construction of the text in their discussion of *rhizomes*.[14] A rhizomatic plant (mint, certain grasses, weeds, and others) depends upon a root-like system that is decentered, spreading in all directions. A more tree-like plant structure, on the other hand, depends upon a central taproot and a more hierarchically organized set of roots of progressing size, centrality, and importance to the system. ("Any point on a rhizome can be connected with any other, and must be. This is very different from a tree or root, which fixes a point and thus an order."[15]) Deleuze and Guattari develop these two metaphors, the rhizome, or grass, versus the root system, or tree, into two guiding models of the text. Hypertext is inherently *rhizomatic*:[16]

> A rhizome ceaselessly establishes connections between semiotic chains, organizations of power, and circumstances relative to the arts, sciences, and social struggles. . . . A rhizome may be broken, shattered at a single spot, but it will start up again on one of its old lines, or on new lines. . . . These lines always tie back to one another. This is why one can never posit a dualism or a dichotomy, even in the rudimentary form of the good and the bad. . . . A rhizome is not amenable to any structural or generative model. It is a stranger to any idea of genetic axis or deep structure. . . . A rhizome is altogether different, *a map and not a tracing*.[17]

As noted earlier, this rhizomatic structure can be seen as both a feature of the organization of hypertext, and as a way of reading *any* text nonlinearly and nonhierarchically. The difference is the degree to which a hypertext, by explicitly representing such a nonlinear, nonhierarchical structure, encourages such readings. A hypertext might still be organized as a sequential, hierarchical outline, but this becomes merely one possible way of organizing it, and one possible order in which to read it. The significance of computer hypertext systems, as opposed to other, more simple hypertexts, lies in the number of associations that can be made and the ease and speed with which they can be accessed. Only by means of a computer network can one have direct, virtually immediate access to every other linked node in a system. (And only with a computer can these linkages be made conveniently with multimedia sources.) When one is reading a book and it refers to a passage in another book one may, if interested, get up, walk to the library, find the book, check it out, return to the office, find the passage, read it, and then (perhaps) return to the original text. But, that book might not be available, or there might not be a library nearby. In a hypertext system, the same reference can appear on the computer screen at the stroke of a key—*as easily and automatically as one can call up the following page or any other part of the original text.* As discussed before, this reference may lead to a third reference, or back to the original material. This seamless shifting from text to text is only possible online. The line between primary and supplemental materials fades and disappears. As Paul Delaney and George Landow describe it,

> the text [in a hypertext] appears to break down, to fragment and atomize into constituent elements (the *lexia* or blocks of text), and these reading units take on a life of their own as they become more self-contained and less dependent on what comes before or after in a linear succession.[18]

Moreover, hypertext throws open the parameters of what can be searched for. In traditional forms of data organization, the search parameters are fixed. In a library's card catalogue, for example, access to textual information is restricted to certain fixed search categories such as author, title, or previously codified descriptors and keywords. Hypertext is able to operate between *any* segments of text, allowing them to be accessed in flexible, customized ways.[19] Moreover, in certain types of hypertext, these links are not only passive (hard-wired into the system) but active, allowing readers to create new links, and new *types* of links, in terms of their own emergent understandings of the material. The immediacy and flexibility of online hypertext are, therefore, much more than matters of degree; something different, and indeed virtually unprecedented, is possible.

HYPERTEXT AND THOUGHT

As Vannevar Bush noted, the structure of hypertext environments parallels and can facilitate the ways in which we learn: dynamically and interactively, through associations and by exploration.[20] Hypertext can allow the user the freedom to navigate courses through the material in a manner determined by his or her own interest, curiosity, and experience, or by the nature of the task at hand, rather than following a course predetermined by the author. Hypertext makes concrete the idea of interactive reading.

This process of actively selecting and assimilating new information in light of personally coherent cognitive frameworks meshes the potential of hypertext with constructivist learning theories, especially schema theory. This link is particularly strong when we consider knowledge domains that are complex and indeterminate; domains requiring a high degree of "cognitive flexibility" and a tolerance for ambiguity.[21]

Learning and understanding operate by making connections. We come to comprehend something when we can bring it into association with other things we already know. Mind and memory are themselves hyperenvironments: we do not learn new information as discrete, isolated facts—or, if we do, we are not likely to remember them for long. The information we learn best is material that can be integrated with knowledge we already have, frequently through complex and multiple links of association. John Slatin captures this idea nicely in discussing the need for writing that "surprises" the reader:

> The informational value of a given document is not simply a function of the quantity of information it presents or the facts it contains. At one level of abstraction, what we call information may indeed consist in numbers, dates, and other information, other facts. . . . At a somewhat higher level of abstraction . . . none of these data can be considered information until they have been contextualized, arranged in such a way that both the significant differences and the significant relationships among them may become apparent to the intended reader. . . . This is when information becomes knowledge.[22]

As we discussed earlier, in this process of establishing active, novel, and idiosyncratic patterns of association, the elements recombined in relation to one another are also seen differently.

In a hypertext, any information point should be seen not as simply an isolated "fact" or a discrete reference point, but as a node of multiple intersecting lines of association. There are lines from literature and elsewhere—

"'Twas brillig," or "Fourscore and seven years ago"—scenes from movies—Humphrey Bogart saying good-bye in Casablanca, and so on—that evoke an entire range of responses, images, and associations, quite apart from the narrative in which they were originally contained. They stand between that text and the nodes of association they evoke. Often we encounter these familiar nodes, or references to them, in fresh and unexpected contexts, and see them differently as a result.

The year 1492 does not only indicate that "Columbus comes to America"—it also refers to "the expulsion of Jews from Spain," "the completion by Michaelangelo of one of his first sculptures, 'The Battle of the Centaurs,'" and many other events, from the momentous to the trivial. This is exhilarating in one sense, mind-boggling in another. What makes Columbus in America more "central" to the importance of 1492 than the fate of Jews in Spain or Michaelangelo's artistic achievement? To whom is it "more central"? By what criteria? How is that same year regarded by the native peoples of North America, who were here before Columbus (although for them, the year was not "1492")? How does our understanding of "1492" change in that context? Why 1492, and not 1493?

In hypertextual representations of knowledge, nodes become "leveled." None are a priori more important, or central, than any others are. This is the poststructuralist dream state: a limitless bricolage of fragments and pieces that can be brought into new and unpredictable associations with one another:[23]

> Hypertext has no center . . . [which] means that anyone who uses hypertext makes his or her own interests the de facto organizing principle (or center) for the investigation at the moment. One experiences hypertext as an infinitely decenterable and recenterable system.[24]

The possibilities of novelty and creativity inherent in this view of reading should be clear, as is its potential for chaos, arbitrariness, and spinning out endless permutations and juxtapositions for their own sake.[25]

But now we begin to see a dilemma (the first of several in this discussion). If hypertexts do make possible the manifold linkage of nodes to different points of association, they *also* have the effect of fragmenting and decontextualizing each node, freed up from its position in some original narrative or line of argument. "Lateral" associations may turn out to be more useful in certain contexts than the original "linear" ones; but the leveling of all associations without privileging any particular one may make every association appear arbitrary. Yet it does not seem arbitrary, for example, to privilege the idea of an historical sequence, or of a literary story line, or of a logical explanation, as particular ways of relating information nodes (even if one might acknowledge that alternative ways of organizing the same information are also possible). Without some such starting point, even a provisional one, the exploration of a rhizomatic system might be simply anarchic—a nice image for *avant garde* literary interpretations, perhaps, but not necessarily for beginning learners. Problematizing given narratives is one thing; proposing alternative readings is another; but the very constructivist theory that encourages these alternatives also explains why a reading with absolutely no center is not reading at all.

WRITING AND READING HYPERTEXT

The production of traditional text tends to be exclusive as opposed to inclusive. Authors spend much of their time when writing in deciding what to leave out. Given finite space limitations, and often finite time, writers need to apply fairly strict self-discipline in authoring a text. Any text can only address certain topics, and not the many others that might be interesting, relevant, and important, but for which there is neither time nor room. Hypertexts remove some of these limitations. Virtually anything that is judged interesting, relevant, and important can be included and made accessible to the reader. In hypertext, the premium can be on drawing more and more sources in, multiplying the number of data points and diversifying the *direction* of meaningful associations to a potentially limitless (and at some point counterproductive) degree.[26] Umberto Eco calls this a process of "unlimited semiosis."[27]

Stanley Fish tells a well-known story, very apt in the present context, in his book, Is There a Text in This Class? *He recounts teaching a class in English religious poetry of the seventeenth century. As students enter the room, Fish notices a vertical list of names/words on the blackboard, left over from the previous class: "Jacobs-Rosenbaum, Levin, Thorne, Hayes, Ohman." He adds the descriptor "p. 43," and tells the English lit class that this is a religious poem and asks them to interpret it, which they proceed to do with gusto. The lesson he draws from this example is that "Interpretation is not the art of construing but the art of constructing. Interpreters do not decode poems; they make them."[28] Virtually any finite set of nodes, it appears, can be subject to some sort of meaningful interpretation. Who is the "author" of the poem on the blackboard: the previous instructor? Fish? the students in the English lit class? Is it a "poem"?*

Authors of hypertexts need to produce their work with an eye toward how it will fit within this transformed system of reading. They may still write out sentences or compose pages of prose. But in the final text, traditional concerns for beginnings, endings, order, and sequencing are vastly complicated, as concerns of navigability through multiple entrance and exit points need to be weighed as well.[29] The process of writing becomes also a process of design:

> The authoring challenge is to design the structure of the hypertext database to match the ways that a user might want to think about the topics. . . . Knowledge must be structured in a way that supports the mental models that readers may create when they use the hypertext system.[30]

However, the author's capacity to impose unilaterally a necessary structure and sequence on a text is undermined as the network of links becomes more and more complex. The relation of author and reader is reciprocal: the "accessing" of textual information influences its "production," and not only vice versa.

A brilliant example of this process of reading as a form of authorship, and a frequently cited precursor to hypertext, is Roland Barthes' book, S/Z, an exhaustively detailed analysis and commentary on a short novella by Balzac, "Sarrasine."[31] *Although the original novella is only a few dozen pages, Barthes breaks it up into more than 500 separate text units, or* lexias, *each of which he discusses at length, then cross-references them in an intricate manner, producing in the process a parallel text that dwarfs the original. Barthes' book, in fact, reads fairly well on its own, without knowing anything about Balzac or his novella; and of course the novella can be read without the assistance of Barthes. Which is the primary text here? Which serves to amplify and illustrate the other? Having read "Sarrasine" through the readerly/writerly interpretive network of Barthes, can one ever* simply *read the novella on its own?*

There is a strange passage in Small World, *a novel by David Lodge, about a literary critic studying "the influence of T.S. Eliot on Shakespeare."*[32] *In a hypertext environment, this can make sense, because the actual historical sequence of producing texts is not the only constraint on reading. The point is not that Eliot (the living person) could have influenced Shakespeare (the living person), of course, but that* our understanding of Eliot *influences* our understanding of Shakespeare. *We cannot read Shakespeare today without echoes of Eliot coloring our readings (compare, in this sense, the "influence of Barthes upon Balzac"). A similar point is made by that most hypertextual of writers, Jorge Luis Borges. In his short essay "Kafka and His Precursors," he suggests that rereading previous authors with a contemporary understanding of their influence on Kafka creates not only a new reading of Kafka but also a new reading of these texts in relation to one another:*

If I am not mistaken, the heterogeneous pieces I have enumerated resemble Kafka; if I am not mistaken, not all of them resemble each other. This second fact is the more significant. In each of these texts we find Kafka's idiosyncrasy to a greater or lesser degree, but if Kafka had never written a line, we would not perceive this quality; in other words it would not exist. . . . The fact is that every writer creates his own precursors.[33]

What these examples show is that *hypertext* is actually a hybrid term, meaning both the particular technological developments that have made textual fragmentation and complex cross-referencing possible and convenient; and a theoretical view of the text as decentered, open-ended, and dependent on other texts, an idea which has been with us for a long time (some call the *Talmud* one of the first hypertexts). What we call *hyperreading* is both the kind of reading that hypertexts tend to encourage, and a more general view of reading as active and reconstructive. Hyperreading is based on the idea that there is never just one way to read a text. The reader effectively creates a version of the text in the process of reading it. Any text always stands in relation to many other texts to which it refers (whether implicitly or explicitly), and in this sense reading is a process that always operates hypertextually, across texts, to some degree. Eco's process of "unlimited semiosis," of playing with multiple interpretations, of questioning any particular authoritative version or interpretation (even the author's own), all situate a responsibility and a power in the hands of readers to read more critically and in an actively constructivist manner. But as we have noted, even if one embraces this model of hyperreading as the mark of the fully mature reader, an important question remains about where readers *begin* in learning to read this way, along a path that might bring them to this point. It is far from clear whether this strongly decentered model is consistent with actually teaching beginning learners to read (a process in which statements like, "This is what this sentence means" must have an uncontested, if provisional, boundary and finality).

Authorship and Design

This hypertextual view broadens the meanings of "text" and "writing" in another way too: more products, textual and otherwise, look like hypertexts. Librarians, archivists, cataloguers, indexers, editors, translators, anthologists, and so on, are not merely in the process of archiving, organizing, or providing access to information, but are themselves producing texts: hypertexts. They create systems that associate new textual information to other textual information. None of these activities is new, but their role has become even more crucial as the volume of information available grows exponentially and as the technical means of accessing and organizing information, especially through the Internet, become more powerful and complex.

These activities, in a technologically driven information system, move from being facilitative (which they always were) to being *indispensable*. In all fields of inquiry, scholarship, literary production, journalism, and commentary the sheer volume of textual material available has exploded. And with this comes an accelerating rapidity with which it is produced, consumed, and becomes obsolete (a problem most clear in certain scientific and technical fields, where by the time a new research article reaches print its information is often already outdated).[34] No one can read everything relevant, and not everything relevant is worth reading. With the enormous growth in volume of textual materials comes a greater need for selectivity; how does one decide what is most worth reading? These changes mean that the selection, evaluation, and organization of new information, in a form that is accessible and useful to readers, has become increasingly the responsibility of people who are intermediary between author and reader. These textual intermediaries (as we saw with Barthes, for example) often do their work by producing hypertexts that compile, relate, and interweave the elements of different texts in a meaningful and useful way.

In such an environment, the new inventions of knowledge will be heuristics: meaningful and useful ways of putting things together in the face of a morass of overwhelming information. So "chronological sequence" might be one kind of heuristic, "causal relations" another, "analogical similarity" another, and so on. These are the kinds of interpretive tools that the typical reader of hypertext will need in order to find and access meaningful information related to the text he or she happens to be reading. Moreover, the question of how the "interface" is designed for a hypertext will influence its usefulness and accessibility. Many readers will need to be able to call up for reference explanatory materials that make explicit to them the implicit structures of the hypertext system. Indexes, charts, maps, glossaries, concordances, search engines, and so on, become more than just guides to moving around a hypertext; they become crucial textual elements themselves, replete with their own interpretive assumptions, emphases, and omissions.

A number of writers have addressed these and similar concerns about the need for a "hypertext grammar."[35] *The forms of connection and argument in hypertext are not limited to the standard methods of logic and supporting a case with evidence. Arguments here may rely more on linking and recombining elements, making juxtapositions that suggest or invite a connection, but do not "argue" for one. They may rely on multiple media to make a case, and not only on explicit verbal reasoning (for example, playing a certain piece of music as a background to a recitation of spoken text; or annotating a video with intercut images from another source). This can lead to creativity, and it can lead to puzzlement (and maybe sometimes creating puzzlement is exactly the point). Because hypertext is both a way of connecting ideas (via links) and also a navigational path through an information space, being puzzled conceptually can be associated with being lost navigationally.*[36]

Delaney and Landow, therefore, identify the need for "stylistic and rhetorical devices" that orient readers to where they are in the hypertext, help them to read and navigate efficiently, indicate where links lead, and assist readers who have just entered the document to feel "at home" there.[37] *One of the best examples in current hypertext systems is familiarly called a "bookmark." A bookmark is a means for readers to tag some important element so that they can return to it directly, rather than by remembering and retracing the exact pathway through which they came across it. This is one simple way in which readers can customize a hypertextual environment. David Jonassen also raises issues of navigation: How does one get about in the document? Where are its entrance and exit points? How does the point at which one enters the hypertext influence the user's subsequent understanding of the material? How structured must hypertexts be? What risks are there that the user will suffer from "cognitive overload," given the potential richness of the hyperenvironment? How can authors anticipate and alleviate this result?*[38]

Active Reading

We believe that addressing such questions of organization and design in hypertext depends upon distinctions between the different sorts of readers who will encounter hypertexts, in educational and other settings: we will call them browsers, users, and hyperreaders.[39] These are not discrete groups of people, so much as three basically different readerly orientations toward hypertext systems, especially in the reader's need for and use of explicit guidance toward specific associations among textual elements and in the reader's capacities to identify and establish novel associations among textual elements in his or her own active processes of reading. Depending on one's purposes, a reader may adopt any or all of these approaches even in a single session of reading. Moreover, people who are users and hyperreaders in certain contexts, dealing with material about which they have a good deal of background knowledge or a high degree of interest, may act more like browsers in other contexts, and so on.

Browsers represent casual, curious readers. The signs or navigational aids that are available may mean little to them because browsers are doing just that, browsing. As Slatin points out, because the pathways of certain hypertexts are nested hierarchically, it is probably less important to anticipate where these types of readers will go than to provide them a means to backtrack when they get lost.[40] Hence an especially important feature in their textual universe is a list or map of the previous selections they have made, in the order in which they made them (most standard Web applications provide such a record). This list or map can be called up by the reader if he or she wants to return to some previous point in the journey. Browsers may look at many text elements, but they are not actively seeking to create associations or patterns among them, nor do they need to know how to make any changes or additions to what they find.

Users, on the other hand, have reasonably clear ideas about what they are looking for. Often seeking some specific information from the hypertext, these users need quite precise directional information. They need signs to indicate where certain branching options might lead and what they will find there. Once they find what they want, they are finished. This raises design and organizational questions about hypertexts and how linking paths can be created that give adequate directions, useful heuristics, and a necessary degree of predictability, while also being flexible enough that more experienced and knowledgeable readers can move more freely between the different sources.

Hyperreaders place much greater demands on the hypertext, since they require not only the resources and guides to move about within the system but also the means to actively alter and add to the system in light of their own reading. As discussed previously, many academic readers do this when they highlight or underline text, write notes in the margins, and so forth. In a hypertext, all of these alterations and additions can become part of the hypertext—if the environment is structured "dialogically," in the sense that it allows for an active response and intervention by the reader (as opposed to a "read only" mode that does not allow modification or custom tailoring).[41] In our view, it is important that hypertexts not only permit authors to establish the context in which information becomes meaningful but also allow active, knowledgeable readers to construct and record their own meaningful links.

Paths, Trails, and Learning

As we have noted, designers make a fundamental choice when creating hypertexts. We have distinguished between texts that are more static, or passive, and those that are more dialogical, or interactive.[42] In the former, the links and paths are set; they cannot be changed, nor can the readers construct new ones. The built-in links of access to other materials may be very complex, and they may be explorable along myriad alternative routes (such as within the World Wide Web), but they are restricted to those anticipated and constructed by the designers. Clearly, this form of hypertext makes the most sense for relatively inexperienced or less knowledgeable readers, those whom we have called "browsers" and "users."

The latter form of organization is more like the trails worn by walkers in a forest: the dynamics of use establish patterns and connections, which gradually get reinforced by further use until they become familiar features of the environment. There is a record of how different people have explored and evaluated the environment, leaving a trail that others may follow (or adapt and add to in their turn). It is far from standard for hypertexts to allow this sort of modification by readers, although some Web applications are beginning to allow a degree of annotation and customization of Web pages by readers (hyperreaders, as we call them).[43]

However, this raises another dilemma for authors and designers (and educators). The manner of design and organization that might be most useful for less experienced users, or that might be most intuitive for them, may not correspond very well with the design and organization that might reflect an "expert" understanding of the subject. Some readers may not want or need very much control over the text if they are the sorts we have called "browsers" or "users" (and all readers are in this mode sometimes). A high degree of customizability and interactivity may actually *interfere* with their purposes. Here again the forms that designers think are most useful may not conform to those most beneficial or meaningful to readers. Clearly, this dispute raises larger pedagogical concerns:

> The organizational structure of hypertext may reflect the organizational structure of the subject matter or the semantic network of an expert. . . . If we assume that learning is the process of replicating the expert's knowledge structure in the learner's knowledge structure, then learning should be facilitated by a hypertext that replicates the expert's knowledge.[44]

It is not within the scope of this project to adjudicate this debate; and as some have pointed out, certain authors seem to advocate both of these views simultaneously.[45] As readers already will have seen, each of these approaches is subject to some dangerous abuses. But we do mean to point out the fundamental tension between them, and the fact that they manifest crucially different conceptions of learning. Once one is committed to a "passive" system in hypertext, this choice reflects a bias toward particular learning possibilities inherent to the type of system being developed.

The theme underlying this discussion is that what we are calling an active, dialogical hypertext has a multifaceted relation to learning: (1) Hypertext can facilitate learning, by allowing the reader to make novel connections that stimulate his or her thinking. (2) Hypertext can be an external representation of learning, by allowing the reader to build into the hypertext a record of the connections he or she is making. (3) Hypertext can be a prompt to metacognition and new learning, as these very modifications and additions to the hypertext system, by representing back to the reader connections he or she has made, help the reader reflect upon and modify them further.

Unfortunately, this desire to structure a hypertext in an open, dialogical fashion encounters a difficulty when we look at concrete problems of the learner, and of the different types of readers who might encounter a hypertext. As noted, a form of organization that only allows a novice reader to search through direct and explicit connections may not facilitate the development of that novice into an independent and autonomous reader who can alter and add to what he or she finds in a hypertext. Conversely, a flexible hypertext system might be too open-ended to be of much use to a novice or to a user who is simply interested in extracting specific and already-organized information from the textual source. Such choices between *flexibility* and *accessibility* reflect implicit decisions about learning styles and about the audiences to whom hypertextual materials will be practically useful. These are educational decisions, but also social and moral ones, because they implicitly engage assumptions about access and equity that tend to be self-confirming. Developing a text with certain readers in mind tends to make it inaccessible or inhospitable or uninteresting to others.

For example, a major concern in the literature on hypertext is with the experience of novice readers getting "lost in hyperspace," following a meandering path of associations into the hypertext field, then finding that like Hansel and Gretel they cannot retrace their steps back. In some cases, the sheer volume of information, and the number and flexibility of pathways that are available simply become overwhelming. A substantial body of research suggests that this experience becomes a major source of confusion and frustration, often discouraging new readers from experimenting further with the system.[46] While, as noted, there are features that can be added to a hypertext system that limit choices and provide an exact record of the trail a reader has traced to arrive at a given node, this aid in itself does not always help readers to understand where they are, or where to go next. As a result, many readers of hypertext end up performing the textual equivalent of "channel surfing": quickly scanning or surveying randomly accessed information, in very short snippets, with no overall sense of coherence or meaning for what they are exposed to.

The educational implications of this issue are profound. Beyond allowing students to proceed through the document by taking prescribed routes, in a specific sequence, at a deliberate pace, hypertext can permit students to focus their investigations on questions informed by their own particular interests and experiences. They proceed through and organize materials in ways that make sense to them, developing their own heuristics. This flexibility has many advantages, not the least of which is a capacity to accommodate different personal or cultural learning styles. But in order to reach this stage, learners need to have experience with explicit tutorials, guides, indexes, and so on, which provide them with models or heuristics that they can learn from and adapt, without becoming dependent upon them. The question is, can a hypertext serve the needs of browsers, users, and hyperreaders at the same time, and can a hypertext designed for browsers and users also have the capability to help them learn to become more autonomous hyperreaders?

In a sense, this dilemma is an updated version of "Meno's paradox." Originally, Plato asked how learners can ever learn anything truly new, since if it is entirely unrelated to what they already know, it will not make sense to them. But if it is closely linked with what they already understand, or can deduce, then in some sense they already "know" it, and are merely recognizing *it. The hypertext version of this paradox is: How do you look for something if you don't already know what it is or where it is? A novice encountering a complex hypertext system for the first time cannot possibly know what information the system contains, without happening to come across it through searching or guesswork. But if there are explicit guides built into the system that direct the novice to particular information points, then the danger is that the novice may become dependent upon this particular system of organization, and not become capable of developing his or her own—may not ever become a hyperreader.*

The dangers of hypertext are not only that they might be too rigidly structured and directive. Others fear that hypertexts may be too *unstructured* to accommodate the needs of learners:

> It's a way of presenting documents on the screen without imposing a linear start-to-finish order. Disembodied paragraphs are linked by

theme; after reading one about the First World War, for example, you might be able to choose another about the technology of battleships, or the life of Woodrow Wilson, or hemlines in the '20s. This is another cute idea that is good in minor ways and terrible in major ones. Teaching children to understand the orderly unfolding of a plot or a logical argument is a crucial part of education. Authors don't merely agglomerate paragraphs; they work hard to make the narrative read a certain way, prove a particular point. To turn a book or document into hypertext is to invite readers to ignore exactly what counts—the story.[47]

This argument is right in showing that learning certain conventions of linear narrative and argumentation should represent an important *phase* of students' learning. But these are not the only useful means of interpreting and organizing information, and for many purposes they can be counterproductive.

Hypertexts are educationally valuable because they highlight possibilities that are inherent to the processes of reading and thinking: allowing the reader to construct a unique, personally meaningful, and useful interpretation of textual materials; and to recognize the susceptibility of information to more than only one form of organization. Yet readers also need to learn that not just *any* organization will do; that there are certain conventions and heuristics that do promote meaningful and useful interpretations. Associating the causes of war with the movements of hemlines may appear frivolous, and it may prove to be just a random collocation; but it might also lead to a novel and revealing understanding of the links between, say, militarism and changing gender roles. It is in learning to tell the difference between heuristics or associations that help to support meaningful and useful interpretations, and those that do not, that the real work of education needs to proceed. Hypertexts with a degree of structure built in, but also the option of customized design, may serve as effective bridges or scaffolds to bring readers to the point where they can create more personal and distinctive organizations of the textual material available. The dilemma is that the design imperatives of providing highly structured and scaffolding heuristics, and of allowing exploration in the pursuit of *new* heuristics, do not always coexist easily. The two educational aims are not intrinsically incompatible, but they imply very different ways of constructing hypertext, and they imply very different degrees of sensitivity to the needs, interests, and readerly approaches of diverse prospective audiences.

Hypertexts have the potential to be used for different purposes than their designers could ever imagine. This is important not only because it allows hypertexts to be read "against the grain," but because allowing texts to be read in multiple ways is one way to involve readers who might otherwise never have or desire access to those texts. The choice between structure and freedom in hypertext authoring and design is not necessarily an either/or matter. Hypertexts can incorporate capabilities for both prestructured and personally structured readings (they are more able to do this because they can include different parallel versions of a text and can allow multiple branching options between them). But doing so effectively and fairly will require thinking of their design not only in terms of organizations of information that represent "expert" knowledge, but also in terms of an access and equity orientation. Hypertext authoring and design must remain sensitive to questions of learning, diversity, and the nonneutral relationship between systems of organizing knowledge and the patterns of involvement or exclusion they promote for varied audiences.

The multimedia and multilayered dimensions of hypertext increase these possibilities, and these dangers, even further. Hypertexts link various texts together, but what counts as a "text" can include graphics, sound, video, and other multimedia sources as well. This complicates the kinds of literacy involved: reading an image, for example, is not the same thing as reading a paragraph; it involves quite different skills; and it may be more effective in communicating ideas or feelings for some readers than for others.[48] It is not just the potential of having multimedia materials to work with educationally (there is nothing especially new about that); it is the ease with which multiple sources can be made available simultaneously, and linked together in ways that contrast, juxtapose, or suggest connections between different kinds of information and different ways of displaying information. For example, some media may strike the reader as more immediate, more "authentic," and in that sense more "real" or more likely to be "true." There may be a tendency to rank different media in terms of their capacity for verisimilitude. When do these expectations need to be challenged, partly by contrasting different versions of the same event or experience, and partly by drawing attention to the ways in which any medium can distort or change the information it represents, or exclude information that other media make more apparent?

There is a great deal of work being done now in graphical forms of representing information (not only charts, but models, simulations, and exploratory virtual environments). What are the new practices and aims of teaching that are possible when learners can hear the speech (as well as read it), watch the flower opening, trace the route on a map, replay the stages of development of the chick within an egg, and so on? What are the new problems raised by hypertexts that link visual, verbal, and other media together in a cross-linked fashion, or include parallel representations of the same information in different forms and media? How do students learn how to move back and forth between these media to extract a more multifaceted representation of things? On the one hand, having multiple media available can accommodate more diverse learning styles; on the other, it makes learning environments much more complex and multidimensional. Does this alleviate access issues, or exacerbate them? Or does it alleviate them for some individuals and groups, but exacerbate them for others?

EDUCATIONAL DILEMMAS

One might dream of making hypertext systems accessible to everyone; but their complexity suggests that this will be difficult. If all things are related to all things, and all relations are of equal value and importance, then even the knowledgeable reader (let alone a novice) can become lost in an undifferentiated morass of information. One might dream of all hypertexts being completely interactive and dialogical, but this runs up against the realistic limits of knowledge, ability, and time in most prospective readers.

The dilemma here seems to be that as an organizing principle and as a potential educational, informational resource, hypertext either can provide too much information, and too loose a structure; or provide too selective a body of information, and too rigid a structure, rife with implicit judgments and potential bias. What makes hypertexts convenient and useful for some, makes them inflexible and restrictive for others. Most readers, especially beginning readers, need heuristics, and in order to make some choices they need to have restricted options about others. But any set of heuristics will privilege particular structures of knowledge, and this exacerbates the stakes involved in deciding who will be creating these heuristics for readers, and who those readers are. Heuristics that select and organize information, define the criteria for relevance and relative importance of information, and hard-wire the most significant associative links into the system. It is essential that educators with an understanding of how different students learn play a role in the design of such materials—for they will be developed (and marketed) with or without such input. Yet it will take a significant change in self-perception for teachers to come to see themselves as designers of information systems—even though, in a sense, this is what they always were. Just as all writing can be seen as a process of hypertextual design (whether the product looks like a hypertext or not), so is teaching a process of representing a set of relationships between information partly to communicate a given set of connections, and partly to facilitate students' learning to make new connections on their own.

The poststructural, decentered state is one in which every element in a hypertext can have equal significance. There is something liberating about this, and something dangerous. Do we truly want a knowledge environment in which individuals can construct entirely personal and idiosyncratic ways of organizing information, without regard to the ways in which communities of culture and tradition have tended to connect and prioritize things in certain ways rather than others? Does the leveling of all information nodes and the decentering of all organizing principles lead to more freedom or less?

On the other hand, does creating explicit hierarchies and organizations of knowledge within a hypertext create the potential for abuse? Hypertexts that are "hard wired," in which certain organizing structures cannot be overridden, or in which there are limits placed on the number and type of associated links the reader can construct, or in which some information sources are restricted, instantiate a kind of hegemony: You cannot ask that question. That information is not available to you. You have to define things this way to make any progress. You cannot get there from here, and so on. Such statements would rarely be explicit in hypertexts; but they would inevitably exist in the choices underlying any particular hypertext.

We have sketched out a number of interrelated (linked) educational dilemmas here. First, if we are to take full advantage of their potential, hypertexts ought to be rich, complex, open, and flexible; yet this may have the effect of limiting their usefulness for all but the most skillful and knowledgeable users. Providing access to the greatest number of readers and involving them in this technology will require making access to hypertexts simple, intuitive, and affordable. Yet this ease of use comes at the cost of comprehensiveness, and entails that a good deal of implicit structure and selectiveness be built in.

Second, hypertexts need to be developed with the needs of very different readers in mind, which we have called browsers, users, and hyperreaders. Any reader acts in one or another of these ways at different times. But the demands of each on a hypertext are quite different; and forms of organization that might be included to help, guide, or engage the interest of some of these, will be useless, misleading, or boring to others.

Third, and similarly, there are the different relations of various readers to the knowledge base that a hypertext might be dealing with. Should the hypertext organize information in a way that makes sense to the author? reflects expert understandings of the material? anticipates the likely readers' understandings, and builds from there? follows some theoretically derived developmental model or pattern? allows a high degree of customized, reader-developed structure (hyperreading)? Hypertexts that rely on content, categories, patterns of links, and explicit navigational guides that serve some of these purposes, cannot serve others as well.

Fourth, there is the issue of different learning styles, ways of reading, and the suitability of different media and content for different cultural, ethnic, or gender groups. As discussed earlier, the capabilities of multimedia and the potential to link alternative forms of representation into one hypertext make it possible for them to accommodate a much broader and more diverse range of readers. But it also makes such hypertexts much more complex and (where this might be a factor) much more expensive and difficult to keep updated. How likely is it that the capability to provide different versions, through different media, will be taken advantage of fully?

Moreover, developing potentials within the technology is fruitless if learners do not have the capacities and opportunities to exploit them fruitfully. The most important of these changes will be a shift away from a consumer approach to reading to a more critical approach to reading, and a shift in one's view of gaining knowledge, away from the passive reception of facts, and toward the active construction of understanding through searching, selecting, and problem solving.

In this regard, designers of hypertext for educational purposes might learn a great deal from the designers of certain computer games, especially those that involve mazes, puzzles, and problem solving in contexts of limited information (for example, the game Myst™). Anyone who has become engrossed in such games knows the challenges presented in finding one's way around an information environment in which some pathways are laid out and others need to be searched; in which the relevance and value of new information may not be immediately apparent; in which alternatives need to be explored through trial and error; in which there might not be one correct solution or goal but several. These sorts of hypertextual game environments, we are suggesting, demonstrate the tremendous appeal that the processes of exploration, discovery, and connection-making can have for learners—if educators can be creative and clever enough to use them for educationally substantial purposes.

In summary, it will be crucial to consider in these educational processes how different readers encounter and respond to different kinds of structured information environments, what kinds of distinct barriers and frustrations they experience, and what kinds of interactions might benefit their learning. There is no reason to expect that any particular form of hypertext will be suitable for all; or that the technological learning environment generally will be equally familiar and approachable to everyone. There is evidence already that the use of these new technologies for learning merely privileges further the groups who can exploit it fully, leaving others who for whatever reason do not or cannot feel as comfortable with the technology even further behind.

One might wish that we could make everyone knowledgeable and skillful enough with hypertext to be hyperreaders in the fullest sense, but this is no more practical than expecting all hypertexts to be completely open and dialogical. Most readers of hypertext will be what we have called "browsers" or "users," not hyperreaders. But there is an intermediate category, *critical users*: readers who will know enough to use the system to find what they are looking for, but will also know enough to realize that what they have found might not be all that there is to know. They can approach the hypertext as an important resource, but maintain some skepticism about its reliability. Critical users will need to understand that what someone else has selected, interpreted, and organized for them may offer a partial and distorted picture of things. Readers at this level might not have the skills to diagnose and find what is missing, or to reinvent fully their own alternative version, but at least they will have a skeptical eye toward what they have found, and remain open to the possibility that there may be more. Eventually some of these critical users may develop the knowledge and initiative to become hyperreaders—people who can actually move around within the hypertext and set up shop for themselves, creating new knowledge, constructing personalized systems, and so on. We might wish that all readers will learn to do this, but this is not likely, we fear. The level of "critical user" may define the level of sophistication that we can expect most readers to achieve in their interactions with hypertext. Yet this is itself a significant educational objective, requiring teachers to develop new skills and understandings themselves, and to be willing to open up certain "authoritative" sources, such as encyclopedias, for critical scrutiny.

At the opposite pole from the critical user is the "surfer," the browser who jumps from information node to node, or from experience to experience, without regard to creating meaningful connections between them. There is some reason to worry that this phenomenological orientation is becoming more widespread in society—not only in computer contexts, but also in switching relentlessly between cable television channels, between samples of music, through pages of magazines, across snatches of conversation. The sheer volume and variety of information can end up limiting attention spans and fostering a lack of reflectiveness about the choices actually made.

One might envision situations in which the technology itself can help students to become more critical users. Hypertext can be used as a tool to teach students multiple strategies for problem solving and information acquisition. In this process there will be an important role for teacher guidance and modeling: students, for example, might follow a teacher through the hypertext, observing and learning how someone with experience searches, collects, and links information.[49] In progressive classrooms, hypertext will allow teachers and students to focus more on the important learning processes of interpreting and organizing information, and less on the trivial acquisition of facts. Teachers could be involved more with scaffolding—engaging learners at early stages with explicit explanation and guidance, leading them through hypertexts, and then gradually removing these supports as the learners become more independent and comfortable with exploring on their own. While we do not favor visions of the future without teachers and classrooms, there is no doubt that some of this instruction (introductory guided tours through a hypertext, for example) can and should become integral parts of the design of hypertexts themselves. There is also little doubt that some students are already able to access as much or even more hypertextual information through computer links in their own homes as can be found in their schools, while others have no such access. As we noted in an earlier chapter, the dangers this raises for a significant new form of educational inequality, one as serious and limiting for learners as illiteracy of other types, should be a pressing concern for any educator interested in opportunity and fairness. The skills and attitudes of being an effective critical user or hyperreader should not become the special domain of certain groups and not others. Part of the very capacity of reading hypertexts critically, diagnosing their distortions, biases, and gaps, will require that they be studied by readers who see the world differently from those who designed the hypertexts. In the next chapter we will explore in more detail what it means for readers to become more critical users and hyperreaders.

We stand at a crossroads where the very technology that offers the means to broaden access to liberating knowledge is just as likely to promote a hegemonic concentration, in the hands of the few, of the "means of production" for shaping and organizing information. Hypertext makes possible some radically new educational possibilities. If educators want to play a role in shaping these possibilities, and to influence them along progressive lines, they will need to develop new skills in information design and interpretation. They will need to take the lead in helping others to develop these skills. And they will need to initiate serious reflections upon the social, moral, and epistemological consequences of technology's influences on teaching and learning. We hope that this chapter has helped to spark such reflections.

NOTES

1. See Jay David Bolter, *Writing Space: The Computer, Hypertext, and the History of Writing* (Hillsdale, NJ: Erlbaum, 1991).

2. An excellent overview of hypertext and its characteristics can be found in Ilana Snyder, *Hypertext: The Electronic Labyrinth* (Victoria: Melbourne University Press, 1996).

3. Like many authors, we will use the term "hypertext" inclusively, referring as well to so-called "hypermedia" environments. Hypermedia refers to a hypertext system that links various media (pictures, sound, etc.) as well as written text per se. While the issue of multiple media as sources of information introduces a variety of important issues, especially for questions of learning and alternative learning styles, all of these media can be considered "texts" in a broad sense of the term, and when organized *as hypertexts*, they encounter many of the same basic issues as purely written hypertexts.

4. The plain text and italicized text in the manuscript do not correspond directly to the two authors' contributions.

5. Several good introductory books on this subject also adopt elements of a hypertext model in the way they present information. For example, see Jay David Bolter, *Writing Space: The Computer, Hypertext, and the History of Writing* (Hillsdale, NJ: Erlbaum, 1991), which is available in both printed and computer disk versions; Robert E. Horn, *Mapping Hypertext* (Lexington, MA: Lexington Institute, 1989); and David H. Jonassen, *Hypertext/Hypermedia* (Englewood Cliffs, NJ: Educational Technology, 1989). Other helpful introductory material is available from George P. Landow, *Hypertext: The Convergence of Contemporary Critical Theory and Technology* (Baltimore: Johns Hopkins University, 1992); a special issue of *Educational Technology*, Vol. 28 No. 11 (1988), edited by Gary Marchionini; Jakob Nielsen, *Hypertext and Hypermedia* (New York: Academic Press, 1990); Ben Shneiderman and Greg Kearsley, *Hypertext Hands-on!* (New York: Addison-Wesley, 1989); and McKnight, Dillon, and Richardson, *Hypertext in Context*.

6. For a discussion of several of these analogies, see J. Conklin, "Hypertext: An introduction and survey," *IEEE Computer*, Vol. 20 No. 9 (1987), pp. 17–41; Robert E. Horn, *Mapping Hypertext* (Lexington, MA: Lexington Institute, 1989); and Cliff McKnight, Andrew Dillon, and John Richardson, *Hypertext in Context* (Cambridge: Cambridge University Press, 1991).

7. J.C. Nyiri, "The concept of knowledge in the context of electronic network," *The Monist*, Vol. 80 No. 3 (1997): 405–422.

8. Michel Foucault, "What is an author?" in Josue Harari, ed., *Textual Strategies: Perspectives in Post-structuralist Criticism* (Ithaca, NY: Cornell University Press, 1979), pp. 141–160. This shift in perspective may also have significant implications for changing views of copyright and intellectual ownership. See Nicholas C. Burbules and Bertram C. Bruce, "This is not a paper."

9. Julio Cortazar, *Hopscotch* (New York: Avon Books, 1966). Another, more recent book, with a strongly "hypertextual" look and feel is Avital Ronell, *The Telephone Book* (Lincoln, NE: University of Nebraska Press, 1989).

10. With hypermedia, "text" here may include not only words on pages, but pictures, music, images, etc.

11. Milorad Pavic, *Dictionary of the Khazars* (New York: Alfred Knopf, 1989).

12. See also Michael Joyce's experimental hypertext novel, *Afternoon*: www.jefferson.village.virginia.edu/elab/hfl0179.html.

13. See Jacques Derrida, *Glas* (Lincoln: University of Nebraska Press, 1986), in which Derrida publishes two essays, on apparently unrelated topics, side by side.

14. Gilles Deleuze and Félix Guattari, "Rhizome," in *On the Line* (New York: Semiotext(e): 1983), pp. 1–65. Thanks to Zelia Gregoriou for this reference.

15. Deleuze and Guattari, "Rhizome," pp. 11, 47–49.

16. In fact, the origin of the Internet as a military-funded communications and computer network was precisely to exist rhizomatically, so that if any portion of the network was destroyed, the rest could continue to operate. There is no "center" of the web.

17. Ibid., pp. 11–25.

18. Delaney and Landow, "Hypertext, hypermedia, and literary studies," p. 10.

19. C. Carr, "Hypertext: A new training tool?" *Educational Technology,* Vol. 28 No. 8 (1988), 7–11. Delaney and Landow, eds., *Hypermedia and Literary Studies* (Cambridge, MA: MIT Press, 1991).

20. Vannevar Bush, "As we may think," *Atlantic Monthly*, Vol. 176 No. 1 (1945), pp. 101–108.

21. See Thomas M. Duffy and David H. Jonassen, eds., *Constructivism and the Technology of Instruction* (Hillsdale, NJ: Lawrence Erlbaum, 1992). See also David Jonassen's helpful discussion of hypertext and schema theory, in *Hypertext/ Hypermedia*, p. 23; David Chen, "An epistemic analysis of the interaction between knowledge, education, and technology," in Barrett, *Sociomedia: Multimedia, Hypermedia, and the Social Construction of Knowledge*, pp. 161–173; M.C. Linn, "Hypermedia as a personalized tool for knowledge organization," presented at the American Educational Research Association meetings (April 1991), in Chicago, Illinois; Rand J. Spiro, Richard L. Coulson, Paul Feltovich, and Daniel K. Anderson, "Cognitive flexibility theory: Advanced knowledge acquisition in ill-structured domains," in *Tenth Annual Conference of the Cognitive Science Society* (Hillsdale, NJ: Erlbaum, 1988), pp. 375–384; Rand J. Spiro and J. Jehng, "Cognitive flexibility and hypertext: Theory and technology for the linear and multidimensional traversal of complex subject matter," in Spiro, R.J. & Nix, D., eds., *Cognition, Education, and Multimedia: Exploring Ideas in High Technology* (Hillsdale, NJ: Erlbaum, 1990), pp. 164–205; and Rand J. Spiro, Paul Feltovich, Michael J. Jacobson, and Richard L. Coulson, "Cognitive flexibility, constructivism, and hypertext," *Educational Technology* (May 1991), pp. 24–33.

22. Slatin, "Reading hypertext," p. 873.

23. On "bricolage," see Claude Lévi-Strauss, *The Savage Mind* (Chicago: University of Chicago Press, 1966), pp. 16–37. The best single source on the relationship of hypertext to poststructural theory is Landow, *Hypertext*; see also Delaney and Landow, "Hypertext, hypermedia, and literary studies." Additional discussions of the affiliation between hypertext and postmodernism are Norman N.

Holland, "Eliza meets the postmodern," *EJournal*, Vol. 4 No. 1 (1994); and Bolter, *Writing Space*; see also a discussion of Bolter's book in *EJournal* by Joe Amato and Doug Brent: *EJournal*, Vol. 1 No. 2 (1991) and Vol. 1 No. 2–1 (1991). Finally, see Michael Peters and Colin Lankshear, "Critical literacy and digital texts," *Educational Theory* Vol. 46 No. 1 (1996): 51–70.

24. Delaney and Landow, "Hypertext, hypermedia, and literary studies," p. 18.

25. For a discussion of this problem and its consequences, see Bernard Williams, "The Riddle of Umberto Eco," *New York Review of Books*, February 2, 1995, pp. 33–35.

26. Slatin, "Reading hypertext."

27. Umberto Eco, *A Theory of Semiotics* (Bloomington, IN: Indiana University Press, 1976), pp. 69 ff.

28. Stanley Fish, *Is There a Text in This Class? The Authority of Interpretive Communities* (Cambridge, MA: Harvard University Press, 1980, pp. 322–327.

29. Jay David Bolter, "Topographic writing: Hypertext and electronic writing," in Delaney and Landow, eds., *Hypermedia and Literary Studies* (Cambridge, MA: MIT Press, 1991), pp. 105–118; see also Bolter, *Writing Space*; Cliff McKnight, John Richardson, and Andrew Dillon, "The authoring of hypertext documents," in Ray McAleese, ed., *Hypertext: Theory into Practice* (Norwood, NJ: Ablex, 1989), pp. 138–147.

30. Shneiderman and Kearsley, *Hypertext Hands-on!*, quoted in Henrietta Shirk, "Cognitive architecture in hypermedia instruction," in Barrett, ed., *Sociomedia: Multimedia, Hypermedia, and the Social Construction of Knowledge*, p. 81.

31. Roland Barthes, *S/Z: An Essay* (New York: Hill and Wang, 1974). For another discussion of this example, see George P. Landow, *Hypertext: The Convergence of Contemporary Critical Theory and Technology* (Baltimore: Johns Hopkins University, 1992).

32. David Lodge, *Small World* (NY: Warner Books, 1984).

33. Jorge Luis Borges, "Kafka and His Precursors," in *Labyrinths* (NY: New Direction, 1964), p. 201. Thanks to Punya Mishra for suggesting this reference.

34. As a result, more and more researchers rely on electronic forms of publishing research results and data. For a discussion of issues in electronic publishing, see Nicholas C. Burbules and Bertram C. Bruce, "This is not a paper," *Educational Researcher*, Vol. 24 No. 8 (1995), pp. 12–18; and Nicholas C. Burbules, "Digital texts and the future of scholarly writing and publication," *Journal of Curriculum Studies*, Vol. 30 No. 1 (1997): 105–124.

35. Delaney and Landow, *Hypermedia and Literary Studies*; Slatin, "Reading hypertext"; and T. Byles, "A context for hypertext: Some suggested elements of style." *Wilson Library Journal*, Vol. 63 No. 3 (1988), 60–62.

36. Nicholas C. Burbules, "Aporias, webs, and passages: Doubt as an opportunity to learn." *Curriculum Inquiry* (forthcoming).

37. Delaney and Landow, *Hypermedia and Literary Studies*, p. 19.

38. David Jonassen, "Designing structured hypertext and structuring access to hypertext." *Educational Technology*, Vol. 28 No. 11 (1988): 13–16.

39. See Slatin, "Reading hypertext," p. 875; and Ray McAleese, "Navigation and browsing in hypertext," in Ray McAleese, ed., *Hypertext: Theory into Practice* (Norwood, NJ: Ablex, 1989), pp. 6–44. See also Punyashloke Mishra and Kim Nguyen, "Readers reading hypertext fiction: An open-ended inquiry into the process of meaning making," unpublished manuscript, University of Illinois (May 1995).

40. Slatin, "Reading hypertext," p. 875.

41. James Levin of the University of Illinois, Urbana/Champaign, has developed an "interactive paper" format that facilitates this sort of reader-writer interaction: www.lrsdb.ed.uiuc.edu:591/ipp/.

42. See also Horn, *Mapping Hypertext*, pp. 11, 26–27.

43. Ted Nelson was probably the first to advocate this; see Jonassen, *Hypertext/Hypermedia*, p. 22. See also Nielsen, *Hypertext and Hypermedia*, p 13.

44. Jonassen, *Hypertext/Hypermedia*, quoted in Shirk, "Cognitive architecture in hypermedia instruction," pp. 82, 85–86.

45. Shirk, "Cognitive architecture in hypermedia instruction," p. 86.

46. See Deborah Edwards and Lynda Hardman, "'Lost in hyperspace': Cognitive mapping and navigation in a hypertext environment," in Ray McAleese, ed., *Hypertext: Theory into Practice*, pp. 105–125; N. Hammond and L. Allinson, "Extending hypertext for learning: An investigation of access and guidance tools," in A. Sutcliffe and L. Macaulay, eds., *People and Computers V* (Cambridge: Cambridge University Press, 1989); and P. Brown, "Do we need maps to navigate around hypertext?" *Electronic Publishing*, Vol. 2 No. 2 (1989): 91–100. See also Horn, *Mapping Hypertext*, pp. 50–59, 150–159; Jonassen, *Hypertext/Hypermedia*, pp. 41–45; and Nielsen, *Hypertext and Hypermedia*, pp. 127, 143–162.

47. David Gelernter, "Unplugged," *The New Republic* (September 19 & 26, 1994), pp. 14–15.

48. Douglas Kellner, "Multiple literacies and critical pedagogy in a multicultural society," *Educational Theory*, Vol. 48 No. 1 (1998): 103–122.

49. Of course, we write this with a full sense of irony that in most classes today it is the students who must explain and demonstrate things to the teacher. How much longer will it be before understanding and experience with information technologies is regarded as an essential part of teacher education?

✑ chapter four ✑

CRITICALLY READING
THE INTERNET

The Internet is growing exponentially. The World Wide Web, e-mail use, the number of, and rate of participation in, listservs, news groups, and other forums for interaction and discussion, continue to draw in more, and more varied, people from around the world. This is, after all, what the Internet promises itself to be: the common medium, open to all, with no barriers to the free flow of ideas and information around the world.

Yet, in a style of analysis and critique that we hope is becoming familiar to you by now, we want to point out that the very success of the Internet in these terms creates new problems even as it opens up important and worthwhile opportunities. The Internet is still far from inclusive, especially viewed from a global perspective. But to the extent that it is becoming more inclusive, to the extent that it does foster unrestricted self-expression, this also creates an opportunity and a problem: the opportunity of having information from millions of sources and points of view, and the problem of having information from millions of sources and points of view. Participants in this environment often need to read and evaluate so much material, from so many sources, that it becomes impossible to maintain a critical and discerning attitude toward it all. Where there is more substance, there is more garbage and chaos. The very volume and number of voices has a kind of leveling effect—everything seems to come from the same place and nothing seems, prima facie, much more reliable than anything else. This makes the need to evaluate the value and credibility of what one encounters on the Internet a crucial skill if one is to be an active beneficiary of the available information and interaction.

In the previous chapter, we distinguished two kinds of critical readers of the Internet: we called them critical users and hyperreaders. As noted, these are not two discrete groups, but two (overlapping) patterns of interacting with new information and communication technologies, into which many of us fit at various times. Moreover, it is probably impossible (and even undesirable) to be a thoroughgoingly critical reader all the time. Knowing when a situation calls for critical analysis is itself one of the skills of doing it well. In this chapter, we want to give more detail about the characteristics of these two kinds of readers, discuss their relation to one another, and explore why criticality is such an important educational goal in this context.

Given the volume and variety of online information, and information sources, a critical reader must be able to make rapid assessments of credibility over and over again. Each new participant to an online discussion, each new Web page, each new e-mail message, gives rise to another potential situation in which something false, dangerous, offensive, or worthless may come across one's screen. As we will explore, some of the skills of critical reading require broad rules of thumb or heuristics, often applied unconsciously, that tell a reader very quickly what sort of material they are dealing with. Certainly these rules of thumb are imperfect, and they always run the risk of leading a reader astray. They may let in too much or exclude too much. But given the volume of material one is frequently dealing with, the necessity of making at least an initial judgment, quickly, even if imperfectly, becomes a sort of Digital Triage.

THE CRITICAL USER

The first sort of critical reader we called a critical user—a "user" because this is a person guided by a fairly specific goal in coming online: a specific question to be answered, a problem to be solved, a piece of information needed for some particular purpose. Hence for the critical user the main imperative is learning how to judge the credibility of online information.

An indication of how important this issue is can be judged by the number of sites on the World Wide Web devoted to "Evaluating Information."[1] Many of these pages look very similar, they contain a good deal of overlapping information, and they tend to refer to one another. This is one of the ways in which the Web is a self-assessing medium. Much of this advice is solid and sensible, and it parallels some of the things we will talk about in this chapter. But there are questions these pages do not address, which we will also discuss. In short, questions of credibility can be asked about these pages themselves: Who developed them, and why? How do we evaluate the credibility of these credibility pages? Where do their criteria come from, and what makes them useful for the different kinds of evaluative judgments readers need to make in the online environment? We hope to shed some light on these questions here (although we expect you to question our credibility also).

Judging Credibility

Judging credibility is not unique to the Internet. Every time one reads a newspaper, asks a teacher a question, or looks up information in an encyclopedia, assumptions are being made about the value and reliability of the information one expects to find there. In many cases this judgment is based on indirect inferences about the source's reputation, reliability, and trustworthiness. Sometimes it is based on a track record of previous experiences with that information source, which has proven dependable in the past. Sometimes it is based on recommendations by other persons of that resource (in which case the credibility judgment is pushed back a level, in judging those persons to be reliable). All of these familiar elements occur in online environments, although sometimes in different forms.

There is a good deal of information that is contained within an e-mail message, a comment to a news group, a Web page, and so on that can tell the reader something about its origins. The address or URL sometimes gives a person's name and institutional affiliation. The ".com" or ".edu" at the end tells something about the source, which in particular contexts might be judged a qualification, based on relevant expertise, or a disqualification, based on bias or institutional self-interest (note that the very same features can often be viewed either way!). Within some online communities, the service provider through which a participant is accessing the Internet is seen as a mark of credibility; users of some of the more popular and widely accessible providers (AOL or WebTV, for example) are seen as "not serious" by other participants. Here is one way in which mechanisms that might increase access are in tension with the aim of achieving credibility as a discussant or information provider (within certain circles, at least). There are many other such "proxies" of credibility that people adopt, whether consciously or not, as indicators that the source of new information is reliable. Some online participants provide a signature file that is attached to all their messages, or a fairly informative home page that tells others who they are, where they work or go to school, and so on.

Yet here we encounter yet another tension or dilemma: in order for this information to be useful as a mark of credibility, the reader has to assume that it is true. One of the chief features of the online environment is that normally we encounter only what a person wants us to know about him or her. Thus there are many opportunities to adopt a partly or entirely fictional "avatar" or online persona. Sometimes this is playful or ironic, sometimes it is fraudulent, and sometimes it is actively malicious (as with online predators). As we will discuss in the chapter on privacy, there are in fact many online resources for learning more about people, whether they want you to or not. But in the ordinary course of events, there is neither the time nor the necessity to check up on the self-identified persona of each and every person with whom one has contact online.

In general, one might make it a rule of thumb that the greater the degree of openness an information source provides about its origins (who produced the material, when, and why, for example), the more credible it probably is. But the very same information that is a mark of credibility, because it can be fabricated, is also a potential mark of deception; skilled fabricators of phony Web pages, for example, work hard to make the content look as good, as well-designed, and as informative as possible. Without reference to information outside the context of that Web page or Web site, a reasonably reliable judgment about its value would be impossible.

What we have called these "internal" measures of credibility largely pertain to evidence regarding the source of the information, and depend on judgments about that person or institution's qualifications, objectivity, or reliability. These are fairly familiar standards of judgment that can be applied in a variety of contexts. But in the context of the Internet, given its hypertextual and networked structure, other, more "external" or relational criteria of credibility also can come into play. In ordinary texts, references and footnotes are often measures of credibility; they show that the author has read other relevant work, and that the author is seeking to substantiate what is written by associating it with other established sources. There are many ways in which a source on the Internet is implicitly or explicitly "linked" to other sources—but some of the most apparent ways arise in the context of the World Wide Web, and so we will use that example here. Almost every page on the Web links to, and is linked from, one or more other pages. How a reader comes across a page is often a significant factor in how it is apprehended: If it is linked from a page that the reader already believes is reliable, there is a "transfer" of credibility from the first to the second. Conversely, if the page under consideration links to other sources that seem comprehensive and relevant, the page gains credibility from those associations as well, and would lose credibility by lacking them. The Web (and other features of the Internet) are in this sense a system of distributed credibility, each part gaining meaning, reliability, and relevance by how it is associated with other parts. Again, this is not unique to the Internet, but in this context, especially the Web, this set of relations is directly instantiated in the hyperlinked form.

Although each Internet node is one and only one point within the larger rhizomatic net, the pragmatics of use over time pass more traffic through particular points, making more links to and from specific sites. This pattern creates foci of importance and credibility because of the number of lines that converge upon these points.[2] Hence, despite the structural decentralization of the Internet, the pragmatics of use create relatively "core" and relatively "peripheral" points within it. It is easier to find certain sites, for example, because they are linked to by many other pages. From the standpoint of credibility, this network of links tends to "support" the credibility of the sources linked to, and of the sources linked from.

A related aspect, again apparent in the Web, is the presence of "counters" that show how many visitors a page has received over a particular period of time. As is true in other contexts, popular appeal and acceptance are hardly perfect measures of credibility. (In some contexts it could be argued that there might be an inverse relation between them.) But such counters, assuming that they are giving an accurate count, provide some information that can be relevant to a judgment of credibility. These ways of assessing what we have called distributed credibility necessarily situate the judgment of each reader in a set of tacit relations with other judges, where the credibility of any part involves judgments about a network of associations. For example, a Web search engine recently developed by Jon Kleinberg of Cornell University searches pages not only by content, but also by the number of links to and from them. In another example, the growth of Web "rings" demonstrates an explicit form of interlinked credibility. By including new sites into a set of mutually referencing and cross-linked sites only when they meet a set of common standards, the quality and accessibility of each site is dependent to some extent on all the others. Conversely, the more that a Web ring includes high quality information as a whole, the more each element within it benefits. Again, this is not without precedent in other contexts as well, but in the context of the Web this structure is made explicit.

Let us summarize, then, some of the capabilities that would define such critical users. In part they derive from traditional sources on "critical literacy" (regarding texts of any type).[3] But they also involve elements that are distinctive to the digital environment. Furthermore, even where the traditional criteria may still hold, the *way* in which they apply to digital sources may be quite different.[4]

First of all, and most generally, a pervasive skepticism toward everything found on the Internet is not a bad starting point.

Critical users will also need to have multiple strategies for finding information on the Internet; not just by using search engines or other technical
means that select items for them, but by developing ways of looking for
what else might be there. Critical users will need to find pages that archive
links that might be pertinent to a particular topic; or seek out relevant Web
rings that collect and cross-reference resources. Even in using a search
engine, issues of critical reflection are important. For example, in how different search engines rank order the importance or relevance of sites; or in
thinking of alternative descriptions of a topic to find material that might
otherwise be missed. For example, searches based on the key word "house-
keeping" and the phrase "domestic labor" will pull up some very different
materials, from quite different ideological positions. Such considerations
underscore the importance of reflecting on the implications of using different descriptions to refer to the "same" thing.

Critical users will need to develop better, multilayered ways of judging
credibility. Having some background content knowledge about a subject
before looking on the Web provides one way of assessing what else is found
(or what cannot be found) there. Cross-checking information through multiple sources will often be important (the Internet can be especially helpful
in facilitating this). Assessing the quality of evidence, the coherence of arguments, and the impact of persuasive rhetoric will be as important in this
context as in any other communicative setting. But the key here is on
adopting multiple measures and procedures of credibility, not relying on
any one. Imperfect as these heuristics are, there is no guarantee of reliability; but triangulating several sources increases the likelihood of identifying
more useful and reliable information.

Beyond Credibility

However, there is another way in which we want to push the idea of a critical user beyond the idea of someone invoking the traditional criteria of
credibility. These criteria, as we have emphasized, are primarily criteria
about judging the truth, accuracy, or reliability of information. But critically responding to the Internet (or other sources as well) requires more
than just judging credibility in these ways. It means asking other sorts of
questions than simply "Is this true? Is this useful to me?" important as those
questions are. In part these larger questions involve judging non-epistemic
factors about the information available: asking social and political questions, asking questions that go beyond the available information, and ask-

ing questions about one's own criteria of judgment, and what they are and are not adequate for.

First, one type of critical slant is to ask, "Whose interests are being served by this information and by this presentation of information?" Sometimes this is a matter of looking at the source of information, when it is identifiable, and asking what stake a person, group, or institution might have in promulgating certain material. But apart from identifying the sources of information, one also needs to question the emphases and omissions of content, how it is organized and represented, and so forth, which may serve particular interests over others. This involves going beyond simply assessing the truth of information, because something may be true but still be harmful or partisan in its presentation or effects. Sometimes these effects might be very subtle; but they are almost never neutral, and with certain kinds of content they are absolutely unavoidable. This will often not be so simple as detecting "bad" effects; more typically, there are multiple effects of information, some potentially beneficial, some potentially harmful, but in ways that are very difficult to separate or trace through to precise outcomes, especially in advance.

Related to this point is that where the information on the Internet is contextless, critical users will need to recreate that context, if they can. This not only provides ways of evaluating its significance, but also potentially of enhancing its meaning. A particular piece of information, again, may be true enough, judged in and of itself; but information as isolated bits of data is often useless, and it can be deceptive to present such facts as if they simply stand on their own. By questioning the context of information, the meaningfulness of that information can be seen in greater depth and complexity. Often this broader picture also reveals the hidden agendas expressed by that apparently neutral "fact."

Second, a very different sort of critical reading will require asking the question, "What *isn't* here?" (like the dog that doesn't bark in Sherlock Holmes), or "Who isn't here?" Such a conclusion will require extrapolating from what one already knows to infer where the gaps might be; or will require a close reading of the organization of information to interrogate the dead ends and omissions. This is one of the most important and yet most difficult dimensions of critical use; since, for all its encyclopedic content, the most striking thing about the Internet is still its silences. Many ideas are not there, many points of view are not there, and many, many individuals and groups are not represented there. In a way this also requires asking questions about the Internet itself, since one of its prime features is an illusion of comprehensiveness; there is so much to it that it is difficult to imagine anything important being left out. When search engines pull up millions of references, the first impression is of a cornucopia of ideas and information. Ironically, it is the people who use the Internet the most who best appreciate what it does not provide. Hence experience is an important guide here. But many lack such experience, and as more people become dependent on the Internet for information, it becomes all the more necessary to remember that other sources of information need to be preserved and respected as well. Here, again, the Internet both supports and interferes with the development of critical capacities, in different ways.

Another aspect of going beyond the information content of the Internet concerns how to apply these faculties of critical reading *across* the media sources that it comprises. Especially on the World Wide Web, a great deal of content is nonpropositional (graphics, sound, video), and so cannot be judged simply by the epistemic criteria of truth and accuracy. Reading and questioning these requires additional skills of interpretation and judgment, and requires skills across a range of different media. Critically reading images, music, video, and so forth, are not all the same as reading written text; and the particular way in which the Web *juxtaposes* text, images, music, and so on, becomes itself a dimension of expression.[5] How are the elements of graphic design, for example, a way of suggesting ideas and relationships? At a deeper level, how does this lead to a blurring of the form/content distinction?

Third, there is the reflexive nature of critical reading: of using discussions about credibility to highlight and reflect upon the procedures and criteria by which we identify information as relevant and reliable, or not. It involves looking at the criteria by which the credibility of information is being judged, and asking what they may miss or conceal as well as what they may illuminate. Where do these standards come from? What authorities recommended them? What sorts of purposes do they assume? This type of critique also involves the critical user in reflecting upon his or her own perspective, potential blind spots or biases, and the purposes that bring him or her to the search for information. In certain ways, reflecting upon how one makes such judgments in ordinary circumstances shows just how problematic these assessments can be. The way that information and communication work within the Internet heightens some of these paradoxes and difficulties. It takes a certain kind of flexibility to examine the assumptions of one's criteria of judgment at the same time that one is applying them; and a certain kind of open-mindedness to reflect on the possibility that things might be otherwise. This, too, represents an important dimension of critical use and, significant for our purposes here, it may be something very difficult to do entirely on one's own.

Critical Judgment as a Social Practice

Criticality is not just a matter of intellectual skill or cleverness. There is an aspect to it that draws also from aspects of personality or character. A critical user is also the type of person who *wants* to exercise critical judgment and who values the skeptical attitude while also recognizing when it is not appropriate. This is a complex constellation of cognitive and personal qualities. But it is also crucial to see that this sort of critical discernment is not solely a property of individuals. In many instances the process will be one of shared judgments: how a group of users share their judgments and information with one another in a way that inspires cooperation and trust. Judging credibility is often a social practice, situated within a group identity and a distinctive set of other, related social practices.[6] This is the virtue of a system of distributed credibility, expressed in such practices as the development of Web rings and other ways of making collective judgments visible to others. The intelligence and resources of the community will often surpass that of any member within it; conversely, the way in which credibility is reinforced through this sort of networking helps to underscore the identity and solidarity of a community.

Thinking of criticality as a social practice both informs a deeper understanding of what a critical user of the Internet is, but also shows how such a capacity inevitably involves activities, relations, and access to information and experiences that go beyond the Internet itself. As we have tried to indicate throughout this discussion, becoming a critical user of new information and communication technologies can draw from and benefit from those technologies; but there are also ways in which those technologies can limit the capacity or opportunity for critical reading practices. It would be a huge mistake to see the Internet or other information and communication technologies as an entirely self-correcting or self-policing system.

When we think about critical use as a social practice, the kinds of communities that support that practice need to be looked at themselves (our final chapter addresses these issues). One dimension of this is the way in which critical judgment does not operate separately from substantive content knowledge in particular fields. Critical standards rely upon the background literature and the standards of evidence defined by particular disciplines, and these vary. One can talk of interdisciplinary perspectives, but these are simply a matter of drawing from more than one set of standards. They still originate within the disciplines. Methodologies of inquiry, testing evidence, weighing arguments, and so on, are similarly linked to content in particular ways. These observations suggest that helping to support more critical use of information and communication technologies will still require substantive content knowledge as well. Some of this might be learned from the Internet itself, but in most fields the bulk of the relevant information and knowledge can only be acquired by reading and learning elsewhere. Another consequence of these observations is that some users will be more critical in certain contexts than in others. This is not because they lack generic "critical thinking skills," but because they have a greater resource of background knowledge and context for interpreting and applying those skills with certain kinds of material. A similar point can be made about the varying capacities of different users to apply critical discernment to certain media, rather than others. Some will be very savvy about interpreting and judging visual images but less discerning about written text, or vice versa, for example. This provides another reason why collaborative groups working together and sharing critical perspectives will generally improve the overall level of critical understanding.

A second point about the kind of social group working together to read and use new information and communication technologies critically is that the diversity of such groups is itself a valuable resource in enhancing the criticalness of their perspectives. It is precisely because people come from different cultural backgrounds, different points of view, different parts of the world, different sets of experiences, and so on, that each might be in a unique position to view information critically and to see in it limitations and biases that may not be apparent to others. Conversely, a lack of diversity (or tolerance for diversity) within a community can be viewed as a serious liability in its ability to reflect critically on what it might encounter in information environments, or in what it might take for granted about its own outlook and assumptions. Here is one of the ways in which Web rings or other online communities can, if the group is too homogeneous and inhospitable to critical perspectives from outside it, actually work against a critical perspective. Here again, access issues interrelate with issues of credibility.

Finally, there is a sense in which the very character of the Internet itself can interfere with critical judgments within it. This is one area in which viewing criticality as a social practice (and not just as a set of abstract criteria) deepens our understanding of the complexity and ambiguity of the judgments at stake. The Internet is a tremendous archive of information and a powerful medium for communication and collaboration. But it also takes shape, not only in terms of its potential, but also in how people actually use it.

In practice, most people let others make judgments of credibility for them. They rely on authoritative judgments by people who seem to be knowledgeable, and they either derive information from them directly, or from sources that those persons create, recommend, or authorize. As noted before, this acceptance of their credibility can be based on more or less carefully thought-through criteria, and it is sometimes well justified. In many ways, new information and communication technologies, including the Internet, as well as other related popular media, make the centrality and influence of these authorities all the more important. To the extent that this has happened, it weakens the capacities or inclination for independent critical judgment by many individuals or groups online. It is easier to leave those judgments up to someone else.

There are many consequences of this. One is that the Internet has become a forum for gossip, rumors, hoaxes, and conspiracy theories on a huge scale.[7] The very decentralization and lack of central control that makes the Internet so exciting and democratic a medium for grass-roots coalition and information sharing, has also opened it up to every sort of wacky speculation and scandal. Sensationalism aside, sometimes these reports or rumors turn out to be true; but even this invites reflection on whether something's being true is a sufficient reason to disseminate it so widely (these issues will arise again in the later chapter on privacy). Moreover, even when "true," the way that these reports often stand without context can be a kind of distortion itself, as we discussed earlier.

The Internet is an enormously rapid and powerful means of dissemination. A message or piece of information can spread through millions of users, around the world, in a very short time. This is what makes computer viruses so dangerous to users, and it is what makes false reports of computer viruses (a kind of virus themselves) so susceptible to spreading quickly. Sensational news reports and scandalous gossip can operate in the same sort of virus-like fashion. But the mechanisms of retracting or correcting these stories can never spread as widely or as quickly as the original "virus."

Yet another feature of the Internet and other information and communication technologies is that they are changing very rapidly. Much information becomes quickly obsolete. This colors all information with a tone of transience or uncertainty; an online fact has a unitary electronic moment, and users are perfectly prepared for it to be gone or transformed in a very short while. This impermanence also tends to discourage careful, rigorous testing for credibility (why bother?).

Finally, the very comprehensiveness of the Internet becomes a problem here. On any issue, a user can find well supported and apparently plausible competing points of view (sometimes several, all mutually inconsistent with one another). What does one make of this when they have no independent or extra-Internet resources with which to judge or compare those views? The outcome is often a certain kind of relativism or casualness toward all points of view.

In each of these ways, the Internet, precisely because of its capabilities to be a medium of sharing, testing, and interpreting new information, also has the capability to interfere with such careful judgments. For many users, the experience of interacting online tends to *reduce* the time or interest in applying a careful filter to everything encountered there. A great deal simply goes by unquestioned.

HYPERREADING

In the previous chapter we made clear that the categories of "critical user" and "hyperreader" were not entirely distinct. These referred not so much to discrete groups of users of information and communication technologies, as to two modes of interacting with information that many of us fall into at one time or another.

We have argued for the importance of developing more critical users, and of seeking to create the kinds of communities, including online communities, in which these capacities can be collectively strengthened and improved. But we have also tried to make clear that these capacities rely to a significant degree on knowledge and experiences that cannot be provided by the online medium alone; and that certain features of the online environment can, in practice, actually interfere with their development and application. Developing more critical users is a very important educational aim in itself, and it may be realistically the level at which most users, at best, will operate much of the time. But there is a limit to the degree of criticality that these sorts of criteria and modes of judgment can support. So we recommend another mode of interacting with new information and communication technologies as well, which we have called *hyperreading*.

Critical users are primarily concerned with selecting, evaluating, and questioning information that they encounter, and with judging it relative to their purposes (hence, we still call them *users* of information). A more critical outlook would include questioning those standards of judgment, and questioning those purposes; but many critical users will be reluctant to do so. (It can be a very upsetting experience, after all.) A hyperreader is more willing to put existing standards and purposes into play; more willing to see the context-dependency, and not the absolutism, of those criteria. Additionally, a hyperreader is more willing and able to act in a creative manner to restructure and reinterpret information and communication environments, and not simply to accept or reject them as they are.

Hyperreading begins with the element that makes hypertext: the link. In the previous chapter we discussed what makes hypertext different from ordinary text, and how hyperreading is a style of reading not unique to hypertext, but facilitated by it. Hyperreading is the process of reading across links, laterally, as well as within the bounds of the "given" narrative or argument. Here we want to explore more deeply the idea of the *link*. Our hope is to invert the order of how people normally think about links and information points, nodes, or texts. Usually people see the points as primary, and the links as mere connectives; here we highlight the importance of thinking more centrally about the links themselves—as associative relations that change, redefine, and provide enhanced or restricted access to the information they comprise. When a hyperreader is critically reading the links, and not only the material joined by them, a deeper level of criticality is accomplished.

Links and Hyperreading

The significance of links within a hypertext environment is often underestimated. The textual points or nodes are taken as givens and the links are regarded simply as matters of preference or convenience. Their ease of use makes them appear to be merely shortcuts. They are seen as subservient to the important things: the information sources that they make available. The speed with which a reader moves from one information point to another across these links makes the moment of transition too fleeting to be an object of reflection itself; the link-event becomes invisible. Their familiarity can be deceptive, and we wish to discuss three important aspects of links that need to be brought to the surface in order to counteract their apparent naturalness or neutrality.

The first is that, although all links in an online HTML text work in the same way, involve the same act, and result in the same effect, all links are not the same, and do not imply the same type of semic relation. Below we will describe a variety of different types of links, coding these different types in terms of some standard rhetorical tropes. Here we simply want to make the point that links are not all of the same type, and that selecting and following any particular line of association between distinct textual points involves a process of inference or interpretation about the nature of the association this link implies. Sometimes this association will be one's own idiosyncratic way of making sense of the connection. Sometimes it will be prefigured by certain conventions that have a familiar significance within the context where we encounter the link (for example, the nature and purpose of footnotes, which are familiar sorts of links for most readers). Sometimes it will be one's attempt to guess at the reason why the hypertext author made exactly this link in this location between these two items.

This leads to (links to?) a second point, which is that in one's ordinary encounters with links, they are already made. Readers can certainly author their own hypertexts, writing their own texts as well as incorporating or modifying material from other textual sources; and, increasingly, Web applications will allow readers to add their own customized links to the hypertexts they encounter that have been authored by others. Nevertheless, the initial contact readers have with hypertext—and for most, even now, the only contact—is with materials created by unknown persons whose reasons, biases, motivations, and credibility are almost entirely beyond discovery. The usage and placement of links is one of the central ways in which the tacit assumptions and values of the author are manifested in a hypertext—yet they are rarely considered as such.

Third, and at a more subtle level, the act of a link is not simply to associate two givens. Links change the way in which material will be read and understood—partly by virtue of the mere juxtaposition of the two related texts. How is a jump from a page on teenage drug use statistics to a page on rock music going to affect how the rock music page is read? There is an implied connection that a link expresses—though it is far from inevitable that the connection an author intends is the one that readers will necessarily draw. Moreover, it is worth noting that links are (generally) only one-way. A reader can return from a page visited to the page from which the link originated, but the semic significance implied by the link from A to B does not necessarily accompany the return from B to A.

This hermeneutic and transformative effect is key to understanding the hidden rhetoric of links: they express meanings, they betray biases, they invite or suggest inferences, and sometimes they manipulate the reader. Their meaning as individual links interacts with—changes and is changed by—the system of meanings in which, and across which, they operate. The link is the elemental structure that represents a hypertext as a semic web of meaningful relations.

In online texts, links define a fixed set of relations given to the reader, among which the reader may choose, but beyond which most readers will never go. Links not only express semic relations but also, significantly, establish pathways of possible movement within the Web space. They suggest relations, but also *control access to information.* The link takes the reader from A to B, but not to C, and sometimes this represents a clear decision by the creator. Hyperreading, therefore, should involve the reader making connections within and across texts, sometimes in ways that are structured by the author, but also sometimes in novel ways shaped by the reader's own ideas and interests. It can mean reading *across* the author's design intentions, not only within them. As discussed in the previous chapter, each new reading (hyperreading) is in a significant sense a new *version* of the text under consideration. But even more than this, hyperreading involves critically reading the links themselves, and reflecting on the changed meanings of knowledge within a linked information system.

Different Types of Links

Developing a more reflective and critical approach to the Internet, including the World Wide Web, and the information found there includes learning to read the subtle and not-so-subtle implications that links make through association. A thoughtful hyperreader will ask questions about why links are made from certain points and not others; where those links lead; and what values are entailed in such decisions. But beyond this, links *create* significations themselves: they are not simply the neutral medium of passing from A to B.[8]

Part of developing this critical discernment is to consider how links are tools of rhetoric. In the same way that links carry readers from text to text, so also do tropes or other rhetorical turns of phrase associate words and concepts (in fact, "metaphor" derives from the Greek words to "carry over"). There are many examples of such tropes, each suggesting a different sort of relation between the elements; and in the same way, different kinds of links suggest different sorts of relations between the text elements they join. A few examples follow.[9]

Metaphor is a comparison, an equation, between apparently dissimilar objects, inviting the listener or reader to see points of similarity between them *while also inviting a change in the originally related concepts by "carrying over" previously unrelated characteristics from one to the other.* Like simile, metaphor asks us to see one thing *as* another: "my beloved is a rose," "the city is a cesspool," "school is jail." Web links can be read as metaphors when apparently unrelated textual points are associated. A link from a page listing Political Organizations to a page on the Catholic Church might cause a sense of puzzlement, outrage, or insight. Or it might be taken for granted unreflectively—but considered as a metaphor it might make a reader think about politics and religion in a different way.

Metonymy is an association not by similarity, but by contiguity, relations in practice. Baseball and football have affinities by both being sports; baseball and hot dogs have a metonymic affinity only because in American culture they often appear together (it would be possible to imagine that, say, hamburgers or tacos would be the food typically eaten at baseball games instead). A Web link, almost by definition, has the potential to become metonymic, with repetition. Most users do not have to have it explained any longer that clicking on a pentagon-shaped icon will take them "home," that is to the index or entry-page of a set of interlinked pages. On a broader scale, the increase of advertisements and clickable icons sponsored by private companies, crowding the screens of pages that have nothing to do with their product, creates a metonymic space that continually reminds the user that the Web is for sale, and that commercial interests underwrite more and more of what is presented there.

Synecdoche involves figurations where part of something is used as a shorthand for the thing as a whole or, more rarely, vice versa: "the blonde came back to the bar and asked for another beer; he already had a six-pack inside of him." In the context of Web links, this trope is particularly influential in identifying, or suggesting, relations of categorical inclusion. For example, a list of "Human Rights Violations" may include links to pages dealing with corporal punishment in schools, or vice versa. This relating of categorical wholes to particular instances, or of parts to wholes, is a matter of key importance. The power to register superordinate categories to which particulars are subsumed is a special way in which conceptual and normative leverage is exercised over how people think. Because different categorical wholes are always possible, clustering and organizing available instances in different ways, and because identifying and adjudicating particulars *as* instances is a way of regulating them, such determinations need to be recognized as such and brought into question. Links make such associations, but do so in a way that often is not made explicit or problematic. Yet because such categorical links are often the gateway through which access to that information is controlled, clustering and relating items in one way rather than another is more than a matter of convenience or heuristic. It becomes a method of shaping and restricting how people think about a subject.

Hyperbole, one of the more familiar forms of figuration, is exaggeration for the sake of tropic emphasis: "my office was flooded with mail." Anyone who spends much time browsing Web sites will recognize these as part of the basic vocabulary by which authors seek to attract attention to their handiwork. But beyond this, and at a more subtle level, the dynamics of the World Wide Web are essentially hyperbolic (starting with its name). There is a tacit implication with each collection, each archive, each search engine, of a degree of comprehensiveness beyond its actual scope. For all its wealth and complexity, the Web comprises only a fraction of culture, society, and politics, worldwide. Its omissions are often quite glaring, but nothing in its self-descriptions, or its link attributes—"Movie Guide," "Dining in San Francisco," and so on—suggest that what is not included may be more important than what is.

Antistasis, a much less-familiar trope, involves the repetition of the same word in a different or contrasting context ("whenever I *fly* in an airplane I feel trapped, as if I were a *fly* in a bottle"). Many Web links work in this way: using a particular word or phrase as a pivot point from one context to a very different one. Keyword search engines are based almost entirely on this principle. For example, in reading an online article describing someone's vacation to San Francisco, the term "North Beach" might be linked to a page of information about Italian Restaurants, on another to strip bars, and on another to the Beat Poets from the 1960s. These are all the "same" North Beach in one sense, but in another sense very different ones, separated in time and spirit. The effect of such links, especially when the differences in context and significance are not made explicit, is to put all phenomena within the same semic space, eliding time, space, and discursive context, making all these information points simply grist for the contemporary reader.

There is a metonymic element at work here as well; as in those encyclopedias or calendar programs that connect together everything that happened on a particular day in history. ("September 24: on this day, the President signed the Budget Act into law; the Baltimore Orioles beat the New York Yankees 4-2; the movie 'Singing in the Rain' opened in Los Angeles; a housewife in Akron, Ohio, won the Betty Crocker Cookoff with her recipe for Upside-Down Blueberry Cake; in Pakistan government troops used clubs to disperse a crowd of protesters; a panda bear in the Peking zoo became the first to give birth in captivity; and so on.") As noted previously, one of the primary effects of the Web is such juxtaposition of apparently unrelated points of information and reduction of all to the same surface level of significance: mixing the momentous and the trivial, the local and the global, the contemporary and the historic; and inviting multiple—and frequently untestable—interpretations of significance that can be as personal and idiosyncratic as one wishes. As such points of information all pivot around a common date, or a particular location, or a given word, they are brought into an association that may, from different perspectives, seem arbitrary or trivial, or on the other hand meaningful and explanatory. At the same time, the pivotal word or reference point shifts and broadens in significance. Antistasis invites such connections by invoking "the same" in a way that reveals difference.

Identity may not seem to be a trope, but it is useful here to include it as a companion and contrast to antistasis. In associations of identity, the "same" linking point is used to highlight points of commonality, not difference. Where other tropes, such as metaphor or simile, invite comparisons of similarity across different items; identity denies difference and emphasizes equivalence ("the woman who came to buy our house this morning is the surgeon who operated on our son last year"). Such relations typically depend on realist assumptions about co-referentiality or on logical tautologies; but here we want to emphasize the tropic effect of such assertions in practical contexts, including the Web. Unlike antistasis, which tends to highlight the ways in which terms or concepts change significance in different contexts, identity tends to hypostasize meanings, to freeze them, by suggesting the resistance of core meaning to changing context. In the context of the Web, such associations tend to draw lines of connection *through* pages, from different people or institutions, different cultures, or different countries, as if these reference points established a unifying net that spans the surface multiplicity of Web content and contexts. For example, many Web pages deal with the topic of privacy, and often cross-reference one another, as if they were undoubtedly addressing the same issue. But it may in fact be that the most revealing thing about these pages is that they conceive "privacy" in very different ways, and that protecting privacy in some respects may involve betraying it in others. Using the same word in every context, as if they were all referring to the same thing, conceals such potential conflicts and paradoxes. Beneath the particular instantiations of such associations of identity is an underlying figure of interwoven unity and commonality; a compelling image of the Web, but one that excludes and obscures at least as much as it highlights.

Sequence and *cause-and-effect* could also be given a very literal and nonfigurative interpretation; that these indicate *real* relations, not simply allusive ones. But without engaging that dispute here, there is a tropic effect of such associations, whether based on "real" relations or not, which may be indistinguishable from the reader's side. Links that suggest "this *and then* that" or "this *because of* that" (for instance, the rock music/drug use example mentioned earlier) do much more than simply associate ideas or information points. They assert, or imply, beliefs about the world outside of the Internet. But because they do not specify or explain such connections, but simply *manifest* them, they are more difficult to recognize and question. They are just followed, in many cases, carrying the reader with them to inferences that often could be drawn quite differently, or could be criticized and rejected.

Catechresis is in some ways the most interesting of all the tropes. Though sometimes characterized as a "far-fetched" metaphor, or as a strict misuse of language ("the belly of the river," which was just made up at random), catechresis is the recognition that such apparent "misuses" are how many tropes originally begin. These novel, strange instances might spark reflections just as revealing and delightful as those one recognizes more readily. (If a river can have a mouth, why not a belly?—perhaps the belly of the river rumbled—perhaps it is the point at which the river bends—perhaps it swelled, pregnant with fish.) At a deeper level, catechresis is the originary form of changes in language generally: "far-fetched" uses of familiar words in a new context; slang; accidental malapropisms; street patter that purposely uses coded terms to mislead authorities. Over time, such uses become "literal" in effect. Is the phrase "the hands of a clock" metaphorical or literal, today? In the context of the Web, catechresis becomes a trope for the basic working of the link, generally. *Any* two things can be linked, and with that link a process of semic movement begins. The connection becomes part of a public space, a community of discourse, which, as others find and follow that link, *creates* a new avenue of association—beginning tropically or ironically, but gradually taking its own path of development and normalization. Two key points follow: first, we never can know which uses will become accepted and standardized, so it is impossible to separate in any strict way proper uses from misuses. It may be simply a judgment made from within a particular time frame. Second, the Internet, because of its global and cross-cultural span, and because it currently requires most interactions to be filtered into and through a common language, English, will become a major new avenue in which malapropisms, slang, and far-fetched associative links will become familiar and, before long, normalized.

There are many other examples of such tropes that could be explored, and readers may question some of the particular tropic interpretations we have offered here. But our central points are that links act to change the interpretation of the elements they join, and that they do this in manifold ways. Reflecting on these effects is, we are arguing, one of the key features of hyperreading: learning to read the links themselves, and not only the elements they connect. Links imply choices; they reveal assumptions; they have effects—whether by design or inadvertently. Reading links is a crucial part of developing a broader critical orientation to hyperreading: not simply to follow the links authors lay out for us, but to interpret their meaning, to assess their appropriateness, and sometimes to suggest new links, new ways of associating and thinking about the material.

Hyperreading as Critical Reading

As we have sketched it here, hyperreading is a critical orientation to reading Internet materials. It begins with an awareness of the linked nature of the medium: linked not only in explicitly hyperlinked ways (the underlying HTML code of the World Wide Web), but in the larger sense in which information points are interdependent with other associations and assumptions that may not be manifested in the information points (taken out of context) themselves. This is clearly a step beyond the attitudes and skills of a critical user, who makes critical and discerning judgments, but largely within an acceptance of the medium itself. Hyperreaders are critically reading the medium as well as the content.

There are several dimensions involved with how hyperreading might be taught. One crucial aspect of developing this capacity is to learn about the mechanics of online design/authoring itself. Just as producers of texts in other fields (from poetry to acting to political speech writing) can be the sharpest critics of other practitioners because they know the conventions, tricks, and moves that elicit particular effects in an audience; so also should hyperreaders know what goes into selecting material, making links, and organizing a cluster of separate pages into a hyperlinked Web site. The more that one is aware of *how* this is done, the more one can be aware *that* it was done and that it could have been done otherwise. This capacity discloses the apparent "naturalness" or invisibility of designer/author choices and grants the hyperreader the opportunity to stand outside the particular forms of information available to question, criticize, and imagine alternatives to them. Links are made, not givens; and specific individuals and groups having their own assumptions, prejudices, agendas, and limitations make them.

Another dimension of this type of critical reading is to recognize that however flexible a hyperlinked structure might be, it is still a structure with particular organizational and connective features. These will not be equally hospitable to all cultural groups and individuals; a medium always advantages certain voices and perspectives and disadvantages others. The Web and other hyperlinked media are no different. Moreover, to the extent that these structures are the outgrowth of certain artificial intelligence assumptions about the way thinking works (or should work), they will not merely represent externally the way (certain) people think. Ironically, and significantly, they will have feedback effects that *influence* and *alter* the way people think. Here again the tool we have created to serve us shapes us in return. Insofar as this way of thinking is culturally particular, it raises issues for those who might think differently: is the price of admission to the Internet a matter of conforming to a dominant mode of thought and expression? To the extent that readers can become aware of this, it can become more a matter of choice or, in other circumstances, a locus of resistance.

Another dimension of learning to hyperread is to see the particular items being examined in the context of the online medium itself. For instance, Cynthia and Richard Selfe present an excellent analysis and critique of the user interface that defines most computers today. It is built around a set of metaphors (desks, folders, files, trash cans, and so on) that define a certain type of workplace and a certain set of primary purposes.[10] Other metaphors could certainly have been possible (a kitchen, a tool shed, a farm). However, by basing design around the model of the office, and of the rather bureaucratic manner in which information is organized within that environment, the interface privileges the mindsets of certain prospective users and anticipates, or shapes, certain sorts of uses over others. This is not to say that other uses *couldn't* be developed (and are), but that they are working against the grain of the medium. Hyperreading is an activity that continually asks these sorts of questions: what are the assumptions being displayed here; why is it easier for me to do A or find B, rather than C or D? If I tacitly accept this way of doing things, how is it shaping or delimiting my options? And so on.

Similarly, learning to hyperread also includes an apprehension of the *limits* of any organization of information. As large and inclusive as the Internet is, important things to know or care about are not included in it. This will be true no matter how "World Wide" the Web becomes. Because the Internet is a complex, interlinked semic network, one can move almost infinitely within it without ever encountering an explicit "edge" or limit: like physical space itself, it curves in upon and contains itself. Yet even though there are no edges, there are limits—limits which are very difficult to determine *from the inside*. It is a special skill of hyperreading to be able to recognize this, to imagine what is not or may not be there, *and* to read the absence as well as the presence of information. In short, hyperreading means being able to stand outside the particular set of associations and assumptions that define the information space one occupies. Every link excludes as well as includes associative points. Every path leads away from other avenues as it facilitates one passage. Every trope conceals as it reveals. Because of the apparent inclusiveness of the Internet and because of the apparent neutrality of the associations it establishes such an awareness needs to become a particular virtue of hyperreading. When a reader has such capabilities, and has considerable exposure to and experience with sources of information and knowledge *besides* the Internet, the Internet can provide an enormous opportunity for discovery and synthesis. Given the lack of such capabilities and experiences, it can be a frightening medium of manipulation and distortion—all the more effective for its flashy, user-friendly facade. As we discussed previously in the chapter, there are important ways in which the Internet, if taken at face value, works *against* the capacities or dispositions for critical reading. By the same token, seeing this fact, and understanding why it is so, is an important dimension of criticality.

Finally, the awareness of, and reflection upon, the hyperlinked structure of the Internet, most apparent in the World Wide Web, but exemplified really across all Internet programs and activities, is that one reflects also on the processes and criteria of critical judgment themselves. These too are "linked." They are linked in the ways in which standards and criteria depend upon communities of judgment and practice, and in the social nature of how many of these judgments get made (what we called earlier a system of "distributed credibility"). They are linked in the ways in which judgments of particular information elements depend upon seeing those elements in relation to others in a networked information system. They are linked in the ways in which judgments of an information object also involve self-judgments (Who am I? What is my relation to this material? and so on). They are linked in the ways that simple judgments of "good" and "bad" or "true" and "false" material are seen as often artificially truncating the range of considerations, consequences, and implications of the matter under consideration. Viewed in a larger, more complex, and interlinked context, such simple judgments often become much more difficult to defend, and the criteria by which they are made become matters for reflection themselves. To what extent are these criteria and judgments themselves the artifacts of a particular set of purposes and assumptions that could be resituated in a context and viewed differently as a result?

To take one example, how does society define and defend standards about what young people or children should and should not be allowed to see on the Internet? Where do these standards come from, and how are they justified and explained? Indeed, *are* they justified and explained in most cases, or are they simply imposed by adult authorities who have the power to do so? Could other standards be possible (in fact, they are, in other societies around the world) and can a hyperlinked medium ever simply impose such standards without creating new paradoxes? If one is trying to teach the critical skill of finding out what is not on the Internet as a valuable dimension of hyperreading the medium so that its silences do not become institutionalized as the boundaries of possible knowledge, then how does that aim fit with the purpose of working to keep readers from accessing certain material that is judged "inappropriate"? Isn't there a paradox here? And might there not be a better way of helping young people identify, judge, and criticize "inappropriate" material than by trying to keep them from ever seeing it? Might trying to keep them from it simply make the temptation all the greater (since the material will always be there to be found)? These sorts of dilemmas will be our main topic of concern in the next chapter.

The educational task we are sketching here is complex and demanding. While it is not essentially different from previous attempts to foster a skeptical and discerning literacy toward other kinds of texts, critically reading the Internet raises some particular challenges. The seductiveness of the technology, its complexity of organization, the volume of its content, the speed with which material comes at the reader, are unprecedented. It partakes of all the features of other media, combines them together, and adds the additional capability of hypertext to them. Yet addressing these issues is unavoidable, because the Internet is unavoidable. For better or worse (for better *and* worse), it will play a larger and larger part in people's educational, social, cultural, working, and political lives. Those who do not have access to it, or who cannot or will not partake of it, will be practically excluded from important opportunities for human interaction, communication, and learning. While not all users may become hyperreaders in the full, active sense, we do think that developing more critical users is a realistic, valuable near-term objective.

Although we have focused here on the hazards of flawed information on the Internet, there is much that is important, useful, interesting, and entertaining as well. The problem is in telling the difference. Hence, these issues of critical use and of hyperreading are important because they illuminate, in a special way for our times, the basic processes of selecting, organizing, filtering, interpreting, evaluating, critiquing, and synthesizing information that underwrite our constructions of knowledge and understanding. This has always been, in some ways, the *central* educational project.

NOTES

1. A long list of these links can be found at Nick Burbules's Web site: www. ed.uiuc.edu/facstaff/burbules/NickB.html.

2. A recent research study by Xerox showed that almost 75% of all Web traffic went through just 5% of all Web sites (*New York Times,* 6/21/99).

3. See, for example, Colin Lankshear and Peter McLaren, eds. *Critical Literacy* (Albany, NY: SUNY Press, 1993); Allan Luke, Barbara Comer, and Jennifer O'Brien, "Critical literacies and cultural studies," in G. Bull and M. Ansley, eds. *The Literacy Lexicon* (New York: Prentice Hall, 1996), 31–44; Allan Luke and Peter Freebody, "Critical literacy and the question of normativity: An introduction," in Sandy Muspratt, Allan Luke, and Peter Freebody, eds., *Constructing Critical Literacies* (Creskill, NJ: Hampton Press, forthcoming); Allan Luke and John Elkins, "Reinventing literacy in 'New Times,'" *Journal of Adolescent and Adult Literacy,* Vol. 42 No. 1 (1998): 1-4; Colin Lankshear, James Paul Gee, Michele Knobel, and Chris Searle, *Changing Literacies* (Philadelphia: Open University Press, 1997); and The New London Group, "A pedagogy of multiliteracies: Designing social futures," *Harvard Educational Review,* Vol. 66 No. 1 (1996), 60–92.

4. Chris Bigum and Bill Green, "Technologizing literacy: The dark side of the dreaming," *Discourse,* Vol. 12 No. 2 (1992): 4–28; Paul Gilster, *Digital Literacies* (New York: John Wiley, 1997); Colin Lankshear, Michele Knobel, and Michael Peters, "Critical pedagogy in cyberspace," in Henry Giroux, Colin Lankshear, Peter McLaren, and Michael Peters, *Counternarratives* (New York: Routledge, 1996); Michael Peters and Colin Lankshear, "Critical literacy and digital texts," *Educational Theory,* Vol. 46 No. 1 (1996): 51–70; and Douglas Kellner, "Multiple literacies and critical pedagogy in a multicultural society," *Educational Theory,* Vol. 48 No. 1(1998): 103–122.

5. See Kellner, "Multiple literacies and critical pedagogy."

6. Allan Luke, "When basic skills and information processing just aren't enough: Rethinking reading in New Times," *Teachers College Record,* Vol. 97 No. 1 (1995): 95–115.

7. Kurt Andersen, "The age of unreason," *New Yorker* (February 3, 1997): 40–43.

8. Nicholas C. Burbules, "Aporias, webs, and passages: Doubt as an opportunity to learn." *Curriculum Inquiry* (forthcoming).

9. Here we have relied on an excellent typology of tropes by Richard A. Lanham: *Handbook of Rhetorical Terms, 2nd Edition* (Berkeley: University of California Press, 1991). For a fuller treatment of this subject, see Nicholas C. Burbules, "Rhetorics of the Web: Hyperreading and critical literacy," in Ilana Snyder, ed., *Page to Screen: Taking Literacy Into the Electronic Era* (New South Wales: Allen and Unwin, 1997): 102–122.

10. Cynthia Selfe and Richard Selfe, Jr., "The politics of the interface: Power and its exercise in electronic contact zones," *College Composition and Communication,* Vol. 45 No. 4 (1994): 480–504.

MISINFORMATION, MALINFORMATION, MESSED-UP INFORMATION, AND MOSTLY USELESS INFORMATION: IS CENSORSHIP THE BEST RESPONSE?

O ne of the major issues we have discussed concerning the Internet is the question of unequal access: who is becoming familiar and comfortable with this new environment for learning and communication, and who is not. There are many dimensions of the access issue—questions of hardware, network access, training, and so forth. But an underdiscussed problem concerns those who have interacted with this new environment and who "by choice" have withdrawn from it. The quotes are meant to indicate that the apparent voluntariness of this decision needs to be questioned in certain cases. If the decision to withdraw was the result of *content* on the Internet, and if this content differentially affects some groups more than others, then the cumulative outcome of these individual decisions is a broader pattern of involvement and noninvolvement that should concern those committed to widespread and diverse participation in all that the Internet offers. Yet these sorts of difficulties seem inherent to the online environment, which continually confronts users with material that they might regard as false, dangerous, offensive, or worthless. The same medium that can provide easy instructions on how to repair your own clock radio, also provides instruction on how to build bombs using readily available chemicals and supplies. You can buy books or CD's at a discount; and you can buy child pornography. You can read newspaper editorial columns from every major U.S. newspaper, and you can find neo-Nazi hate tracts. You can get up-to-the-minute weather information, and you can watch people sitting in front of their "web-cam," typing at the keyboard in their underwear. The spectrum of material on the Internet runs from the useful, fascinating, and important, to the pointless, bizarre, and frightening. The problem arises, of course, when different people characterize the same material in radically different ways.

In this chapter we discuss four types of content that elicit these sorts of responses: some users find them irritating, frustrating, or worse. While our labels for them (misinformation, malinformation, messed-up information, and mostly useless information) are somewhat playful, the actual experience of encountering such content, and its effects, can be far from humorous. And content can be an access issue if it drives away prospective participants to (and beneficiaries of) the online environment. Ironically, improving access for some people, and bringing greater diversity of perspectives and interests online, creates an access problem for others who are frightened or offended by such material, and so choose to stay away. For users who stay and continue to use the Internet, the actual benefits of what they stand to gain will be affected by how well they can make discerning judgments about what they find.

TROUBLESOME CONTENT: THE 4 M'S

Misinformation

The first category of information that troubles users is *misinformation*, information judged to be false, out of date, or incomplete in a misleading way. Because there are so many providers of information and opinions on the Internet, in so many forums, and because there is no practical check on people putting out whatever they might, there is sure to be a high percentage of unreliable content mixed in with what may be more credible. The problem is when a user cannot distinguish which is which.

As we addressed in the previous chapter, it is hardly a new issue to wonder about the accuracy of the information we encounter in texts (books, newspapers, television, or whatever) or in the discourse of everyday life. There is nothing unique about the electronic universe in this regard, except that the people who are creating and putting out the information are usually even more invisible. People generally assume the reliability of certain providers of information (the *Encyclopedia Britannica* or the local telephone directory). In some areas, they may know enough to evaluate that credibility against their own expertise in certain matters. But often they will rely on indirect proxies of credibility, such as a professional degree, an institutional identification, or—in face-to-face encounters—elements of style, appearance, or manners. In the context of the Internet, as we have discussed, some of these indicators may still be usable; others have little meaning at all. The providers of information on the Internet, even more than in other media, operate through surrogates of representation. Users see of them only what they choose to represent about themselves and users may have very little additional information against which to judge their claims. Moreover, the origins of information itself may be indirect, as people forward or link to information provided by others, so that a relatively reliable person may be repeating an assertion from an (unknown) unreliable source, or vice versa.

Already we have seen that the Internet has become a special haven for rumors, gossip, hoaxes, and conspiracy theories. These ideas can be circulated very quickly through multiple cycles of forwarding. They are therefore difficult to trace back to any original, accountable source; and can have a surface credibility that looks just like "real" news and information. In a decentralized information system with few formal gatekeeping mechanisms, how does a user prevent the "noise" from drowning out worthwhile material?

A special category under misinformation is *disinformation*, knowingly false or malicious information transmitted purposely to discredit an organization or an individual. For example, some people find that e-mail is sent by other people, under *their* name and with *their* return address, containing embarrassing or insulting content. False Web pages have been posted, looking for all the world like authentic ones, with believable URL addresses, but with false, misleading, or derogatory information just close enough to the edge of plausibility to reflect badly on the putative source. (The 1996 Bob Dole presidential campaign was the recipient of this.) The line here between satire and libel becomes blurry. How "obvious" does the prank need to be? How can the person or group disavow the page as a reflection of their views? What are the appropriate margins in public political discourse between challenging opposing positions and distorting or misrepresenting them (a problem that does not pertain solely to the Internet, of course)?

At the other end of the political spectrum, a leading progressive political theorist was castigated in an e-mail manifesto written by a student group at her university, ostensibly for failing to support them in a protest they had posed against their administration. This message was sent out on various mass-distribution lists, and took on as these things do, a life of its own. But as to the particulars of the protest, what the professor's actual stance was, what her reasons might have been for not supporting them (or not supporting them enthusiastically enough), these were not available to the recipients of the manifesto. This feature of Internet information standing without context, from unknown points of authorship, transmitted or repeated from source to source until its origins are virtually impossible to recover, is not fundamentally different in kind from gossip or rumors or hand-printed fliers that have served similar purposes in the past. But the apparent credibility of Web pages or other electronic documents, which can be from all evidence of appearance as authentic as any official publication in the same medium, begins to shake conventional assumptions about what "credibility" or "authenticity" mean for the casual Internet denizen.

In part, these difficulties arise because Internet users have not settled the status of e-mail along the continuum between written and oral discourse. It has the print character of letters or other documents, but the spontaneity and informality of a telephone call. Ordinarily, if one hears a rumor by word of mouth, or via an anonymous phone call, or through an unsigned handwritten note slid under one's door, one might grant credence to the assertions or not, but would certainly maintain a bit of skeptical distance from the claims. If the same report is written on official letterhead stationery, and signed, it appears more credible. People have experience with judging certain media for reliability, and though imperfect indicators to be sure, their assumptions about formality of presentation and identifiability of authorship usually help in making judgments of credibility. Various forms of electronic communication occupy a middle space in terms of these measures of formality and identifiability. As a result, when it comes to e-mail and other forms of electronic communication, users—especially new users—probably tend to grant too much credibility to what they see on screen.

Malinformation

A second type of information is what we are calling *malinformation*, what some users will consider "bad" information. This includes sexual images or material, potentially dangerous or damaging information, political views from militant fringe groups, and so on. Of course, what some consider "bad" others consider extremely important and interesting. All of this information may be true enough; it isn't necessarily *mis*information—in some instances it is all the more dangerous because it *is* accurate (for example, bomb-making instructions). Even free speech purists will feel uncomfortable with some of what is in openly accessible circulation on the Internet, either in topical discussion groups, chat rooms, or on open Web pages.

Such content has received disproportionate attention in the media. The media's love of crisis and alarm is perfectly tailored for sensationalistic stories about ten year olds looking for naked pictures on the Web, or the more bloodthirsty pronouncements of neo-Nazi groups, or the bomb-building instructions just mentioned. The fact that all of the same can be pulled off the shelf in any well-stocked bookstore, and in many libraries, is a comparison rarely made. Yet the fact is that the Internet *is* different, in the sense that it can be accessed without restriction. It is not just a repository of information, but also a medium of communication and connection among the producers and fans of such materials.

It is revealing to consider why this sort of material has been so over-represented by popular media coverage of the Internet. In part, we believe, it constitutes part of a larger moral panic over youth who are less subject to parental supervision and control when they are out of the home—the fear of what they might be reading, seeing, thinking, or doing when there is no one to check up on them. This reaction to the Internet is also part of a larger set of concerns over the media and popular culture generally; although, revealingly, while few would argue for strict censorship of books, movies, or magazines, censorship has often been the *first* response in dealing with the Internet. We will return to this issue at length later.

Messed-Up Information

The third kind of information is *messed-up information*; poorly organized and presented, to the point where it really is not usable. Questions about the organization of information begin to introduce questions about how "information" becomes "knowledge." Raw information, lists of facts, and so forth, is what the Internet is very good at offering, because it can be quick and relatively cheap to take data from other sources and slap it into an e-mail message or a Web site for others to sample. But the problems of selection, organization, interpretation, and synthesis of information—what one could call, in shorthand, turning information into knowledge—is the more time-consuming, intellectually challenging, and potentially controversial process that actually allows people to do something with that information. And because it is more time-consuming, more intellectually challenging, and potentially more controversial, the natural inclination for some people is to say, "Here, you take it. Make of it what you will." Now messed-up information, poorly organized information, raises only some of these issues, but it does make us think about the responsibility of providers of information to choose, select, organize, and filter information—which someone, somewhere, is likely to take issue with. So it is easier not to do it at all.

Another element of this process is sloppy Web page design: long lists of links with no organizers or annotation to tell people what they will find from them, or links that are no longer active, indistinguishable from working links. Badly designed pages with poorly organized and undependable links often lead to the problem that users feel "lost," uncertain of their position within the relational network of links that make up the World Wide Web. How did I get here? Where can I go next? Why is this link here? This becomes a major source of frustration for new users.

Another aspect of poor design is gratuitous logos or other graphics that clutter and distract. The multimedia potential of Web pages can provide multiple forms of information, through multiple channels of access, with flexible user interests in mind. Sometimes, legitimately, it can be for entertainment or amusement. But in the increasingly noisy environment of the Internet (and the media generally) some features are added merely to attract attention to one source rather than another or to show off the designer's programming skills or flash for its own sake. The result is overburdened (and to some tastes, aesthetically horrific) design.

Yet another element of this process is indiscriminate inclusion of material. E-mail distribution lists that proliferate unsolicited junk mail. Discussion groups where nine out of ten comments are off topic and of interest to no one but the author. Web pages that for the sake of comprehensiveness do not discriminate quality or relevance. Given our earlier comment that the networks of dissemination of information provide one of the few potentially reliable procedures for evaluating the credibility of material, when people simply pass along material indiscriminately it denies users of one of the measures they rely upon in evaluating it.

Another, related issue (discussed in David Shenk's *Data Smog*[1]) is that too much information can be as paralyzing as no information at all. As the Internet becomes more compendious, a user seeking information to guide personal or public policy decisions has three sorts of problems, two of which have already been mentioned. One is *finding* relevant information, another is *evaluating* what is credible information. The third issue is that where there is an *excess* of information, much of it apparently credible, much of it supported by plausible arguments and persuasive evidence, pulling in multiple, incompatible directions, it offers little or no guidance to decisions and actions. One can support almost any point of view in an apparently data-driven way. Does one then simply select information that reinforces pre-existing preferences and inclinations? Does one follow the most apparently popular or prevalent views? Or does one accept what accords with conventional wisdom within their particular community?

Messed-up information, then, becomes yet another source of frustration, confusion, and even cynicism about the value of the Internet and what it can offer. In an era where people are already deluged with stimuli, information, opinions, and other claims on their time and attention, the Internet becomes yet another unwanted complication and distraction. The hype promoting the Internet has been about the potential of this new technology to provide useful, entertaining, liberating information that can help to inform choices. For many users, however, especially beginning users, it is experienced as simply chaotic and overwhelming.

Mostly Useless Information

Finally, the category of *mostly useless information*. There used to be an entire Web page that was a collection of "Useless Web Pages." It contained items such as real time photos of the coffee machine on the first floor of a large research building. Anyone could see on his or her own screen exactly how much coffee was left in the pot. Or the fellow who provided an exhaustive, detailed, and regularly updated inventory of every item in his desk drawer ("three felt-tip markers, one red, one blue, one black, and so on"). Or the page where one could type in a word or phrase and it activated a speech synthesizer on the owner's home computer, where it spoke those words to the owner's cat, if the cat was in the vicinity of the computer. Some of these pages seem clever and whimsical; some just seem silly.

But there are a few important things to say about apparently "useless" pages. One is that my "useless" page might be very useful to someone else. It turns out, for example, that the "coffee pot page" was actually created by people on the top floor of the research building, who simply wanted to save the time of walking all the way down to the first floor to check to see if there was any coffee left in the machine. Now, why, you ask, don't they just buy their own coffee pot? This just shows that you don't understand how computer geeks think.

Another point is that sometimes an apparently useless page can actually be illustrating a principle, or a technological capacity, that in other contexts might be extremely useful. Saying "hello" or "eat the mouse" to Steve's cat, halfway across the world, might seem pretty trivial, but without much effort one can imagine uses of that same technical capability that might in fact prove invaluable (for example, for speech-impaired users).

Finally, and at a different level, the apparent triviality of such pages highlights in a satirical way some of the larger concerns we have been discussing here. How a technically impressive medium does not in itself insure the importance or quality or reliability of what it delivers. How what is important or interesting to one person may be trivial to another. How the "truth" of certain information is only one way of evaluating its importance or worth. How what some find amusing others find irritating or offensive. How the remarkable diversity of content on the Internet sparks many ingenious ways of attracting attention *for its own sake*. How the very volume of material, dispersed across a global Internet, *creates* a degree of uselessness by transferring information from the context that made it meaningful and useful into other contexts. In each of these instances, the very success of the Internet, in one respect, gives rise to a difficulty, in another respect.

What to Do About the 4 M's

These considerations pose some special educational challenges. If one believes in providing access to the Internet as an important medium for communication and accessing information, then there are many kinds of practical barriers that inhibit prospective users. This chapter has described some of them: issues of content that frighten or frustrate or discourage people before they have explored enough of the Internet to gain skill in finding what is worthwhile to them and learning how to avoid what is not. They raise, as we noted earlier, questions of *quality* as well as of *quantity* of access. They also, as we have tried to show, reveal some of the paradoxes of access.

Hence the challenge of providing access includes not only technical information about how to use computers, e-mail programs, and Web browsers; it also means providing users with critical skills to assist them in making discriminations about misinformation (what to believe); malinformation (what is worthwhile); messed-up information (what makes sense); and mostly useless information (what is relevant). As users gain experience in using the Internet they can develop some of their own strategies for finding and evaluating information. The challenge is to provide workable arrangements that help them to get started without getting lost, frustrated, frightened, or discouraged.

In the next section, we will talk about five basic approaches that educators and others have proposed. Our account here derives from the assumption that, although it is important that designers and providers of information on the Internet understand their obligations to quality, accuracy, and fairness, and while authorities may have a role to play in regulating certain kinds of content on the Internet, that any strong attempt to enforce such limits is more likely to impose too much restriction than too little. Either an over-regulated or a totally unregulated information environment poses important hazards. In the end, there will be a high proportion of junk (or worse) on the Internet whatever authorities might try to do. In general, then, it seems to us a better approach to strengthen the capabilities of users of the technology to make these discriminations for themselves.

FIVE RESPONSES

Censorship

As long as there has been formal education, there have been parents, citizens, governmental groups, and school people who have attempted to limit what students can see, hear, read, or say. Even before the advent of new information and communication technologies, such as computers, censorship in schools was on the rise. More and more groups, from a variety of political agendas, have been challenging standard curricula, textbooks, library materials, and so forth. These moves toward censorship have been most visible recently in the coordinated efforts of interest groups such as the so-called Religious Right, but they have often gained wider acceptance as well. Some so-called progressive groups have also called for censorship in the name of "political correctness." As schools have made heavier use of new technologies, there have been more calls to censor digital content even among groups who have not traditionally been pro-censorship. The most common rationale for such efforts is the fear that children will have ready access to pornographic or "indecent" materials.

One approach has been to attack the problem on the side of supply. This was the approach, for example, of the Communications Decency Act of 1997, later ruled unconstitutional. With that ruling, censors began looking for new ways to restrict access to objectionable materials on the Internet. But there are good reasons to doubt whether the problem can ever be solved on the supply side, given the vast, decentralized nature of the Internet, and the speed with which new provider sites can be established. Furthermore, the internationalization of content places many suppliers outside the grasp of national laws or regulations. The predominant response among censorship advocates in this country has been merely to look for ways to rewrite the CDA to see if it can withstand constitutional review. We consider this to be a typical technocratic response, looking for a simple fix to a complex problem, and responding to the failure of one "solution" by thinking that with a little tweaking it could work in another form.

The Communications Decency Act was not a proposal to censor material per se but a provision allowing users to sue providers of "indecent" materials.

This law would have had two chilling effects. One was to replace the relatively well-defined term "obscene" (in the sense that there is ample statutory precedent for demarcating what should and should not be included in that category) with the much more inclusive and vague term "indecent." The other was to allow any user anywhere on the Net to apply suit to anyone else, so that a person in a very conservative and religious area of one part of the country could sue an online discussion group among, say, HIV-positive gays in the San Francisco Bay Area, because *they* find it offensive. Previously, the standards of such regulations were restricted to the standards of particular communities. Now, the way that Internet users can access information across any distance has raised new questions about whether a localized group can proclaim a protected space for its own consensual interactions, regardless of whether or not that information or material can be found or accessed by others.

But censorship on the supply side is only one form censorship can take. Censorship may take place at any time, before or after the objectionable act, and either as prior restraint, or as a punishment meant to deter other such acts. Sometimes censorship is based on an explicit legal threat, in which case it can be subject to judicial review on constitutional grounds. But very often it is based more on political pressure or the threat of boycotts—an individual or group's attempts to suppress "objectionable" material or expression by means of withholding economic support (for example, a refusal to support new funds for schools because parents and community members disapprove of what is taught there). These sorts of responses, while possibly even more devastating in their consequences, are not subject to challenge on legal or constitutional grounds. They are political in nature and can only be contested in the same manner.

Our concern here is not to wade too deeply into the current censorship/ free speech debate—a debate that will never be resolved to the satisfaction of all. Rather, our interest is with resituating censorship on the supply side as only one possible response to concerns about Internet use in schools. Here we want to introduce a wider range of meanings of censorship, which we will explore further in the rest of this section:

(1) Censorship, foremost, involves suppression—a limiting or narrowing of choices or opportunities. It is a constriction of the expression of ideas and access to them. Censorship always begins with clearly dangerous or controversial material—bomb directions or dirty pictures—and invariably gets expanded over time to include the suppression of materials for other reasons such as dubious quality or questionable accuracy. In other words, the definition of "malinformation" is highly flexible and context-sensitive.

(2) Censorship usually takes place without regard to principle. Instead, it relies upon the degree to which the suppression is supported by an individual or an entire community. Yet the concept of simple majority rule, while a common justification for censorship, is not sufficient in a democracy, where there are many safeguards to prevent majorities from trampling on the interests or rights of minorities. Invoking "community standards" is ultimately a device to censor minority opinions and suppress materials that appeal to only the few. And besides, as we will discuss in a later chapter, when dealing with the Internet the question always needs to be asked, *Which* community?

(3) The suppression caused by censorship can occur at any time in the communication process—from conception and initial expression through the point of reception. If censorship is effective, the parties involved might never know their access to information had been denied. How would children know, for example, that there was a better book they could have read but which was withheld for some reason? When censorship is most effective, individuals never even know what they might have missed.

(4) Censorship involves much more than just protecting individuals or society-at-large from some perceived harm, although it is often couched as such. Explicitly or implicitly, there is an ideological component to most censorship acts. It would be naive to believe that censorship challenges are only designed to protect individuals, usually young people, and not to protect existing social and economic privileges and power relations. Similarly, many religiously based censorship challenges seem to be less about removing objectionable materials than to create vacuums (for example, by excluding talk about sexual activity in school curricula) into which they can then interject their own preferred positions.

(5) Challenges to censorship may come from many types of individuals or groups and for many reasons. Censorship is typically not described as such: parents censor by preventing their children from being exposed to certain kinds of materials. Supermarket chains may censor by not carrying certain issues of magazines because of customer complaints. Newspapers may censor by refusing to print certain installments of a cartoon series, and printing reruns in their place. Individuals may engage in self-censorship because they fear punishment, ridicule, or unwanted exposure. Opinions and content on a Web page might not be accessible because they fail to pass through some automatic filtering software.

(6) Another example of censorship that is often not characterized as such is censorship by cost. Material that has been made very expensive will only reach a small audience; fees to be paid for the privilege of accessing certain

material can constitute a powerful disincentive to people taking advantage of it, even though there is no other "barrier" preventing them from doing so. This problem is becoming salient for the Internet, as more and more online material is available only after payment, and as the rates charged are subject to no regulation whatsoever. Where quality of information is a premium, and where quality is made to equal expense (as it is in many other domains), access to ideas and information becomes another dimension of privilege that differentiates the opportunities for some over those of others. These can include educational opportunities, as in the case of educational programs offered (for a fee) online. And, as noted above, because this form of censorship is not based on *legal* exclusion, there is no avenue of appeal for those who have been effectively blocked from reaching what might be interesting, useful, or beneficial to them.

Our definition of censorship, obviously, is more encompassing than current usage dictates. From this perspective, the issue of what constitutes appropriate and inappropriate material from the Internet in educational settings, and what to do about it, becomes more complicated and problematic than it has usually been considered. We find it ironic, though not surprising, that an increase in the amount of accessible information and opinions in an educational environment causes an increase in attempts to suppress that information. The answer, we believe, lies in conventional views about the nature and function of schools. In any society, an important part of schooling is to socialize the young—to inculcate the values, norms, and culture of the society into the next generation. By definition, schools are not neutral; they are not value free. Schools teach and communicate a host of values and attitudes along with facts and skills that reflect a particular cultural perspective.

The problem, of course, is that in a free and diverse society, there will always be contention over *whose* values are taught. These disputes are sometimes expressed as arguments over teacher qualifications and training, curriculum, testing, and instructional methods. Few subject areas are not in some way touched by controversies over what is to be taught and how it is to be taught. The arguments have revolved not only around what should be included as part of a complete education, but also in terms of what should be *excluded* from one. As schools increasingly move into cyberspace, the traditional camps of contention will find these debates exacerbated and censorship will take on new dimensions. On the Internet, as we have noted, there is something to offend nearly everyone and to contradict nearly every view about life, politics, and morality.

But the approach of censorship on the supply side flies in the face of the basic structure and organization of the Internet. (This is why the CDA focused not on banning material, but on encouraging lawsuits that seek to punish purveyors of controversial material.) There is no central worldwide authority that could define or implement any such restrictions (an exception is child pornography, against which a global consensus exists, but even in this case the enforcement of this rule is selective and ineffective). Here again the highly interlinked nature of Internet resources complicates a seemingly straightforward problem. There can be many routes of access to the same material, and it does not matter on the receiving end where the point of origin of material is (in many instances it is impossible to identify the point of origin). No simple process can block transmission of information or material. Censorship can be enforced upon particular groups whose access to computers can be regulated and limited (for example, students in school); but as a general approach it cannot address the problems that people have with encountering unwanted material on the Internet. And even with students such policies end up having counterproductive effects, as we will see.

Filters

If restrictions on the supply side do not work, one alternative is to turn toward restrictions on the demand side. This is also a kind of censorship. A currently popular approach is to install software that blocks reception of certain categories of material at the point of reception: this allows parents, for example, to prevent their children from accessing certain types of materials. These software packages are often updated periodically (like anti-virus software) to include new addresses or categories in the continually shifting terrain of what people find dangerous or undesirable.

However, early returns with this approach have revealed myriad cases of filters knocking out too much. For example, filtering out all pages mentioning the keyword "breast," so that people cannot access pages with information on breast cancer detection and treatment. Another example is when filtering criteria have other unintended effects, as when an access provider in Vietnam picked up tonal marks in Vietnamese, rendered as the letters "sex," which knocked out 85% of all messages and overloaded the software. The predominant response has been that such software is in its infancy and can be expected to improve with further development. (This is the typical technocratic response.)

On one level, the use of these filters produces ironic and ineffectual results like those above. More importantly, however, we believe that the use of technological filters as a panacea will have many undesirable consequences, including anti-educational consequences.

It does not matter how much the software improves. Because of their capriciousness and unpredictability, filtering software will always block students' access to certain sorts of worthwhile and useful information because of that information's tangential relationship with subjects or terms that some believe to be objectionable. A filter whose purpose might be to prevent access to material of a sexual nature might inadvertently block access to information about gender in general, women's health care issues, or equity issues in women's sports. Worse, filtering software is designed to be customized or "fine-tuned" by those in authority—teachers, school officials, principals, parents, and librarians. This means that the scope of what is included and excluded will often be modified in an unaccountable manner, without any explicit justification or explanation of what is being shut out and why. Don't ask who did it, the "software did it." Not only does this create an arbitrary and idiosyncratic pattern of censorship, but the end result is that students will be denied access to information and not even know it. For example, a student searches for references to abortion and finds none. What can this mean to the student? Perhaps she believes the information has been blocked. But finding no reference to a subject may also leave the impression that the subject is not of sufficient importance to warrant any coverage. To suspect that information may have been filtered leaves the user in the perpetual quandary of not knowing whether some information does not exist or whether it has been blocked (and if so, at whose order and why).

The practice of filtering, of blocking targeted information, tears holes in the fabric of knowledge and understanding. Knowledge, creativity, critical thinking, discernment, wisdom—these are not about the accumulation of facts. They are about the relations between ideas, information, ethics, and culture. As one searches the Web, points of information are not merely destinations, they are also gateways—hyperlinked points that are intrinsically connected to and provide access to other points of information. It is not only that someone cannot find information about "abortion"—he or she also cannot move through "abortion" on the way to other important or pertinent information. If authorities close the door marked "abortion" (whatever the justification), they are also closing off a hallway of other possibilities.

There is little debate that parents, concerned about their children's access to material in their homes, should be able to impose any restriction on access, through any means, that they decide is prudent. And certainly there are things on the Internet that any parent would feel uncomfortable with a child seeing or hearing about. But the reasoning that schools or other public institutions should act *in loco parentis* has led too easily to the policy that if filters are suitable for the home, they are suitable in other contexts as well. Yet schools and libraries are different sorts of institutions, with broader responsibilities, and the concerns than might justify the use of filtering software in homes do not automatically translate into these spheres.

Filtering is a practice that is antithetical to the sorts of educational and democratic ideals we hold for schools and other public institutions. How can students learn to discern, discriminate, or evaluate? How can students learn to make good choices, social and intellectual, if choices are made for them by filtering out things they can and cannot see? We believe that filtering software will create more problems than it will ever solve, and that attempting to restrict access to the Internet because a student might see a dirty picture is like closing a library because some pervert once exposed himself in the stacks. It is the wrong response to the problem it attempts to solve.

What school children do, see, and collect on the Internet is an educational and a moral question, not a technological one. And although this distinction does not solve the fundamental problem surrounding the debate about what is educationally appropriate, its recognition may help prevent a vast watering down of the educational potential of the Internet. We believe that arguments for restricting access to students because they might be exposed to "indecent material" is often either a manifestation of an exaggerated preoccupation with sexual matters, or a red-herring that distracts attention from the actual reason some want to censor the Internet: to keep students from encountering a whole host of material that is not harmful, but merely controversial, unconventional, or upsetting to the local community's values. It is less about the putative issue of sexual material, and more that many adults are not willing to grant children the opportunity to learn to make up their own minds based on their own investigations of the world.

Finally, the dirty little secret about filtering software is that it only works for users who lack a certain level of skill with the machines. Worse, it has unintended consequences and "revenge effects" that may make the very problems it is intended to "solve" worse. Filtering software can only block sites that either contain keywords that explicitly identify sexual material, and so forth, or can be identified in advance so that their URLs can be added to the list of blocked addresses. But the purveyors of such material are not stupid, and these barriers are easily circumvented. A common approach is to create a "Trojan Horse" site, one that is identified nowhere by a tag that identifies its content; often the cover name is of cartoon characters or other topics of appeal to children. Then when they go to the site, unexpected material pops up on the screen. This makes it *more* likely that young people will be unwillingly exposed to such material. In many respects, this situation is worse than one in which everyone knows where certain material is, and then decisions can be made about whether to go there. Furthermore, with Trojan Horse sites parents or educators may never be sure if a child came across such material accidentally or intentionally. The important problem, the *educational* problem, is not simply about keeping young people from going to certain material, but for them to learn why adults think it is not a good thing, why it might be harmful to them or to others, and to learn to make better decisions. Blocking the materials for them never teaches the capacity to learn self-control and the discerning standards of judgment they will need when they are separated from their parents' or other authorities' supervision and control.

Beyond this, as we noted, filtering software simply does not work for skilled computer users who can find ways to circumvent or disable the software. (There are, in fact, numerous Web sites that tell them how to do so—should these be blocked by the software too?) Here is the simple fact: *There is no way to prevent determined youth from finding their way to "inappropriate" material if they are motivated to do so, especially when they are pooling their skills and sharing things that they find with one another.* Once one accepts this fact, the focus must clearly shift toward the questions of why young people are motivated to do so and how to talk with them about what they are doing and the harmful consequences that may result. In short, the only response that can reliably "work" in the long run is an educational response, not a technological one.

Partitions

A variation of the filtering approach is to restrict access only through pages (archives or "portals" as they are sometimes called) that are themselves lists of approved sites. This allows some other person or group to filter out unwanted materials and select desirable ones in terms of the values of the group concerned—certain religious groups, for example. A related approach to this issue, as took place in Germany with CompuServe (and occurs on some university campuses in the U.S.) is for a service provider to block access to certain sites for *all* users, because it has decided that it does not want to condone the provision of certain sorts of materials through its servers. Users do not have to use that service, but if they do they tacitly agree to the restrictions imposed on them (assuming that they are told that these restrictions exist). If they do not like the restrictions, they will have to find some other service provider, assuming that they have an alternative. Some users, of course, may *prefer* to use (and subsidize) such providers. Yet another related approach concerns online Web communities, such as those on Geocities or Tripod, which attract users to the group only when they agree to abide by certain norms and standards that define that group. So long as participants limit their involvement to interactions within the community, and to materials that have been screened by group members, they can reliably avoid anything that does not suit their values. These online groups rely on partitions that they assume define a "safe space." They are similar in some ways to the "gated communities" that attract new home-owners who want to live in a neighborhood sheltered (to the extent possible) from external threats and inconveniences. Of course, limiting one's activities and associations to such communities also places significant horizons on what can be found or learned that may surprise or challenge one's values—but, really, that is partly the point, isn't it?

Now, what sorts of buffers people will want in place to prevent either accidental encroachment across such partitions or, in the case of young people, intentional exploration that adults consider inappropriate, is yet to be fully worked out. (Although, increasingly, some of these buffers will be commercial in nature; access to certain materials will be by fee only or will require a credit card, which young children, presumably, cannot obtain.)

The best that can be said of this approach to censorship (and censorship it certainly is) is that it is more or less consensual. People choose to limit their own or their family's online interactions, accepting avenues of access that they know will not provide them with unrestricted flows of information in and out. They also, whether they know it or not, frequently make themselves subject to various sorts of surveillance, since many of these closed communities also maintain the right of policing their own members.

Clearly, granting to others the right to decide what is or is not going to be available for one's own online interactions raises serious questions. Who are these authorities? Who selects and authorizes them? What accountability do they have to the online group or community? How might potential abuses of that role be detected and corrected? In other areas, the role of librarians, editors, and archivists have traditionally entailed some similar risks and responsibilities: but these actors are also situated typically in professional contexts of training and accountability that make them subject to some restrictions on their prerogatives. They are often visible and public in their activities, or at least can be identified if they are not. The online equivalents of these roles are often carried out by people or groups who may have little accountability to anyone, and are subject to no higher court of appeal for decisions they make that might be deemed capricious or unfair.

As a way of keeping out the misinformation and malinformation that participants wish to avoid, such an approach is deeply flawed. The Web page selected as appropriate today may be very different tomorrow. In fact, if a page is a good educational resource, it probably will change—and possibly not to the liking of the original selector. An additional dimension to any cyberspace selection policy is that materials that are "rejected" by one group remain available within the broader Internet nonetheless. Many censors are concerned not only in limiting access to these materials for themselves or their own children, but for people in the general society. Placing intermediaries between one's self and the unwanted material creates a buffer that protects the consenting parties, but not those who remain outside that compact. When this sort of policy is applied to schools, of course, it is not the affected parties (the students) who are normally involved in the decision to create, in effect, a closed Intranet that only includes "approved" materials. Finally, creating a partition of any type always creates with it an exaggerated sense of curiosity and temptation (especially for the young) about what might be on the other side.

Labeling

One approach involves establishing a rating system or some other procedure for creating zones of coded content that provide the user with fairly consistent indicators of what they might find distasteful, either on their own behalf or for their children. This is roughly the process already followed with films, television shows, CD music disks, telephone sex lines, and certain publications. If one knowingly enters into and browses such materials, then consent is assumed. The capacities to build "meta-tags" into the code of Web pages, for example, allows search engines to identify (or avoid) certain sorts of material—which shows how easily a labeling approach can be modified into a filtering, censorship approach. As a result, some providers will simply not cooperate with the labeling system.

This raises an interesting problem. Some of the foremost advocates of free speech in modern society have not been civil libertarians or people motivated by an abstract commitment to political principle. Rather, it has been commercial vendors who have a stake in being able to market certain types of material and who favor the broadest scope of publishing discretion (and hence the broadest scope of potential customers and markets) possible. The irony here is that *voluntarily* accepting some restrictions can actually be good for sales; for example, a labeling system for raw content on music CD's probably *attracts* certain juvenile buyers. To put the point in the context of the Internet, any "Truth in Content" rules or standards will serve simultaneously as a way of protecting people from not encountering what they want to avoid, while also allowing others to find what they are looking for more easily. Here, as elsewhere in this chapter, there is no way to avoid the question of where these motivations and interests come from, particularly for young people.

The labeling approach seems to offer the best compromise between allowing consenting participants to view, discuss, and experience whatever they wish on the Internet, while not confronting unwilling parties unexpectedly with materials they find undesirable. It does not address the issue of where some groups or individuals do not want *others* to be sharing or discussing certain topics or materials at all, because they are considered dangerous, immoral, or politically threatening. As we noted, this was one of the major threats of the CDA: that it allowed people in distant locations to file charges against Internet sites, even when they involved only adult and consensual participants, because the material was viewed as offensive, dangerous, or immoral by those distant parties. (Of course, this potential application of the law was fully intended by the bill's sponsors.)

Until policy makers become more clear about whether their motives really are to "protect children" and to shield those who do not want to be exposed unexpectedly to something that will frighten or offend them, or whether their purpose is to prevent *anyone* from doing, saying, or seeing something that someone, somewhere, disapproves of, it is unlikely that any progress will be made on reaching reasonable compromises on these issues. Where children and young people are concerned, policy makers need to consider the possibility that while the prerogatives of parents, teachers, and others in authority need to be respected, young people *do* have certain rights, including the right to be curious, to want to learn things about adult life, and to express and consider controversial points of view.[2] Far too often, the discourse of "protecting" children from "obviously harmful" material slides easily into including more and more "inappropriate" information into the restricted category. In many contexts, schools and otherwise, the tendency is to err on the side of excluding too much rather than too little—which raises serious issues about invading the rights of young people as well as interfering with their development and growth into responsible and discerning Internet citizens themselves.

We have described these first four approaches to dealing with unwanted material (censorship through threatening providers, through filtering, through partitioning, and through labeling) as related forms of censorship based on either restricting supply or restricting demand. The latter forms seem less onerous because they are at some level censensual. They involve placing voluntary limits on what can be accessed at the receiving end, and so avoid the dangers of an imposed authority deciding what people can and cannot access. In fact, of course, these forms of restricting demand are often *not* consensual, particularly in schools, because they involve some accepting limits on behalf of others (limits that they often would not accept for themselves). Moreover, the problem with both the supply and demand approaches is that they abstract the technical problems from a larger social context. They analyze the problem as one of filtering out the "bad" to protect the "good"; and they see the failure of technical solutions as simply requiring more and better technical solutions. Some-times the results are merely laughable in the ways that they give rise to unexpected and counter-productive consequences. On a deeper level, however, we have suggested that such approaches to censoring access to information reveal a deeply anti-educational bias and have the potential to cause real harm. The remaining approach is quite different.

Critical Readers

We offer a modest proposal: to place a much greater emphasis on fostering the capacities of critical Internet use and what we have called "hyperreading" as a basis for giving students the tools to identify, criticize, and resist what is dangerous and undesirable on the Internet. This approach is far more practical than trying to protect them by pretending that these things do not exist, and thereby running the risk that when students do encounter them (as they likely will) their appeal and effects have been made even more dramatic because they have become forbidden fruit. The philosopher Plato favored a strong view of censorship and assumed that if certain ideas and material were never exposed to young people, they would never think of them on their own. This notion is probably false as a matter of psychological fact; but in the context of the Internet it is particularly self-deceptive. The Internet is rife with misinformation, malinformation, messed-up information, and mostly useless information; even learning how to avoid these requires learning that they are there, why they are there, and what to do about it. Preparing more critical and discerning young people is a kind of "vaccination" against threats and temptations they will certainly encounter (and, as sometimes happens with vaccines, the treatment to protect can occasionally end up causing the very illness it was supposed to prevent). For the very young, it makes sense to think in terms of supervising or filtering their online activities. As children grow in independence (and in their skill with the information and communication technologies), such approaches become increasingly ineffective and, indeed, counterproductive.

In schools, there are additional issues raised by the very notion of trying to supervise or scrutinize every student's online activities. Although we discuss such surveillance in more detail in the following chapter, it is important to raise the issue of surveillance in the context of censorship. Surveillance is certainly not new. Nearly everyone knows about two-way mirrors, tapped phones, surveillance cameras, intercepted memos, purloined letters, and leaked documents. Technology adds two new dimensions to surveillance. (1) Not only does it increase the ease and sophistication of surveillance, it allows for the accumulation and analysis of vast amounts of data resulting from that surveillance. (2) Because of its power, real or imagined, technology functions like Bentham's Panopticon—it constrains by the mere threat of surveillance (if you never know when you might be being watched, it has the same effects as if you constantly were).

Most users of information and communication technologies actually know very little about what these technologies can and cannot do. Is their e-mail stored? Can others read it? Is it true that their e-mail is passed through filters that search for certain words? What happens if inadvertently one of those words appears? When they navigate on the Internet, can their wanderings be tracked? Recorded? Passed on to authorities? Can others see what is on their own computer's hard drive? The fear of surveillance, of being found out, may prevent surreptitious visits by students to sites on the Internet that authorities might deem inappropriate for the educational task at hand. But the price paid for controlling the few becomes great when it limits the access of others.

It is important to see, moreover, that just because the individual user is making the "voluntary" decision to stay away from certain material, this too might be considered a form of censorship—self-censorship. Self-censorship is not the same as not reading a news story or paying little attention to a television report; it can mean conforming to peer pressure or the conventions of a particular group to which one belongs. It can mean a fear of disapproval. Learning to critically judge and select what one wishes to pay attention to, or not, is a positive, even necessary, educational aim. It advances the goal of personal freedom. But making the same sorts of choices out of fear or shame does not. This argument suggests that purportedly "voluntary" decisions need to be viewed within the conditions of choice under which they were made. Once again we return to the question of access. People who are excluded from participating in an educationally beneficial activity, even if it appears to be because of their "free choice," are disadvantaged unless we scrutinize the conditions under which those choices were made (and whether these people had any discretion or choice about those conditions).

CONCLUSION

We live in a world that is at times unpleasant. Understanding and learning to deal with some of the educational and societal problems of our times, problems of equality, democracy, freedom, and personal dignity, will often require the examination of a certain amount of that unpleasantness. If students are to attend seriously to understanding and improving themselves and the world in which they live, they will sometimes need to pursue educational inquiries wherever they lead. Censorship does not help students learn to ask questions they need to learn to ask; interesting lines of inquiry will not be followed; and creative answers will not be expressed. It is a far better approach to anticipate that students in fact *will* traverse into dangerous or upsetting material, and that what they need from parents and educators are better ways of questioning what it is in themselves, or in society, that gives rise to these incidents. Trying to ban such materials does not work, first of all, and by imagining that such bans could work, parents and educators leave themselves and their charges ill-prepared for the temptations and incitements that the Internet presents them with. Relying upon a technological filter or fix so that you can avoid talking about it does not help. Forcing young people to do what they will do anyway, only in private, or furtively with peer groups, is an abdication of responsibility by those who should take it upon themselves to help young people become prepared to deal with grown-up problems; even if it makes the adults very uncomfortable.

As with any important educational choice, context, purpose, and serious judgment play an unavoidable role in deciding, as a parent or a teacher, where and when certain material can give rise to a "teachable moment" that can serve a positive purpose. For example, the nudity that occurs in a film like "Schindler's List" is an indispensable aspect of the mood, message, and historical accuracy of the tale it presents. Taken out of context, a snapshot of one image from that film might be the sort of thing a teacher would confiscate from being passed around the classroom; in the context of the film, it might make the students weep, or realize the humiliation and horror the concentration camp victims were being put through. When are young people ready for this sort of experience? How should they be prepared for it? Should parents be told in advance, so they can request that their children not be allowed to see it? These are important questions that require serious reflection *from an educational point of view.* But few educators, we suspect, would accept a blanket ban that would prevent them from even considering the value of showing such a film. Yet these same educators might not see the parallel of imposing a similar ban on Internet use, or of adopting filters that make the same kind of decision invisibly, automatically, without any discussion about it at all.

There is another educational benefit of encouraging critical reading of the Internet instead of imposing censorship upon it: using discussions about misinformation, malinformation, messed-up information, and mostly useless information to highlight and reflect upon the procedures and criteria by which people identify information as "mis," "mal," "messed-up," or "mostly useless." These are clearly matters of debate and disagreement, as our discussion has shown, and crucial educational issues grow out of reflecting on these judgments, how they are made, and by whom.

To our way of thinking, the major current responses to the problem of "infoglut"—too much information, of too mixed and uncertain a quality and reliability—typify the technocratic mindset. The equation is typically framed in simple, straightforward cost/benefit terms. Access to the Internet is a benefit because it connects students to enormous amounts of information; but the cost is that some of that information is inappropriate at best, dangerous at worst. How can we have the good without the bad? What are the appropriate balances between the benefits of free access to information and the costs of potential harm to children? Having defined the problem in terms of benefits and costs, the next step seems simple: eliminate or minimize the objectionable material without abandoning what is beneficial. The only question is a technical one: *How?*

As we have argued, it is not that simple. While the desire to protect young children from accidentally encountering crude or dangerous material on the Internet is entirely understandable, as is the desire more generally of people not to have to deal personally with upsetting or offensive content, there is no general shortcut to solving these problems. The risk of exposure to unexpected and unwanted material is inherent to the structure of the Internet itself, and learning to deal with it inevitably includes actually experiencing it and then responding to that experience. While there are specific things that informed users can do to limit such nuisances, they are as much a condition of this public space as are foul graffiti, overheard profanity, exploiters of children, or hucksters in any other public space. For very young children it is possible to erect fairly effective barriers to limit their access to broad categories of material, but this is mainly due to the limits of children's abilities to exploit the technological resources, not the reliability of these protections themselves. It is a temporary solution at best. As we have said, there is no way to prevent motivated, sophisticated adolescents from accessing such materials if they are determined to do so. This means that the only intervention that can have any significant impact on this issue is an educational approach. This approach requires parents or teachers to talk with young people about their curiosities, interests, peer relations, feelings, and how they act those out.

Furthermore, as discussed earlier, the attempt to demarcate neatly "good" and "bad" (or "useful" and "indecent" material) is fraught with difficulties. Part of the problem is with the vague and subjective connotations of terms like "indecent" or "inappropriate." Such language inevitably brings in substantive social and political assumptions that are not merely technical in nature. But the problem goes even further than simply calling for better-defined criteria. The Internet is a hypertextual, fundamentally relational information environment; its defining feature is the *link*, the association of material and the opening of multiple pathways of getting from point to point within the information space. Restrictions on any portion of that system, therefore, will inevitably (and often unpredictably) constitute restrictions on some other, unintended portion of the system.

The attempt to restrict "indecent" materials on the Internet through imposing limits on supply or on demand will create many more problems than it will ever solve, because these are the wrong kinds of responses for the problems they attempt to address. These problems, in fact, cannot be "solved." The blanket approach of trying to weed out the bad while retaining the good cannot take into account the complexity of learning and knowledge, and the diversity and diverse needs of learners. This, then, is the educational challenge: helping students learn to operate in an environment that is inherently "dangerous," to deal with what may be unexpected or unpleasant, to make critical judgments about what they find. Such a task cannot be framed as simply sorting out the "good" from the "bad," and excluding all that is "bad." Educationally, we need some of the "bad" in order to create some of the "good." The development of skills of discernment, judgment, criticality, and so forth *require* that one encounter and deal with materials that are unpleasant, misleading, and offensive. It is through engagements with such materials that one can become more resistant to them: by making a *choice* that they are unworthy, dangerous, or immoral. Naturally, one consequence of having a choice, a real choice, is that sometimes it will be made foolishly or against one's own best interests. This too can be a necessary learning opportunity. In an open society with widespread media, an enormous diversity of viewpoints in public spaces, and the myriad content of the Internet at its disposal, any attempt to deal with these problems solely by censorship strategies must fail.

These issues represent, we believe, one of the deepest, most intractable dilemmas raised by the Internet. The evaluation of information and communication technologies continually presents society with issues that cannot to be analyzed in terms of simple choices or dichotomies. Such thinking promotes technocratic solutions that preclude the important questions that need to be asked when discussing the educational potential of the Internet. But, in the end, these disputes are not fundamentally about the possibilities and dangers of new technologies; they are age-old debates about freedom, morality, and responsibility—and how to teach them. What children and students will do, see, and collect in cyberspace raises issues beyond the capacities of the technology itself, and it creates potential problems that the technology itself is ultimately inadequate to handle or solve. Rather than discuss how to censor information from young people, we believe, parents and educators should focus their attention more on how to help young people become more responsible and learn to exercise critical judgment. Beyond this, we believe that few discussions in this area have ever taken seriously the idea of young people's rights to access some information whether adults want them to or not. It is not difficult to understand why most educators have shied away from these controversies; but in shying away from them, they have shied away from the deeper educational issues at stake.

NOTES

1. David Shenk, *Data Smog: Surviving the Information Glut* (San Francisco: Harper Edge, 1997).

2. Jonathan Katz, "The rights of kids in the digital age," *Wired* Vol. 4 No. 7 (1996): 120–123, 166–170. See also the "Blue Ribbon" site: www.eff.org/blue-ribbon.

chapter six

Surveillance and Privacy: Can Technology Protect What Technology Takes Away?

As we discussed in the previous chapter, censorship often entails a degree of surveillance to enforce it. Indeed, surveillance is itself a kind of censorship, in the sense that it can force people to avoid accessing certain materials (whether they are legal or not), for fear that they might be observed in the act. And as with censorship, surveillance is commonly described as a policy intended to "help" people, or "protect" people—especially the very young. In this chapter we will discuss the rise of surveillance in technological environments and the spread of these environments to encompass more and more of what people typically have considered their private space. We will reconsider this notion of privacy as it has changed in educational and other contexts. We will also interrogate the matter of who actually is being helped or protected by policies that erode the sphere traditionally designated as private.

The Shifting Meanings of "Privacy"

From recent popular films such as "The Net" or "Enemy of the State," to countless news features in the media, there is a growing sense of awareness of the vast implications of digital technologies for traditional assumptions about privacy. The volume of information that is instantly recorded whenever one uses a credit card, travels the Internet, visits a hospital or pharmacy, files a tax return, rents a film on video tape, and so on—information that can be accessed by authorized and unauthorized persons alike—has changed the speed and ease with which much of one's personal life and activities (including the circumstances of one's very body) can be recorded and observed by others. Most people have only recently become aware of how ubiquitous such digital record-keeping is. At the same time, cameras as local as the lens on an ATM machine to as distant as satellite imagery record the activities of individuals and groups in an almost constant, overlapping manner. Most people do not even notice any longer the almost seamless way in which their activities are being recorded through one mechanism or another wherever they are and whatever they are doing, once they are outside the home—and, as we will discuss later, even that domain is no longer very private. As these different systems of surveillance and record-keeping have become more numerous, pervasive, and interlinked, we will argue, the very notion of a discrete private sphere is disappearing.

The central premise of "The Net," that a young woman's entire life and identity could be erased and replaced with another by altering her digital records, plays off of a popular suspicion that the Net we use is also the net in which we are caught. Real and disturbing as these concerns are, however, the facility of certain digital means of access only has made more apparent changes that have been at work for more than a century (with the advance of bureaucratic organization, record-keeping, files, and lists). Furthermore, the idea that private space is being "invaded" suggests that we can easily sort out the legitimate from the illegitimate sources of observation and recording that reach into our personal lives. This essay will question such notions of privacy and invasion.

This topic is of special concern for educators. Children, and especially children in schools, have frequently been among the first to be examined, tested, charted, and evaluated, their performance tracked over time. Such techniques, once perfected and legitimated in their use with the very young, have often found their way into more and more areas of the general society.[1] Students typically have had very little privacy: from having to announce to the entire class when they need to use the toilet; to being observed through one-way mirrors; to having their desks, lockers, and persons subject to search; to having their property subject to confiscation; to having their correspondence (such as notes to one another) subject to seizure and scrutiny by authorities; to having few opportunities aside from the hallways, the toilets, or the playgrounds to engage in conversation with their peers. Students in most schools have had to accept encroachments upon their personal activities and social interactions that few adults would tolerate without outrage. The fact that these "invasions of privacy" have usually been justified as well-intended and practiced in the students' best interests must be seen as part of the process by which such practices come to appear innocent, legitimate, normal features of social life.

As classrooms enter the digital age, these two broad trends come into contact with one another: the capacity of computer networks to record and survey personal information, and the long tradition of schools to examine and discipline students "for their own best interests." One of the main benefits of digital technologies is in promoting new and more rapid forms of communication and information-sharing among users. Where these users are students, however, it is easy to anticipate some of the ways in which their communications and other uses of the Internet will be subject to screening if not outright censorship—as is already becoming apparent. But as we peel through the layers of this problem, we will come to see that "invading privacy" is not the most disturbing aspect of this process at work. By the end of this essay, the very meaning and value of "privacy" in schools (and in general society) will be viewed in an inverted fashion: less as a haven from state surveillance, and more as a confirmation and legitimation of it.

PRIVACY AND YOUNG PEOPLE

With networked computers in which certain kinds of file sharing have been activated, it is possible to survey everything from the text of users' e-mail correspondence, to the World Wide Web sites they have visited, to the contents of their hard drives. School students are not the only ones subject to such scrutiny. In the United States many states and private businesses have mandated that computers used in work environments cannot be used for games and that hard drives can be searched to find and expunge such software. The same can be done with "pirated" software that is not registered to the user. Of course, the rationale goes, these are "illicit" uses of the technology, which justifies such surveillance and intervention. Yet the very possibility of such scrutiny might have a chilling effect on other, perfectly legitimate, activities (like complaining about your boss with your co-workers over e-mail).

Nor are schools and workplaces the only sites where these interventions take force. In the U.S. the previously discussed Communications Decency Act sought to establish broad-ranging powers to limit what some consider "indecent" materials on the Internet. The law was a major initiative by conservative politicians, undertaken, they said, to "protect the children" (although its effects would restrict everyone's access to certain materials, not only children's). At what might be called the opposite end of the political spectrum, many have called for screening e-mail and Web site content to eliminate sexually harassing material, for example. It is easy to see the rationale for such policies: Do we want children to have free access to pornographic materials? Do we want adults using the Internet to solicit sexual liaisons with underage youth? Do we want to allow threatening, pornographic, or racist e-mail to be sent to individuals for the sole purpose of harassing them?[2]

However, many uses of surveillance do not seem to be so obviously matters of "protecting" children or others. Many of the commercial Web sites that cater to young people are among the most intrusive in gathering information about the children who visit them. Much of this data-gathering happens automatically, in the background. In other instances, the information is solicited, but in a context that makes it unclear what the information will be used for, and so it is doubtful whether it can be said that children are providing such information consensually or in full awareness of the consequences. Not incidentally, these sites are often also rife with advertisements, promotions, and other attractive enticements. It is a remarkable irony, in our view, that parents, teachers, and other authorities who are adamant about the threats to children being exploited by sexual predators or by purveyors of pornography (understandable concerns, without a doubt) are either oblivious to, or relatively unconcerned with, the implications of other ways in which young people are taken advantage of on the Internet, because they represent "legitimate" forms of solicitation and product marketing. The fact is that the average child is much more likely to be manipulated or taken advantage of by an online marketer than by a sexual predator.

Such questions seem to be more salient because we are talking about young people who may have fewer resources to protect themselves from unwanted materials and may exercise less experienced judgment in how they use digital technologies. However, in many instances these assumptions might be debatable since some young people are much more savvy and discerning in their understanding and use of the Internet than the adults who worry about them are. (Indeed, this may be part of the underlying problem: that adults who do not understand these technologies assume the most insidious uses for them and assume that young people are more vulnerable to offensive materials than they may in fact be.)

In the decentralized and globally linked context of the Internet such material cannot be effectively censored or banned at the point of production, so the currently evolving approach seems to be a heightened degree of surveillance and filtering at the point of reception. Here, again, the discourse of "protecting" young people easily blends over into the discourse of surveying and disciplining them. As we discussed earlier, several software programs allow users (or their parents or teachers) to block access to different categories of Internet materials. Even students' *attempting* to access such materials can be recorded and used to punish them. Individual e-mail messages sent and received by students can be screened and censored. The Web pages they visit can be reviewed by others. We believe that such interventions should be seen less as an invasion of some privacy that students once had, than a continuation of attitudes and practices that have always governed how young people in schools are treated.

Thus the central questions arising at this stage of the discussion are not, How do we avoid invading students' privacy? but, What kind of privacy have students ever had? What circumscribed notion of privacy are we trying to protect? Is protecting it—that is, maintaining its boundaries from further encroachment—also, ironically, a way of maintaining its boundaries from further *expansion*? By accepting certain tacit institutional practices and circumstances that have become so commonplace that we have stopped questioning them, are we in fact conceding a notion of privacy for students that is already so narrow that it is more worthy of critique than of preservation?

TECHNOLOGIES OF SURVEILLANCE

Perhaps the most-discussed section of all of Michel Foucault's writings is his description of Jeremy Bentham's dream (or nightmare) of the Panopticon, a system of surveillance originally designed with penal institutions in mind, but one that has become a metaphor for the much broader and subtler intrusion of observation and record-keeping techniques into more and more areas of social life.[3] The basic idea of the Panopticon is straightforward: a central tower or structure has windows on all sides, and it is in turn surrounded by a ring of cells occupied by the inmates, the open sides facing inward. Observers can look out in any direction, at any time, to see what any inmate might be doing. Furthermore, since the inmates cannot see into the central observation tower, every window or observation point does not, in fact, need to be staffed all the time; the *possibility* of being observed has a deterrent effect even when inmates are not in fact being observed. As inmates become accustomed to this environment, and to the routine of assuming that they are being observed at any/every time, it becomes less important for the observation tower to be staffed at all. The structure of the environment is what exerts control, as people internalize changes to their habits and movements without remembering the original circumstances that necessitated them. The panoptic condition becomes part of the identity of an inmate ("a madman, a patient, a condemned man, a worker, or a schoolboy").[4]

Several deeper conclusions follow from Foucault's discussion. The first is that such mechanisms of surveillance tend to become more pervasive. For example, few people notice how frequently they are monitored through partially hidden video cameras (from the bus or subway, to the bank, to the store, to the parking lot, to the elevator). All sorts of activities, and not only illegal activities, are inhibited by such surveillance. Now, everyone knows that such observation is supposed to protect people from assault or robbery, and in many communities people are up in arms because they want *more* protection, not less. But this is one of the central themes of Foucault's book: that as the mechanisms of surveillance and control become more subtle and "humane," they become more extensive; they actually become more controlling in their effects, but with less complaint.

For example, in schools, it is a commonplace that sitting in a circle is a more humanistic, egalitarian arrangement of persons in a classroom than the old row-by-row seating design. Progressive educators have pushed this idea for years. Yet, ironically, from a Foucauldian standpoint, a circular arrangement is in fact a more effective Panopticon, since every member of the circle is continuously visible to every other member, all the time. No skulking in the back row to sneak a candy bar into one's mouth! And again, even when one is in fact not being observed, at any moment one might be, and that is all that matters. Furthermore, all members of the circle become conspirators in the Panopticon, observers and observed; what the teacher might not see, others will.

The Panopticon, then, is not a simple physical structure, machine, or spatial arrangement: it becomes a way of life. As people accept the inevitability of being observed and recorded, their habits change; *they* change. As people become *more* visible, the omnipresent circumstances that observe and record their lives become *less* visible. As the "private" domain (the space of activity that is in principle unobservable, unrecordable) has become more and more circumscribed, an alarm about its now being "invaded" seems ironic, for the real issue is with how that domain has become already so compromised. Yet these restrictions, because they are often consensual, implemented gradually and with good sensible reasons, are actually more pervasive and insidious and hence harder to resist.

Finally, and at the extent where the Panopticon ceases to be a discrete physical structure or mechanism, but simply a feature of ways of living together, what does the distinction of "public" and "private" spaces mean any longer? For the ancient Greeks, this distinction actually corresponded to discrete physical locations, the *agora* and the household, two separate realms of activity and human relation. This chapter is not the place to engage the larger question of the status of such public and private spaces; but in a panoptic society people carry many of the attitudes and self-imposed restrictions of activity from the surveyed public into their private life. So in what sense is it still "private"?

What this discussion shows is that restrictions on privacy may be considered consensual in the sense that people give up certain degrees of freedom for the sake of protections that they believe preserve or enhance other freedoms. What is not seen is that this apparent tradeoff commits society to a basic dynamic that inevitably means a gradual diminishment of freedom and privacy in any sense at all. Spaces of free action are increasingly circumscribed by restrictions on freedom. These paradoxical tendencies come together in the idea of an *architecture*—not merely the physical architecture of buildings (or Panopticons), but the social architecture of ways of living. An "architecture" can be seen as the locus where capabilities of creativity and mechanisms of control come together. Architectures both contain and exclude, and the analysis of distinctive architectures (again, not only physical architectures) can reveal important dimensions, and limitations, of human freedom. As we will explore in greater detail in the final chapter, the Internet is such an architecture. While it is a medium that is enormously powerful and susceptible of quite varied uses, it includes constraints (as does any medium) on how information is shared, what sorts of information can be shared, and how people can communicate. It both enables and inhibits.

Within educational contexts and others, this paradox is of fundamental importance for thinking about the relation of new technologies to learning and human freedom. The *very same* devices that allow the creation, exploration, and sharing of new knowledge and information, that spark new possibilities of action and interaction, also facilitate a heightened degree of observation and record-keeping about what people actually do. The dynamics of simultaneous production and recording are clearly linked within communications media, especially computers (as noted, for example, whenever one visits a Web site, that server automatically records one's own address). One can avoid using such devices, in order to resist having one's freedoms compromised in one sense—but only at the expense of giving up the other kinds of freedoms and opportunities that those new technologies make available. A life without computers, without credit cards, without a passport—without schooling—may in one sense be less panoptic, and more "free"; but this freedom is obtained only at the cost of forgoing a number of other opportunities.

PUBLICITY AND THE INTERNET

As we have discussed in different contexts in previous chapters, the Internet is a medium for incredibly rapid and dispersed sharing of information. Some of this information may concern individuals: previous examples have shown how rumors and gossip can spread exponentially. As with other open media, the Internet raises questions about the proper boundaries and protections that should apply to individuals. For example, are existing libel and slander laws adequate to cover the particular ways in which Internet communication can spread information about someone that might be damaging to that person's reputation, or hurtful to him or her personally? *Is* the truth of such gossip a defense, as they say?

But the problem is much more complex than this, because unlike other media (unless one happens to work in that industry), the Internet is a place in which people act, write, and speak as denizens of this domain. It often is not a *separate* channel through which reports about people are circulated with or without their involvement. To the extent that the subjects of rumor or gossip are already participants in this medium, they have chosen a certain kind of publicity about themselves simply by virtue of logging on. This costs them certain kinds of privacy they may have been used to in other sorts of contexts. Society is having to deal more and more with such issues as: Are the contents of one's local hard drive a private space? Does one give up a degree of privacy by being part of a networked system (a LAN or an Intranet, for example)? What are the appropriate uses of cookies and other record-keeping devices that Web sites use to keep track of who is visiting them? Should a computer at work (or school) be subject to fewer privacy protections than a computer at home? And so on. What we are trying to illustrate here is a central theme of this chapter: that it is the very same decisions and choices about technology that promote certain types of opportunities and conveniences for the user that *create* certain privacy problems.

These issues of apparent choice and consent always need to be examined in the context of circumstances that people may *not* be choosing; from this broader standpoint, the apparent voluntariness of certain choices might be questioned. But there can be little doubt that within a surprisingly broad range of activities *people choose to lose their privacy.* To take a whimsical example, most people know about "web-cams" that individuals have posted on their home computers, transmitting shots of themselves at any time of the day or night, whatever they happen to be doing. If someone did this to another person without his or her knowledge or consent, it would be seen as a horrific invasion of privacy (although many workplaces do this, for "security" reasons, all the time). Web-cams appeal to a certain voyeurism on the part of the viewer, of course; but at a deeper level it needs to be asked, "Who is being exploited by whom here?" The web-cam provider may feel very strongly that the publicity gained serves his or her interests (by selling advertising space on the web-cam site, for example). Until a recent court decision, "reality-based" television shows involved police bringing film crews into homes to film suspects being interrogated or arrested. Remarkably the subjects must have signed release forms allowing this footage to appear on television. When people agree to have their privacy exposed, does this make it no longer a privacy issue? If they actively seek out, or consent to, a certain kind of publicity, for whatever purposes, do they thereby abandon their rights to complain later that their privacy was abused? And why is going to a workplace, or attending school, treated as if it involved that sort of consensual, if implicit, acceptance of publicity at the expense of privacy? Where young people are concerned, who is making these decisions, and what rights of consent or refusal should even young children be able to retain?

CONSENT AND IDENTITY

The language of "tradeoffs" suggests that these changes in publicity, privacy, and freedom are primarily matters of choice, choices that could be made otherwise. But as we have seen often a true choice is not possible because the very terms of social participation involve restrictions and encroachments upon personal life. Moreover, in many contexts, including school contexts, people are *not* asked if they consent to observation. Indeed, all of us are, in many circumstances, *already* surveyed with or without our knowledge. William Bogard's *The Simulation of Surveillance* provides a detailed and discouraging picture of how this happens.[5] Moving beyond a Foucauldian "panoptic" thesis to the ideas of Jean Baudrillard's *simulacrum* and Donna Haraway's *cyborg*, Bogard argues that we already inhabit a world constituted by simulations (through new virtual technologies, the media, the representations of advertising, and so forth). The spaces ("public" *or* "private") that we occupy are already constructed as imaginaries. They are to a large extent defined for us by cultural circumstances that we do not choose, that we can hardly see beyond, since they predominantly define the horizons of our understanding and our sense of ourselves. Hence, when we think that we are choosing between different possibilities, the options from which we can choose are themselves *not* chosen.

Moreover, the "we" who choose are partly defined by such technologies as well. We are, as Haraway says, cyborgs, humans with a technologically constituted identity. Bogard offers a perceptive analysis of how this happens: of how technologies of simulation and surveillance come together, of how the very processes for exploring or creating a sense of self inherently contain the conditions of surveillance and control as well. We have already mentioned the extensive data collection that takes place, with or without people's knowledge, and the kind of publicity and compromises to privacy one accepts (implicitly) as soon as one goes online. Still further, the increasing use of focus groups, survey techniques, and sophisticated computer modeling have enabled advertisers, marketing agents, pollsters, and politicians to become increasingly adept at developing audience or consumer profiles and predicting the preferences of persons *before they have even considered the choices themselves.* Such highly effective social science and psychological techniques are used for everything from helping police to decide which cars to pull over on some pretext and search, to helping politicians select the homes and neighborhoods on which to focus their "get out the vote" efforts. Such efforts at profiling and prediction are not new, but through the use of various digital technologies they have become much more sophisticated and effective, and extend through more and more areas of our lives.

It is sobering to think that when one enjoys a movie, a politician, or a breakfast cereal, it is often because a demographically correct test audience of people very much like us previewed the product and advised the producers on how to change it so that they (we) would enjoy it even more. The product is a simulation designed to fit the audience's expectations. The audience is already-examined consumers whose preferences and reactions have been predicted and shaped in advance. We seem to be making a choice as consumers (or as voters), but it is a choice that was prepared for us to make—of course, we like it; how could we not? Furthermore, as these choices are prepared for us, our tastes and attitudes are changed by them. These "public" incursions predict and shape our reactions even in the "private" sphere (what we read, what we eat for breakfast); they are constitutive of the people we are.

Such dynamics are clearly involved in schools. For example, when teachers identify student "needs" in terms of examinations normed on assumptions, based on previous representative samplings, as well as learning objectives, the loop of self-confirming identities closes in upon itself. When a test is *validated* on the basis of a certain percentage of students not doing well at it (a percentage that happens to comprise disproportionate numbers of certain racial and ethnic groups), then how do we judge the outcome when members of those groups do "fail" that test in large numbers? What Bogard wants us to see is how such processes—common practices in schools and elsewhere—are simultaneously acts of simulation and surveillance. They create knowledge, they create categories and norms, they create identities, and they constrain and direct human behavior. In the terms of this chapter, these are privacy issues. Privacy issues because they survey and constitute the identities that we carry with us throughout our lives, and because they represent attempts to shape, through modeling and prediction, the horizons of hope and possibility within which we act. Like the Panopticon, but even more pervasively, such interventions make us feel that what we do (or fail to do) has been observed and anticipated already.

THE DEVIL'S BARGAIN

To return to the question in our title, Can technology protect what technology takes away? There is a paradox in relying on the very mechanisms that have allowed increased and more sophisticated surveillance, record-keeping, and profiling of persons to also be the means of safeguarding this information. If it were not being collected in the first place, it would not need to be protected. But framing the question this way also puts the onus on society, and not only on technology: because that is where the decisions to collect this information originate.

To frame this question in a provocative way, do people really *want* privacy? There are many reasons to suspect not, whatever people might say. Most people accept the rationale of "protection" as a reason for being surrounded by video cameras much of the time they are outside the home. Of course, the same cameras that "protect" them from muggings also "protect" store owners from shoplifters, so it is not entirely clear whose interests are most seriously being considered here. In many schools and daycare centers, parents insist on having video cameras (which they can access via the Web) trained on their children all day long. Consumers ask companies to keep their credit card number on file so they do not have to re-enter it each time they make a purchase (especially in online commerce). A more accurate picture, we think, is that people often think they are trading their privacy for the perceived safety, convenience, or benefits they associate with publicity (including online publicity). To press the issue, we suspect that even today few people would give up the perceived advantages of this panoptic society, to return to a more robust sphere of privacy. The issue is no longer the protection of discrete "spheres" that have some meaning or existence apart from human choice and practice; it is the distinction between what people agree to, and what they do not agree to (or do not agree to in full knowledge of the consequences).

This is the Devil's Bargain. Look at the operations of commerce, again. The gathering of information about consumers (for example, collecting data from online transactions) can be—and is—justified in various ways. Companies say that this information allows them to serve customers better. Customers say they like the convenience of having customized information or advertisements sent to them, which anticipate their buying patterns and needs. ("Our records show that your car is due for an oil change. This is a friendly reminder, and we have included a coupon for you to use on your next service visit. We value your patronage!") Designers and manufacturers say that profiling information allows them to understand consumer preferences and shape products to better serve their wants and needs. Marketers say it allows them to anticipate the prospective market for products and to promote efficiencies in pricing and delivery of goods and services. Online prices are, correspondingly, lower. Banking and credit card companies like it because e-commerce is enormously faster and more convenient for them. Who loses? Privacy, shmivacy.

To take another, even more difficult, paradox, current proposals to create a National Health Database would undoubtedly be a boon to improving the quality of health care. Doctors could access an easily-searched database of a patient's entire medical history, checking for previous symptoms or maladies, watching out for harmful drug interactions, and so on. Diagnosis and treatment would be improved. Patients could travel or move across country without worrying about the loss of continuity for their health care. Time and record-keeping staff would be reduced. Costs would be lowered. Lives would be saved. But there is also no doubt that when such a system is established, it will be abused, hacked-into, and combed for information that will be used against public figures, celebrities, and even ordinary people applying for jobs. So, is such a database a good idea or not? Could a cost/benefit analysis ever help us in answering such a question?

These are the sorts of Devil's Bargains we make in schools as well. In our view, it is much too simple to justify actions that compromise the privacy of students in schools because they are a special population, because they are younger, or because the school experience is intended to be "good for them." Without denying that in fact the intentions of most educators are benign, it needs to be seen how these processes of surveillance and control operate behind the scenes (indeed, teachers are often subject to them as well). The ethos of the liberal state and its institutions and policies is fraught with good intentions; they are the internal as well as external thread of legitimation that allows its daily practices to continue.

But this chapter has attempted to show that the "privacy" one might seek to protect for students in schools has long been compromised. Moreover, the boundary of "public" versus "private" spheres generally that such concerns rest upon does not exist. In a panoptic society, students and the rest of us carry with us, in our own identities, the tacit restrictions, the categories, the very sense of being observed (examined, tested, surveyed, polled, modeled, predicted) *before* we act or choose. So what does "protecting privacy" mean any longer?

Bogard makes an excellent point about this as well. The system of digital record-keeping and examination prevalent in schools is merely the extension of a larger mode of operation typical of state institutions generally. Maintenance of precise records and ostensibly benign surveillance are integral parts of the process by which state agencies seek to "help" their clients. The dual imperatives of *bureaucracy* (maintaining detailed files as part of orderly business) and of *therapeutic practice* (observing and recording information to be used in diagnosis and treatment) coincide, reinforcing and legitimating one another.

Collecting mountains of information itself, as well as having legal access to all sorts of information collected by others, the state *creates* a problem of privacy by its own means of operation. Having collected such information and used it for its purposes, the state then presumes to undertake the responsibility of "protecting" such information and defining what will constitute legitimate and illegitimate uses of it. Yet the potential for "misuse" is inherent in the very fact that such information is collected and maintained in the first place. Here the scope of privacy, and its protection from "invasion," is nothing more than the self-defined limits that the state allows in the use of information and surveillance data that it has authorized itself to collect.[6] The state may seek to protect this information, but in the realm of digital technologies no protection is entirely secure, once the information is gathered and stored online. Moreover, in deciding itself what will constitute use and misuse, the state cannot readily recognize when its own (possibly well-intended) conduct may itself be a species of misuse.

To be sure, states often do adopt laws (Privacy Acts, and so forth) that exert real restrictions on their information-gathering activities, and on who can access certain information, and for what purposes. Such laws are not trivial, and they constitute a major area for political contestation and resistance. These restrictions, though real, are restrictions that the state writes, interprets, and imposes upon itself (including the exceptions it grants itself to those restrictions). The actual scope of their application is an outcome of the extent to which citizens allow their own horizons of freedom to be defined for them. This is one way in which the scope of privacy can be rethought as the *outcome* of a process of consent, contestation, and resistance, not as a given to be protected.

In the context of public schools, state policies and procedures of record-keeping and examination are supposedly justified by a concern with the best interests of children, protecting them from indecency, harassment, exploitation, or their own illicit conduct. (As noted before, one cannot deny that this motivation is frequently sincere.) Activities of testing, examining, and categorizing, on the one hand, and activities designed to protect students through surveying or screening their communications *both* are redefined and facilitated by new digital technologies. In many circumstances, they become indistinguishable. They become more effective, more pervasive, and more difficult to recognize and resist. And thereby they become more accepted as a part of the institutionalized environments to which we are all subject at one time or another.

The free exercise of communication and information-sharing by students has often been regarded by educators as mildly subversive. This is a domain in which students do contest the sphere of privacy that is defined for them. From passing notes surreptitiously, to whispers, to graffiti in the bathrooms (and now in their uses of the Internet) students have always sought to resist surveillance and to find alternate avenues for communication and interaction. Such resistances seek to create a sphere of *unauthorized privacy* that is explicitly not dependent upon the approval of authorities or state "protections." This is a second way in which the scope of privacy can be rethought as the outcome of a process of consent, contestation, and resistance.

In communications between teachers and students information is often elicited for the purpose of "helpful" diagnosis of student problems, for the routine examination of student performance, or for the prevention of "illicit" conduct. Such activities, however well-intended, need to be seen as manifestations of how the state operates at the ground level. This interaction exists against a background of unequal power (a power dynamic that bears upon different students and groups to different degrees). It *creates* privacy issues by collecting information that then must be protected from misuse, by shaping attitudes and constructing identities that students carry with them out of the public school and into their private lives, and by drawing out from students their thoughts and feelings in an asymmetrical relation where the student ends up exposed, and the teacher does not. One response to such requests for information is *silence*. This is a third way in which the scope of privacy can be rethought as the outcome of a process of consent, contestation, and resistance.

The erosion of privacy has happened through a series of gradual compromises. The promise of good intentions, on one side, and the promise of trust, on the other, create the mutually sustaining fiction that one can safely trade off the privacy of one's personal life and activities for the sake of greater protection in an increasingly estranged social world. The tradeoff occurs through the acceptance of surveillance, in the expectation that it will only inhibit illicit conduct; through the acceptance of new constraints, with the belief that some freedoms must necessarily be limited so that others might be preserved; and through the tacit assumption that these are freely made choices, when the very terms of choice are themselves constituted in ways one does *not* choose. And, when dealing with young people, in schools particularly, they are given no choice in the matter at all. In all of these ways, we have found ways to accustom ourselves to the gradual erosion of privacy, to come to accept that increased state interventions are the only way of preserving the "privacy" that remains. We hope to have made this contradiction explicit.

What we have tried to sketch here is a tension between "authorized" and "unauthorized" senses of privacy. The notion of an authorized sphere of privacy, in which the state, having gathered information about nearly every aspect of one's life that it can, promises to protect it and use it only for legitimate purposes, is in many respects a contradiction. Instead, privacy needs to be thought of not as a sphere, certainly not as a "protected" sphere (protected by whom?), but as an *outcome* of a process of consent, struggle, and resistance. The instance of student communication in schools, including the use of digital technologies, helps to reveal several general ways in which this resistance might be manifested: (1) by contesting the self-defined restrictions that the state does impose upon itself; (2) by maintaining a scope of *unauthorized privacy* that circumvents, to the extent possible, the well-intentioned limits and "protections" that state authorities seek to impose; (3) by silence, by withholding trust in certain cases, and by refusing whenever possible to provide information that can be used for the ordinary business of record-keeping, categorizing, modeling, prediction, profiling, and intervention into the choices and decisions, not only of one's self, but of unwilling others. In other words, delimiting a meaningful sense of privacy often entails *resisting* the mechanisms society has set up to "protect" it. In this, as in many other respects, students may have something to teach the rest of us.

NOTES

1. See Michel Foucault, *Discipline and Punish: The Birth of the Prison*, trans. Alan Sheridan (New York: Vintage Books, 1977) for the different senses of "examination" at work here.

2. An excellent overview of privacy issues and computers can be found at the "Cyberspace Law" web site. Its URL is www.counsel.com/cyberspace/privacy.html. See also the Electronic Privacy Information Center: www.epic.org, The Center for Public Integrity, "Nothing sacred: The politics of privacy," www. publicintegrity. org/nothing_sacred.html, and Jerry Kang, "A privacy primer for policy makers," www.law.ucla.edu/Student/Organizations/BLT/01/KangJ.html.

3. Foucault, *Discipline and Punish*, 200–209; see also Mark Poster, *The Mode of Information: Poststructuralism and Social Context* (Cambridge, England: Polity Press, 1990): 69–98.

4. Foucault, *Discipline and Punish*, 200.

5. William Bogard, *The Simulation of Surveillance: Hypercontrol in Telematic Societies* (New York: Cambridge University Press, 1996).

6. Bogard, *The Simulation of Surveillance*, 125–126, 131–133.

chapter seven

INFORMATION FOR SALE:
COMMERCIALIZATION
AND THE EDUCATIONAL
POTENTIAL OF THE INTERNET

In 1934, the U.S. government gave television broadcasters free and exclusive use of the public airwaves on the condition that they serve the "public interest, convenience, and necessity."[1] To the disappointment of those who, at the time, saw the possibility for television becoming a national educational resource, the new medium was almost immediately taken over by commercial interests. Television quickly grew into a vehicle whose primary purpose was to deliver viewers the real "product" of the enterprise, to advertisers, using programming as bait. In 1961, Newton Minnow, President Kennedy's Chair of the Federal Communications Commission, in a speech to network broadcasters, described television as a "vast wasteland."[2] By 1995, according to Minnow, the situation had only gotten worse: "No other democratic nation has so willingly converted its children into markets for commercial gain and ignored their moral, intellectual, and social development."[3] At a time when serious consideration has been given in the U.S. Congress to cutting the funding for noncommercial public television, the pretense that television is anything other than a commercial enterprise has been dropped. Television's educational potential is clearly a secondary consideration to the concerns of corporate profits and economic growth.

The computer is not a television and cyberspace is not the space between channel one and channel one hundred and one, but there are parallels to be drawn and lessons to be learned. The enormous educational potential of television was compromised for the interests of commerce. To what extent, we ask, will this same phenomenon occur on the Internet? What will be the price of admission for educators and educational institutions? As we think critically about the educational promises and pitfalls of new information and communication technologies, we need to examine not only their costs, in terms of capital, but also in terms of the consumer and commercial messages that become embedded in the education provided to children and young people. Hardware and software, wired schools, corporate sponsorship and logos that adorn school web pages, the proliferation of unwanted solicitation and advertisements in cyberspace, the gathering of "marketing information" over digital networks—these all create a tension between economic and educational considerations, which we believe is a contradictory relationship.

HARDWARE AND SOFTWARE, UPGRADES AND DOWNTIME

The most obvious commercial interests associated with new information and communication technologies are those related to the sale of hardware and software. Taking a page from the marketing genius of Detroit, and aided by rapid advances in technological innovation and manufacture, hardware and software companies have given new meaning to the term "planned obsolescence." Detroit relied on marketing and the influence of fashion and style to sell new cars to individuals who had perfectly good older cars. But at least there was backward compatibility—you could drive to the store just as well in the new car or the old one. Things are different on the "information superhighway." Not only do hardware and software companies draw new business (as well as create a great deal of repeat business) with claims of new features and increased speed, but in what amounts to a conspiracy of constant improvement, we can no longer drive "the old car." The almost unimaginable shortsightedness of the Y2K problem aside, software programs that are perfectly adequate for the tasks that many people wish to use them for, no longer run on the newest computers. As operating systems change, adding features that are sometimes useful but as often as not either arcane or simply gimmicky, previous generations of software become incompatible and obsolete. Worse yet, software manufacturers often charge for an "upgrade"—a euphemistic term for having to pay for essentially the same product over and over. An upgrade may add a few new features but mostly fixes problems that existed in the older version. In other words, first generation purchasers of a new application or operating system are often subsidizing development costs for the version (2.0 or higher) that finally works the way it is supposed to. Too often consumers serve as a test audience for software that manufacturers know is imperfect and incomplete. After receiving feedback on problems and on how to make their product function properly, the companies then resell the product back to the same users as an upgrade.

And by changing file and data standards with new versions of their software, manufacturers force holdouts back into the fold. Individuals perfectly happy with Word Processor 1.0 soon find that they cannot exchange files with those using Word Processor 3.0. Not only must they upgrade at their own expense, but they must also invest time into learning the operation and features of a program they may not need nor want. This seriously undermines the autonomous choice of any given consumer to decide his or her own needs and purchase accordingly; the consumer market is interlinked in the same way the networks are.

All this "improvement" creates havoc in educational settings. Given the sizable initial investments needed to adopt new information and communication technologies at a school or district level, it can be backbreaking to then have to spend a comparable amount of money just a year or two later. Without constant attention, servicing, expensive upgrading, and frequent replacement cycles, the computer lab in a typical public school soon deteriorates into an incompatibility nightmare. Expensive machines that were purchased just a short while ago are now only good as planters, fish tanks, and doorstops for the "educational needs of the 21st Century." In an effort to keep up, schools feel pressured to spend their limited resources replacing perfectly good equipment and software for the sake of currency and compatibility.[4] The deeper threat is that if institutions do not grow gradually with each upgrade, the cost for the wholesale change that will inevitably come will be even greater. If they don't keep up, they may never be able to catch up.

The demands of ever-shortening replacement cycles have human and instructional costs as well. Schools, teachers, and students are caught in a tension between staying current and up-to-date or making do with what they have, a situation that can result in their being able to do very little at all. Many educators feel a sense of professional responsibility to stay current. But as they look forward to high capital outlays and commitments of time they are faced with daunting challenges. Considering the requirements in time and effort for new training and the political battles to be waged with skeptical taxpayers and those inclined to blame schools and the Internet for all that is wrong with American youth, the price for continual innovation may seem too high.

Given the cost of access to the educational resources made possible with information and communication technologies, schools with the fewest capital resources will face the untenable choice between remaining unconnected to a world of learning and occupational opportunities, or choosing to invest in technology and making severe educational sacrifices elsewhere. Where are resources better spent—a few dozen computers with Internet connectivity or an additional full-time teacher in a classroom? Bathrooms that work? Asbestos removal? A metal detector to keep guns out of the school? Even when they can make some minimal investment in new information and communication technologies some schools may be forced to settle for using the pedagogically bankrupt CAI practices of the previous generation because they are unable to exploit the full technological resources of a higher-end system. While students in some schools create and maintain Web sites and use the Internet as a research and presentation resource, students in other schools, if they are able to use computers much at all, spend their time with learning-to-type programs and running ancient computerized drill and practice exercises. And quite predictably, the latter will happen in certain segments of society much more frequently than in others.

Information and communication technology changes the very way individuals do their work. People do not type anymore, they word-process. Many libraries have abandoned their card catalogs in favor of online databases. In many schools people who do not get e-mail are out of the "information" loop, and so fall even further behind. The determination of how individuals work, in turn, influences the expected nature of that work.

For example, the expectations for a student essay start to change when the essay is produced on a word processor rather than a typewriter: format, font, charts and illustrations, grammar, even spelling are all evaluated differently because of the capabilities of new technologies. On one hand these capabilities, these new features, provide a greater range of options for the user, but on the other hand, they are not simply options—their use becomes expected.

These changing expectations are not, or should not be, lost on teachers. Where a generation ago teachers competed with television for the *attention* of their students, today they compete with the World Wide Web for the *instruction* of their students. As school districts need to justify large expenditures for information and communication technologies, the pressure for teachers to incorporate these technologies into their teaching increases. On one hand, the computerization of attendance records, grades, and assessment measures maintained on a centralized database, or memos and announcements sent via e-mail represent minimal intrusions into the work of most teachers. But the expectations to use new technologies in instruction are another matter. At a time when most teachers are already preoccupied with demands for higher test scores and increased accountability, the effort required just to keep up, let alone stay on the "cutting edge" of technology, is nearly overwhelming.

A similar concern that affects teachers is that in a market-driven world of continual upgrades and innovation, individuals are forced to surrender to others the decisions about the technologies with which they will work. Upgrading becomes a dynamic with its own inevitable logic: If individuals want to participate in new arenas (such as the Internet), then they are pulled along by the inevitable logic of development in the network as a whole. If schools expect a certain degree of technological participation, this cannot be left up to personal choices. District and school administrators, often with little knowledge of an individual teacher's work, will make decisions about which platforms will be purchased, what features individual's machines will have, and which software will and will not be supported. With this loss of individual choice comes a loss of control over how an individual works, and a loss of control over the content and nature of that work. Computer labs in schools, if they are to work at all, must be standardized with the same software, the same operating systems, the same filtering schemes. And while this may work well for the maintenance of the facility, it severely undermines the autonomy and discretion of the faculty.

Finally, for many users the "information superhighway" is a toll road: the longer you ride, the more it costs. Antithetical to the rather sloppy and serendipitous way the Internet works, where a search for something useful and relevant to one's needs may take some time, pecuniary concerns in cyberspace create concerns of efficiency. There is pressure to get in, get the information, and get out. "Pay as you go" services create a situation where individuals are discouraged from exploring—just the sort of behavior we believe makes the Internet so potentially educative. People would be infuriated with libraries that charged admission, and then charged use of library materials by the minute. Yet this is just the way many schools must connect to the Internet. And once again, those that need the most can probably afford the least.

Getting connected has other costs as well. For nearly everyone, the gateway to the Internet is controlled by a commercial provider or an educational institution. Many such providers impose restrictions that affect the content and utility of the Web for the user. Users may need to use specific software that privileges certain companies (in commercial arrangements, where some sites can only be accessed with a specific company's browsers). There might be a restriction on what sites can be visited, or which newsgroups can be read. The e-mail an individual sends or receives may be filtered or monitored.

Likewise there may be restrictions on the content of the Web pages that individuals create.[5] The hidden cost of many providers is the restrictive price of censorship—restrictions on what can be sent, received, or viewed. As we have argued, censorship can come in many disguises, and sometimes the mere fact of not being able to bear certain costs keeps another potential learner out of the loop, another potential Internet denizen silent.

First of all, then, the Internet needs to be seen as a commercial environment at the level of a set of consumable products that must be purchased as the price of admission. Such products include computers, software, monitors, printers, modems, network cables, Internet service, new electrical wiring and outlets for the lab room, security systems, and so on. The simple fact is that the providers of these products stand to make enormous amounts of money as a result of adoption decisions by districts and schools. Marketing to these audiences is aggressive, often well-intended and creative, but has very high stakes commercially.

ADVERTISEMENTS, SPONSORS, ENDORSEMENTS, AND LOGOS

If it is true that you get what you pay for, then the Internet seems almost too good to be true. For many users, it provides a low-cost cornucopia of information, entertainment, and diversion. Cyberspace appears to be a learning resource of almost unlimited potential—an unregulated, dynamic space in which to explore and learn (although, as we discussed in a previous chapter, this openness creates educational problems as well). But a closer examination shows that cyberspace may not be as free or as unregulated as it first appears. The commercialization of the Internet may ultimately impose a kind of systemic regulation and pecuniary sensibility that will transform the current notion of cyberspace as a decentralized, free, and open information resource.

Americans live in a culture where advertising is so ubiquitous in public spaces that they take it for granted. Advertising has become equally ubiquitous in cyberspace—often in the form of banner ads that appear on a Web site long before any real information appears. Such advertising helps to subsidize the development of some valuable Web resources: search engines, portals, access to free Web pages for users who do not have access to their own server, and so on. What is so wrong with advertisements, even if they are placed on Web sites that young people and their teachers are most likely to explore and use?

Alex Molnar points out in *Giving Kids the Business* that the desire to advertise to young people in and out of schools is nothing new. As an example, Molnar discusses at length Chris Whittle's Channel One, the enterprise where, in exchange for free video equipment including televisions and VCRs, participating schools agree to require students to watch twelve minutes daily of Whittle programming—ten minutes of youth-oriented news and two minutes of commercials.[6] The money, big money for Whittle, is in the commercials. Whittle's intrusion into schools is a very large and very public endeavor, but as Molnar points out, Whittle's enterprise is simply one of many strategies corporations have used in their attempt to advertise to the captive audience of children in school.[7] As long ago as 1963, Jules Henry's *Culture Against Man* made clear the profound and irrational effects advertising has on our culture. It focused specifically on how corporate advertising targeted children—not so much for their current buying power, but as part of their education, their cultural inculcation into capitalism, consumerism, and the goal of lifelong product loyalty.[8]

Not unlike television, advertisements in cyberspace turn students into products. The site delivers the student to the advertiser, and the more visits per site, the more lucrative the relationship between the advertiser and the site provider. This commercial arrangement creates the pecuniary impetus for site providers to create popular, attractive sites that will be visited often. But what is the cost of this popularity? From an educational standpoint, we believe the cost is significant. The price paid for such a commercial relationship is the disadvantaging of sites that offer specificity, depth, and attention to topics of limited appeal: controversy, minority opinions, unconventional views, and critical analyses.

Advertisements foster a culture of seduction where popular appeal and appearance can become of greater concern than content. This is the lesson we should have learned from television: accessibility, approachability, and lowest common denominators become paramount. It is not that quality and reliability must necessarily be compromised for popularity—a source of information that totally lacks credibility will most likely receive few return visits. Our concern, as we have discussed previously, is that in balancing considerations of style and content, all too often style emerges victorious. According to AdKnowledge Inc., a "provider of Internet advertising management strategies": "Advertising is a buyers' market. The advertisers and agencies dictate how business is conducted in all other media and the Web will be no different. Web sites that believe their 'content is king' will find themselves on the difficult side of negotiation."[9]

Advertisements influence content and thus credibility in other ways beyond giving greater import to style over substance. Naturally, advertisers are selective about where they advertise and what they sponsor—concerns as true in cyberspace as they are in other public spaces. Corporations are concerned with placing their advertisements where individuals most likely to be interested in their products or services will see them. And certainly the practices of targeting audiences and of strategically placing ads are not lost on those who create sites in cyberspace. Some educational Web sites are designed from the very beginning with advertising potential in mind. This means, of course, that they are specifically created in order to attract the kinds of targeted audiences that corporations find attractive for their advertising pitches.

Not only do corporations target specific audiences, they want to appeal to the broadest number of potential customers, without offending or alienating anyone, if they can avoid it. Knowing full well the importance of corporate identity and image, and understanding the proclivity of certain political and ideological groups to mount boycotts against advertisers and sponsors of content they disapprove of, most corporations are very conservative when it comes to advertising. This creates a situation where advertisers want to have at least tacit approval over the content of what they sponsor. This may be a situation society is ready to live with when it comes to an entertainment medium such as commercial television, but it becomes an entirely different matter in cyberspace when we are dealing with a medium that may become the backbone of educational opportunities. Commercial, for-profit interests are often at odds with the aim of free and open inquiry wherever it may lead. Credibility is suspect when there is the understanding that the ideas expressed, the information provided, or the views propounded have received some sponsor's tacit approval.

The commercialism of cyberspace imposes the Darwinism of the market on a medium that, until now, has encouraged the flourishing of myriad possibilities, whether profitable or not. Popular sites attracting sufficiently large audiences may be able to support themselves with advertising revenues alone. But as we have discussed, these sites may be less credible, yielding to the commercial and ideological concerns of sponsors and containing only the mainstream content necessary to attract large audiences. On the other hand, more "discriminating" sites may need to begin some sort of fee-for-access arrangements. Some of these sites will fall into the realm of "Adult Entertainment"; others will be "need to know" information providers (stock quotes or medical information, for example); still others will be sites that deal with topics and issues where demand is too small to generate sufficient advertising revenue. In some cases, these sites, independent from external constraints, will have the possibility of being more credible. But their prominence on the Web and their accessibility for those who may not have the resources to pay for them will certainly be diminished. The educational danger is that in such a two-tiered system, sanitized but free information will be the only information available to many.

We are not suggesting that the Internet should become some sort of charitable zone where people are not remunerated for their time, effort, or expertise. We are not suggesting that the Internet be made analogous to the Public Broadcasting System, its content subsidized by the government. Certainly, government intervention raises its own dangers of ideological control. What we are suggesting is that in the commercial environment developing in cyberspace, credibility and quality of information, and access and openness of information, will be in an inverse relationship.

Furthermore, the presence of the commercial and the educational existing side by side in cyberspace has the potential to form troubling new relationships that seem only to exist in cyberspace. These are the relationships formed by the capability in cyberspace to link sites together. When an advertiser or sponsor is associated with a Web site, each potentially benefits from its associations with the other. As in the discussion of the rhetoric of links, earlier, each is seen differently in view of its connection to the other (a tobacco company that sponsors a Web site about motorcycles, for example).

Moreover, most advertisements or banners are also links. It is one thing to have an educational site contain an identification of its sponsor—with the implicit approval of content that this implies. But what are we to make of a link on an educational site that takes users (here, students) directly to the commercial site? Some cases in point: The Web page for a county school district in Virginia contains links to Amazon Books and Barnes & Noble. Well, okay, books and education seem to go together. But the same site also contains a link to QVC, a home shopping cable television station. An elementary school site in central Washington includes a link to a commercial site that claims to be "family friendly" but hosts dozens of advertisements for items ranging from educational toys to luggage tags to automobiles. A charter school in Georgia prominently lists its corporate partners including McDonald's, a local bank, and a national realty franchise. A cursory search of the Internet shows that many school sites either display corporate logos, contain links to commercial sites, or proclaim themselves something like a "Discovery School"—a designation that identifies them with the Discovery Channel. The Discovery Channel is a commercial television station that provides much less educational programming than, in its own words, "informative entertainment." "Educational" or "Resource" links on many school sites connect to corporate sites such as Crayola, Disney, and so on. All of these corporate sites contain interesting and often imaginative activities (remember, they are trying to attract and retain attention, too), but they function primarily to advance the image and ideological concerns of the sponsor. Now, nearly every adult, every teacher, who has been awake for the past few years knows that there is software to filter out obscene or dangerous information on the Internet; and many schools and libraries are now required to install such software. But how many of them know that there is similar software, such as WebFree, that can be installed to block all advertising from downloaded Web sites? And how many schools are being asked to install *these* programs?

What is the educational lesson here? Buy from large corporations rather than locally, shop at QVC, and eat at McDonald's? Certainly that is one lesson. But the other, deeper lesson is that education and capitalism go hand in hand.[10] For a number of reasons that we discuss in this book, this is both a good thing and a worrisome thing. Corporate sponsorship and private investment in Web endeavors can support innovation and high-quality sites. But if sources of information and opinions will require sponsors to maintain a voice and presence in the Internet of the future, who will sponsor the unpopular, the challenging, the critical voices that disagree with the interests and outlook of the sponsors? Who, for example, will sponsor the anti-McDonald's site?[11] To what extent is the Internet playing a role in instilling users with a more commercial mindset themselves, becoming more enmeshed in the operations of capitalism (for example, through sites like eBay, that let every user become a small capitalist; through personal investment sites, that let every user be a player in the stock markets; and so on)? Are schools in the business of inculcating students with the spirit of unbridled capitalism? Who gave them this charge?

The censorship and shaping of opinions that result when commercial interests coexist too closely with educational interests are clearly of deep concern to us. But there is little evidence that the public worries much about the proliferation of commercial influence on the Internet. First, there seems little differentiation to many between free civic speech and free commercial speech.Although this is a much broader issue than can be addressed in depth here, it is our sense that there is no strong argument for why commercial speech should be given the same protection and access to children in schools afforded other types of free speech.We see the right of young people to express themselves freely and to have access to a broad spectrum of materials and ideas as different *in kind* from the rights of a beverage company to try and persuade students to buy their brand of soft drink.

Second, as Molnar points out, society seems to have come to the conclusion that corporate involvement in schools represents an acceptable trade-off. If advertising to young people results in more computers, free software, and so on, good. If corporate sponsorship and advertisements allow for even more sites in cyberspace, all the better. For schools with inadequate funding (because taxpayers balk at funding schools at the level of their needs), we understand perfectly well the attractiveness of such deals. So do the corporations offering them. What we would argue, however, is that these gains come at too high a cost—force-feeding students with the implicit educational message that good citizens are good consumers.

What we find troubling is the prospect that the concerns of commerce, the requirements of those who financially support the infrastructure of cyberspace, will ultimately bring a great leveling and mediocrity to the Internet. If cyberspace evolves into something like modern television to the nth power, it will not be primarily because of government regulation or notions of political correctness or misguided censorship, but rather by a broad-scale capitulation to the economics of what sells. Do we really want to build our educational programs around "informative entertainment?"

THEY KNOW WHERE YOU LIVE

Just as the commercialization of cyberspace can taint credibility and limit access, market interests on the Internet also can exacerbate the serious issues of surveillance and privacy that we discussed in the preceding chapter. At what point does the collection of marketing information for the purpose of targeting advertising become an affront to privacy and a constraint on educational opportunities? At what point do fears of surveillance or of becoming the target of unwanted solicitation begin to limit where individuals go and what they do in cyberspace? Navigating through the Internet, browsing through Web sites and looking in on discussion groups certainly has the feel of anonymity—rarely is one required to divulge one's identity or purpose. But despite the feel of anonymity, cyberspace is not as anonymous as it seems. When you have access to others, they have access to you.

An important part of the educational potential of cyberspace is that it is anonymous. But this is at odds with the interests of commercial entities who wish to know as much as they can about the individuals who visit their sites on the Internet. To that end, technologies have been developed and the capabilities of browsers exploited to maintain a record of who surfs the Web and where they go. As most readers of this book will know, many Web sites have the capability of writing a small text file on a user's hard drive when a connection to that site is made. The file, called a "cookie" (an innocent name—though we tell children not to accept them from strangers!) can be sent from the site itself or from one or more of the banner advertisements located on the site. Cookies are also sent by some search engines, keeping track of the keywords or topics accessed by the user. There is much misunderstanding about cookies; briefly, this is what cookies can and cannot do.[12] Cookies were originally developed so that certain sites could store information such as user ID numbers and passwords and users would not have to retype certain information each time that they visited the site. Cookies can also track users' activity on a certain site, recording which pages were visited and which were not, for example. In this way, they can be used for purposes of site design and maintenance. Advertisers can use cookies to track which banner advertisements a user has seen on a particular site, thus allowing them to send a greater variety of advertisements.

Until recently, the primary objection to cookies has been that they are placed on the user's computer, often without the user's knowledge or consent.[13] Currently, however, the use of cookies has become more sophisticated. The ability of banner advertisements to send cookies, and the existence of several companies that place advertisements on many Web sites, raises the power and possibilities of these small, seemingly innocuous files. A cookie sent by an advertising agency that places a banner advertisement on a site (rather than a cookie sent by the site itself), can be used to create a profile of a user's browsing across all the sites that also use that advertising company's banner advertising. This allows for the targeting of ads across many Web sites. It also keeps track of the user's travels across cyberspace. Likewise, certain search engines construct profiles of users based on what they search for—search words or topics. This can be used to construct a more individualized tailoring of searches based on past searches. It also provides a detailed record of the kinds of information a specific individual seeks out.

Understandably, this technology raises some frightening surveillance and privacy concerns. The data collected by cookies can be linked with the information that all browsers reveal when connecting to a Web site: the computer's IP address and the browser type. Since many computers have static IP addresses and are assigned to individual users, it is only a small step to connect a user's identity to the profiles developed by the extensive use of cookies. Cookies can be written that are even more intrusive: looking at the user's hard drive for information and sending it back to the Web site managers.

Our concern is that as long as market forces play a dominant role in the operation of the Internet, there will always be the push to obtain more rather than less information about users and their activities in cyberspace. How this will play out technologically is hard to predict, but as AdKnowledge states: "Frequency of exposure to advertising messages is the key to its effectiveness. Advertisers must be able to target within each Web site for repeat visitors, for given ad banner exposure frequency. Whether the technique to measure frequency is cookies or some other method, it is an essential component of the mainstreaming of Web media."[14] And for all that this "measuring of frequency" may do to threaten privacy, we believe it will have serious educational implications as well. We will focus on two: the targeting of information and the fear of surveillance.

Targeting is the commercial practice of focusing on individuals' interests and then presenting them with advertisements that address those interests. "Push" technologies accomplish much the same thing. After users establish interest profiles only information relevant to those interests is "pushed" to the user. But with the practice of targeting, this profiling is done apart from the user's awareness or consent. Advertisers, the purveyors of search engines, and others interested in collecting such data place individuals into predefined and necessarily simplistic, one-dimensional categories. They then can target, and thus limit, the information that an individual receives (as in the case of censorship, the person might never know what he or she is *not* seeing). The collection of data on individuals, exacerbated by the demands of commerce and advertising and for the purpose of targeting information, can only serve to limit and restrict access to the wealth of information available in cyberspace, which is its primary educational appeal.

It is particularly troublesome that search engines might conduct such practices. Several search engines are now offering a service to the owners of commercial sites: for a fee they will prioritize the search criteria so that these sites will be the first ones pulled up in a search. Now, most users have no idea what the parameters are that determine the order in which different search engines rank sites. But they generally assume that it is roughly the order of relevance to their search topic (no one runs a search and then starts reviewing sites by starting at site #100). It is clear why companies want their sites listed first; but this change would enlist search engines (supposedly neutral "tools" for finding information) in actively promoting certain sites, certain points of view, and certain products. The price an individual pays for a more *efficient* search is a more severely *restricted* search. As we have discussed, problems of "info-glut" do plague the Internet, but from an educational perspective students should be taught how to develop their own search criteria and parameters, not simply letting search engines or "portals" do this for them.

Our second concern has to do with the extent to which it is possible for most individuals to understand fully the constantly changing capabilities of these technologies. The primary function of these technologies is to collect, store, and manipulate data. And the extent to which they can perform these tasks changes exponentially with the increasingly sophisticated capabilities of the software and the hardware. As the required knowledge to understand and use these information and communication technologies to their full capabilities becomes more complicated and esoteric, few users will be knowledgeable about just what their computers can and cannot do. In doing research for this book, not only was it difficult to discover exactly how intrusive networked computers could be, but the debates and new developments in those areas have changed over the course of the writing, and will almost certainly change again before this book sees print!

One result of this lack of relevant knowledge is that most individuals do not know the degree to which they are under the surveillance of information and communication technologies. To some young people this might be the license of blissful ignorance, but to many, including teachers, educational choices get made in light of the possible (probable) surveillance one may be subject to at any given moment online. Concerns range from teachers who worry that they might accidentally stumble into an X-rated site and have to publicly explain themselves to students who shy away from research into certain areas not explicitly approved by their teachers. Unfortunately, computers will always have a panoptic effect on users. It is not so much what computers can do; it is what individuals worry they *might* do that controls behavior. Such controls inevitably limit the full use of cyberspace as an educational resource. Despite the appearance of anonymity, there will persist for many the feeling, not ungrounded in reality, that a user's movements in cyberspace are constantly being tracked, recorded, and ultimately offered for sale.

As we have argued, the increased commercialization of cyberspace will likely result in even greater surveillance because the collection and use of personal data has become so important for commerce to continue to grow and operate successfully. But increasing surveillance will reduce the educational potential of the Internet (to say nothing of its effects on personal freedom and safety). Whether by offering fewer choices because of targeted advertising, by raising the cost of educational resources that are currently free, or by implicitly creating a wariness for many in pursuing lines of inquiry because of possibly being found out, commerce will constrain educational opportunities for many users.

CONCLUSION

Clearly, given our approach in this book, we are not claiming that all corporations on the Internet are bad or that there should be no commerce online.

Most users (including the present authors) *want* the convenience of online purchasing and product information. Here is another instance where conditions that give rise to important possibilities (including educational possibilities) also, at the same time, give rise to counterproductive trends and dangers. We see the potential of sponsorship to *increase* the quality and variety of materials available on the Web. We see that corporate involvement might promote a greater commitment to widespread access and participation online, not necessarily due to any deeply held commitment to equity, but because corporate self-interest is to encourage the largest market base possible.

The strength of the Internet, especially from an educational perspective, is that so far it is decentralized and unregulated, and some amount of free enterprise clearly fits within that unregulated approach. Unfortunately, the pattern evident from other media and telecommunications corporations is that "free enterprise" leads to greater consolidation and centralization over time. Because the Internet is both a cause and a manifestation of a globalized economy, it has become a very high-stakes terrain for capitalist competition: the potential customer base is so huge; the possibilities of worldwide marketing and promotion so within reach. There is every reason to worry that the Internet will become increasingly structurally commercialized, with areas of resistance, localism, and noncommercial information relegated to the margins of use. This is akin to large department stores moving into small towns and driving out the small local businesses that cannot compete for cost, inventory, or brand-name recognition.

Clearly there are levels and degrees of commercialization at issue here, and at each level the dangers and the costs are different. There is the cost of capital in machines, software, upgrades, and connections to the Internet. There is the cost of credibility in corporate logos, sponsorships, and advertisements. There is the cost of blurring the boundaries between educational interests and business interests. There is the cost that the Internet gives impetus to commercial enterprises of marginal legitimacy: online gambling, dangerous products (guns, pornography, alcohol, prescription medications) available for sale with minimal screening of purchasers, and a whole host of other marketing scams and spams. And there is the cost in personal access, privacy, and freedom—three conditions essential to the educative process, we believe—because of the surveillance and targeting strategies increasingly adopted by profit-making enterprises. In the commercialized world of cyberspace, users do not just pay once; they pay again and again. Over time, these transactions are compromising the educational potential of the medium.

NOTES

1. Newton Minow and Craig Lamay, *Abandoned in the Wasteland* (New York: Hill and Wang, 1995).

2. Ibid., p. 3.

3. Ibid., p. 19.

4. Ironically, with all the pressure to stay on the cutting edge of the newest technological innovation, a possible solution to this problem might be found in the past. Network computers, basically dumb terminals connected to a very fast central server or just to the Internet itself would eliminate many of the compatibility problems schools face today.

5. We anticipate that this will become a major First Amendment issue in the next several years.

6. Alex Molner, *Giving Kids the Business* (Boulder, CO: Westview Press, 1996).

7. Molner, *Giving Kids the Business.*

8. Jules Henry, *Culture Against Man* (New York: Random House, 1963). A current controversy is the use of brand named products in textbooks. For example, a McGraw-Hill mathematics textbook names specific products such as Nike's, M&M's in assigned math problems.

9. AdKnowledge Web site: www.focalink.com.

10. Henry A. Giroux, "Education Incorporated?" *Educational Leadership,* Vol. 56 No. 2 (1998): 12–17.

11. There really is (for the time being) an anti-McDonalds site: www. mcspotlight.org. It has no advertisements.

12. This section draws from the thorough explanation of cookies and the controversy surrounding their use in "The Cookie Controversy" by Lori Eichelberger www.cookiecentral.com/ccstory/cc2.html.

13. Newer versions of popular browsers have the option of notifying the user each time a cookie is sent and allowing the user to refuse that cookie. The default, however, is to allow the cookie without notification, and our concern is that the majority of users do not even know this is happening.

14. AdKnowledge Web site: www.focalink.com.

❧ chapter eight ❧

WHAT KIND OF COMMUNITY CAN THE INTERNET BE?

The Internet is a vast, complex, and flexible information and communication medium. But it is not entirely neutral in structure. Certain features, such as the hypertextual character of the Web and other elements in cyberspace, promote or encourage certain ways of organizing and accessing information, or communicating, and discouraging others. Still, on the whole the Internet has a remarkably broad and open set of capabilities, only some of which are being taken fully advantage of at present. Educationally, it is the most promising innovation since the invention of the book, and perhaps even longer back than that.

We live in a time of open horizons and great expectations surrounding new information and communication technologies. At the same time, policy decisions are being made that will determine to a significant extent what sorts of educational uses and purposes these technologies will serve. Unfortunately, not all of these decisions are being made with *educational* considerations foremost in mind, we believe. Repeatedly in this book, as we have discussed issues of access, credibility, critical readership, free speech and censorship, privacy and surveillance, and commercialization, we have returned to the issue of which communities have a stake in, and should therefore be involved in, making these decisions. What sorts of communities does society want to foster and maintain as a result? What does it mean to foster and maintain the Internet as an educational community, and what barriers is society erecting, in the very present, that by intention or not are preventing that potential from being realized? These are our concerns in this concluding chapter.

The Great Community

"Community" is one of the keywords of American education.[1] American educational policy and practice continually invoke this term to conjure support for schools and to foster a sense of collective responsibility for what happens in them. For example:

> The move away from the dominant ethic of bureaucracy and competitive individualism and toward more democratic values of support, diversity, and community is most possible within a political climate of shared responsibility and trust. Projects aiming to create learning communities, therefore, attend to establishing new political relations among teachers, administrators, parents, students, and community members.[2]

Today, phrases like "community control," "community standards," "learning communities," and "communities of practice" are widely used in education, expressing the underlying, unquestioned idea that schools should be communities of some sort and should be closely integrated with larger communities of which they are a part.[3]

This nostalgic vision of community rests upon a recollection, also, of a time when affiliation was based upon proximity, relative homogeneity, and familiarity: the community of a small town, a neighborhood, an extended family.[4] We see this nostalgia quite clearly in the influential ideas of John Dewey, who recalled the town hall meetings and small-town bonhomie of his childhood in rural New England, while seeking to reconstruct a vision of community that could sustain the modern urban contexts of schooling that he was analyzing in his later career.[5] For Dewey, the challenge was to reconceive "community" in contexts where proximity, homogeneity, and familiarity no longer held. He called this vision the "Great Community," and for him it underlaid the conception of citizenship within the modern nation-state. His remembrance of, and faith in, the virtues of a local, face-to-face community carried over to his vision of democracy. In *Democracy and Education*, he argued that citizens are simultaneously part of two sorts of communities: communities based upon like-mindedness, to which members hold one sort of allegiance, and those based upon broader civic obligations and a sense of common interest, to which members hold a different sort of allegiance. In one of the most memorable passages of his book, he argued that it is how democracies manage communication within *and* across these groups—two values that are by necessity often in tension with one another—that the vitality and self-governance of a democratic public can be maintained. Dewey (famously) notes in this context the related roots of the terms "community," "communication," and what is held in "common."[6] Hence even as he acknowledged the pluralism of modern urban contexts, his vision of community rested upon the idea of recognizing (or creating) elements of commonality that could sustain a sense of "community." At its broadest level, the Great Community, this meant a politically constituted public that rested not only upon "conjoint activity," but on the recognition of consequences of collective actions and decisions that were of import to all, of common concern to all.[7]

As noted, Dewey understood that this collective sense of community was often in tension with local senses of community. Citizens often have to balance split loyalties between their affiliations based upon proximity, homogeneity, and familiarity, and those based upon a more rational calculation of the long-term, aggregated consequences of personal and local decisions, the shared interests of a larger community. Today we see this sort of conflict in debates over censorship in schools. Local groups, often motivated by religious sentiment, want to exclude from "their" school's curriculum content that brings students in contact with cultures and values that exist within the larger society, but which are repugnant to their own local values. Dewey recognized such tensions, but seemed to believe that they were generally reconcilable. Dewey believed in the force of reason to persuade citizens of their larger obligations and interconnectedness, and in the mythic force of the ideal of the nation and of the democratic public sphere.

Hannah Arendt had a very different vision of this problem.[8] For Arendt, the public space is fundamentally identified with plurality, not with commonality. The political constitution of public decision-making often will not rest upon identifying real or perceived similarities, or commonalities of interest, but upon reaching provisional conclusions that contending groups agree to accept. Such outcomes of political deliberation may rest upon some rational assessment of common interest or common purpose (Dewey's vision). Or they may rest upon quite different considerations, each group for their own reasons, but balanced against one another in a compact acceptable to all. If this is a vision of "community," it is one much more attenuated and provisional than the idea of the Great Community. Yet another situation is one in which even this level of agreement may not obtain, and in which the only ground for co-existence within a pluralistic context is one of tolerance and co-existence, despite unreconciled difference.

This is the view, for example, of Iris Marion Young, one of the foremost critics of the ideal of "community" as it has come to us from liberal democratic theorists such as Dewey. Young writes:

The ideal of community . . . expresses a desire for the fusion of sub-jects with one another which in practice operates to exclude those with whom the group does not identify. The ideal of community denies and represses social difference, the fact that the polity cannot be thought of as a unity in which all participants share a common experience and common values. In its privileging of face-to-face relations, moreover, the ideal of community denies difference in the form of the temporal and spatial distancing that characterizes social process. As an alterna-tive to the ideal of community, I develop . . . an ideal of city life as a vision of social relations affirming group difference. As a normative ideal, city life instantiates social relations of difference without exclu-sion. Different groups dwell in the city alongside one another, of necessity interacting in city spaces. . . . Different groups . . . dwell together in the city without forming a community.[9]

From this standpoint, we must always ask *who* is seeking to foster a sense of community, among which groups, and for what purposes? Who is being included within this community, and who is being left out?

The ideal of community has been similarly questioned, particularly in the context of the formation of the modern nation-state, by Benedict Anderson, who argues that communities, particularly at the national level, are always *imagined* (or to use alternative language, "constructed" or "con-stituted"), not givens.[10] "Community" is imagined, or constituted in spe-cific historical conditions and against a background of political interests. The analysis of Young, or Anderson, belies the connotations of "commu-nity" as something based solely on warm feelings of affiliation, and views such ascriptions as something experienced by various "others," excluded or marginalized by communities, as a judgment or a threat; indeed, as some-thing often meant precisely to do so. Hence, it is important not to read Anderson as stressing the term "imagined" as meaning something merely made up and ephemeral. Even "imagined" communities are "real" in their effects on people.

The dichotomy of real or imagined obscures the actual dynamics of belief and action, which motivate and reinforce one another. Believing that something is true makes people act and treat one another in certain ways. These actions and influences can come to create realities that (retrospec-tively) confirm and support those beliefs. This may be nowhere more clear than in the case of communities, where imagining certain affinities rein-forces and is reinforced by ways of speaking and acting together, and by practices of inclusion and exclusion that reify the borders imagined. Thus, communities that may be formed initially merely on grounds of efficacy or convenience, can over time take on stronger feelings of affiliation and commonality, even when (previously) these would not have been thought to exist. Conversely, commonalities (of character or interest, for example) that one might argue "really" exist may in fact *exacerbate* conflicts and heighten the feelings of competition and opposition between groups. According to this line of argument, then, commonality and difference are not the sole driving conditions of the politics of community, and identified communities may exist along multiple dimensions and forms, often based more in who they are excluding as "other," than in what binds them together.

This, in turn, raises a fundamental question that always needs to be posed in the face of ascriptions of community: *What are the conditions under which this "community" is being secured?*

With this background in place, we can turn now to the issue raised at the start of this chapter: whether the Internet is becoming a sort of community (or "virtual community") itself and what it would mean for the Internet to become an *educational* community.

THE CONDITIONS OF COMMUNITY

The idea of community, as discussed in the previous section, rests between two sets of values. On the one hand, the idea that cooperation and shared responsibility provide the best context for human effectiveness in accomplishing social goals; and on the other, the idea that close ties of affiliation are beneficial and supportive, if not necessary, for the living of a good life. This makes the notion of "community" uniquely flexible in being able to appeal to very different sorts of groups and value systems. It is, in short, an *ideology*. To call it ideological is simply to point out that it unifies and motivates social reform agendas that arise from quite different premises and intentions. It is the very vagueness and open-endedness of the term that allows it to be used in these different ways but always wrapped up in what Raymond Williams calls a "warmly persuasive" mood. As Williams says (not having Young's work before him), nobody has anything bad to say about the value of "community."[11] We believe this faith can be seen especially, though not uniquely, in contemporary discourses about American education, across the entire political spectrum.[12]

But today, the developments of post-Foucauldian theory cause us to ask a different, more skeptical set of questions about this ideal. We are more aware of how ascriptions of community, either as a description of a state of affairs or as an ideal to work toward, are based not in natural commonalities but in mediated relations that are politically constituted in specific historical conditions and spaces. The existence of a "community" is not a given, therefore, but a claim, a proposal that is bounded by a set of conditions and practices that have given rise to it. Hence it is a very different perspective on community to ask, *under what conditions* is it thought to obtain? A corollary question, in light of Young's concerns, is to examine the dynamics of exclusion, as well as those of inclusion, necessary to the formation of any particular community—to appreciate that there can never be, so to speak, a "Great Community." The very conditions that include some, exclude others (sometimes inadvertently, though often quite intentionally).

In this section we introduce three sets of conditions that are part of the dynamic of creating and identifying a community: mediating conditions, political conditions, and conditions of space and place. We will then use these three sets of conditions to examine the sorts of communities the Internet seems to be fostering, and their meaning as educational communities.

Mediating Conditions of Community

All human interactions are mediated, even apparently "direct" face-to-face interactions. As Erving Goffman's work explores, even the most *immediate* social interactions are in fact still *mediated* by a variety of performances, gestures, and rituals that do as much to keep the participants opaque to one another as to facilitate some degree of understanding and cooperation. It is a myth to imagine that the more immediate interactions are always the most honest, open, and intimate ones. In other contexts, these mediating conditions may be more visible to people, but this does not in itself grant them more import or influence.

One type of mediating condition is the medium of interaction itself: through face-to-face conversation, different types of writing, or telephone or some other distance medium (including the Internet itself). It is important to see that these are not *degrees* of mediation, or contrasts between mediated and unmediated (face-to-face) interaction, but alternative forms of mediation, each of which works in its own distinctive ways to disclose and to conceal. Any medium acts as a type of frame, highlighting certain elements of interaction and making them more visible, while at the same time serving to block out elements that fall outside the frame. Some media have costs associated with them, sometimes quite material and economic costs, sometimes psychic ones (such as the risks of making one's self "public"); these costs have differential effects on persons. In comparing media, it is important to contrast their distinctive inclusions and exclusions, not to attempt to rank them on a single, simple scale from more to less revealing. Social interactions, as in a purported community, take on particular features because of the media through which they take place.

Overlapping with these questions of media are the forms of communication available to social actors. As Dewey said, the kind of community one strives to foster, and the kinds of communication that are encouraged and made possible among its members, are intimately (and dialectically) related issues. As in the case of media, there is a tendency in much social theory to want prescriptively to define and sort different forms of communication, to rank them along some continuum of desirability, rather than to see them as multiple forms, each with characteristic purposes and effects. Different forms of communication, like media, foster modes of interaction that reveal *and* conceal. They frame what is and what is not open to discussion; encourage certain types of interaction (certain forms of community, if you will) and discourage others; and hence have effects of inclusion and exclusion that affect different prospective participants differently. These factors include a broad range of practices and relations, including the language in which communication happens; the way in which parties to communication are positioned in relation to one another (what Elizabeth Ellsworth calls the "modes of address"[13]); the roles of questioner and answerer; and so on. As should be clear, these factors have significant educational consequences.

A third set of mediating factors are a variety of social practices that govern the ways in which social participants act toward each other and act together for concerted purposes. Obviously, these factors are closely related to the first two, and they are similarly multiple in kind. One of these sets of practices is of special relevance here—identity practices—because they are, as we have seen, one of the crucial dynamics of how people exist and interact online. "Identity practices" refers to the many individual and interactive moves that social actors make as a way of forming, expressing, and defending their identities (plural), in response to and in relation to one another. Sometimes these identity practices are relatively personal, private, even internal to people's thoughts and feelings. Sometimes they are collective, public, and negotiated in conscious relation to (and sometimes in opposition to) the practices of others. They are, moreover, frequently dynamic, as people play out changing identities over time; and they are frequently multiple, as people play out more than one dimension of identity, and work out the frictions of conflicted alternative identities that they are endeavoring to maintain at the same time.

Political Conditions of Community

In addition to what we have been calling mediating conditions (media, forms of communication, and social practices) that shape and constrain the possibilities of community, there are broader political and historical conditions that precede and overarch the choices and activities of participants. We would argue that these political factors are rarely determinative in any simple sense, and that these conditions (like all the others we are exploring here) take on a differing significance depending on persons' and groups' responses to them. Nevertheless, they are not simply matters of personal choice, and they are factors that must be responded to, even if the response is one of resistance. In short, community rests upon ascriptions and sentiments of affiliation; some of these we choose, and some we do not choose. For we are born into certain communities (nation, family, or religion, for example), and while we can act in various ways toward them, even rejecting them, *that we must deal with them* we do not choose. This is the condition Arendt calls "natality." Not all communities are purely voluntary.[14]

Here we return to the contrast between Dewey and Arendt. Both recognized that any public space fundamentally presents actors with the condition of difference, and that a central challenge to forming a democratic public is in dealing constructively with this condition. For Dewey, and progressive liberal theorists since him, difference is conceived primarily as diversity, as a condition with the potential for disagreement and conflict, but also as a condition with the potential for fruitful engagement precisely because of that difference. Indeed, for such theorists, democratic vitality *requires* such differences, to insure that the broadest range of views is heard and that the broadest range of social actions, and their possible consequences, is given consideration. Hence the fundamental weight given in liberal societies to such ideals as free speech and tolerance.

For Arendt, difference is also a condition of public spaces, and it also poses a deep challenge to democracy. But it is a different sort of challenge. For Arendt, difference is conceived as *plurality*, not a range of alternatives that can be simply articulated, compared, judged, negotiated, or combined in some set of social compacts or compromises (so that those who are different become, in certain respects at least, less different over time). It is an ongoing condition, in which even compacts and compromises, when they can be achieved, might retain fundamentally different meaning and significance for their participants—and in which many issues of fundamental importance may never be bridgeable at all.

Dewey clearly understood that broader democratic affiliations could not usually be based on the same elements of proximity, homogeneity, and familiarity that characterized local communities (and that they would often be in direct tension with them). But from the Arendtian perspective the conditions of proximity, homogeneity, and familiarity are actually *incompatible* with community within the public sphere. The attempt to recreate those values in a public space leads to (what is for Arendt) a distortion of publicness, a space that she calls the "social." In the social there is an immersion of distinct identity for the sake of belonging, an inappropriate and unhealthy (in her view) transferring of the virtues of the private onto the public sphere. The social space involves a re-construction of proximity, homogeneity, and familiarity on the basis of a desire for conformity and avoidance of deep conflict in the face of plurality. This social sphere is not the true public sphere, and it retains none of the virtues of public engagement (the possibilities of personal growth and change through encounters with the strange, the difficult, and the challenging). It is a relatively safe space, where "safety" is conceived as the minimization of risk to identity and private affiliations. In this sense the "social" is antithetical to the possibilities of democracy and, as we will discuss later, to the possibility of education in a full and open sense.

Space and Place as Conditions of Community

A central theme in Arendt's view of public and private spheres is her analysis of the distinctive *spaces* that characterize and accommodate each mode of interaction: drawing from ancient Greek concepts of the *agora*, or public square, and the household, or domicile (and arguing, as just noted, for the gradual emergence of a third, social space).[15] As we discussed in a previous chapter, it is important today to go beyond characterizing the public and private in terms of distinctive (and discrete) spaces, to talk more broadly about how spatial arrangements and spatial practices constitute our very ideas of publicness and privacy (including online). As in the case of previous conditions, these spatial arrangements and spatial practices can be viewed as ways of shaping and constraining the possibilities of community.

The first question here is how a *space* becomes a *place*. "Place," and a sense of being in a place, develops from a sense of familiarity and recognizability: one has been here (or in places like it) before.[16] This sense may not be pleasurable. The recognition of danger is also a characteristic of certain places. At the other extreme, a home or homeland is a place where memory, familiarity, and the rhythms of daily life bring a sense of belonging or, for dispersed persons, a nostalgia for return to that place. Hence, place can be a condition for the formation and maintenance of communities (communities of family, neighborhood, or nation). Both public and private spaces are *places* when persons recognize where they are and know how to act there. The familiarity of the space and the familiarity of the activities characteristic of it create and support one another. We know where we are when we know what we are supposed to do, and vice versa.

People also sometimes transform spaces into places, by acting within and upon them to make them their own (what Norberg-Schulz calls a "lived space"). Mapping is an example of trying to turn a space into a place.[17] Another example is the adaptation of a space to the patterns of daily use (and not only the adaptation of use to space). For example, many college campuses lay out a pattern of sidewalks, designed in advance, to connect various buildings, only to find that the grassy areas in between are often worn down by new paths that the residents of the campus actually use in getting from building to building. Some campuses have learned to follow a different strategy, letting people use the campus for a while, looking to see where the pathways of use are, then laying sidewalks down there. The formation of *trails*, artifacts of personal use, convenience, and sense-making, is another way in which people make spaces into their own places.[18]

The encompassing term for the transformation of space to place is *architecture*. It is crucial to see that architecture is not fundamentally about building boxes to keep the rain off one's head; it is about configuring spaces that both anticipate and direct activity. Residents of an architectural space adapt their activities to fit the space, and adapt the space to fit their activities—the relation is always both ways, and it is in this reciprocal adaptation that a space becomes a place. The "architecture" is not only the initial design or building, but also the transformation of it over time. In this sense, people always help build the buildings they occupy, and the buildings are not fully finished until they have been used for a while (in one sense, then, they are never "finished"). In part, of course, this may mean quite literal rebuilding: tearing down walls, moving doors, adding rooms, and so on. But at a more subtle level, it is the pattern of daily choices and activities that reconfigure an architectural design: where people sit, move furniture, try to become comfortable.[19]

Theorizing these dynamics, it can be suggested that architecture is a way of anticipating and directing activity along a number of dimensions, including:

- movement/stasis
- interaction/isolation
- publicity/privacy
- visibility/hiddeness
- enclosure/exclusion

Again, however, the dialectical character of architecture should not be viewed in only one way: architecture anticipates and directs these activities, but the pattern of these activities also transforms and reshapes the architecture. Henri Lefebvre calls these "spatial practices," the activities through which spaces are experienced, perceived, and imagined.[20] In living their daily lives, people seek out spaces and reshape them according to the patterns of their needs and desires, though it is also true that these needs and desires are reshaped by the spaces available to them.

It is, then, one step further along this argument to consider architecture as the design of spaces generally: public spaces, private spaces, textual spaces (the layout and size of a newspaper, for example), agricultural spaces, educational spaces (classroom arrangements, for example), and online spaces.[21] The design of such environments shapes, intentionally or inadvertently, the conditions for activity and interaction within them: conditions for the formation and development of communities. The five dimensions listed above can be seen as the polarities along which specific communities develop their character. Communities are manifestations of the places in which they settle (while the places change also to fit the community).

THE CONDITIONS OF ONLINE COMMUNITIES

With this framework in mind, it is possible now to turn to the central concern of this chapter: the ways in which, and the conditions under which, online communities are being formed. There is nothing natural about such communities; they are as "imagined" (and as "real") as any communities are. But they are formed under conditions that shape and constrain the kinds of communities they can become, and directly affect the kinds of educational activities they can support. We will explore these issues under the same three headings as before: mediating conditions, political conditions, and spatial/architectural conditions. Numerous features of the online environment shape and constrain the educational possibilities within and across different communities.[22]

Mediating Conditions of Online Communities

The Internet is, of course, itself a medium. In fact, it comprises numerous media, all operating over the network of wires and computers that constitute it: the World Wide Web; e-mail; file sharing and transfer; listservs or other asynchronous discussion groups; IRC, or real-time "chat"; teleconferencing and videoconferencing; and so on. While each of these media has distinctive characteristics (some are text-based, others allow for voice or video transmission; some are synchronous, others are asynchronous; and so on), there are some general characteristics that typify the online medium generally.

The Internet has both facilitative and inhibitive effects on the formation of communities within it. On the one hand, the Internet has become a medium where collaboration happens and where people can create networks of distributed intelligence. This point is crucial because it means seeing the Internet as more than a repository for, or a means for the dissemination of, "information," and more than simply a medium of communication. It is also an environment that instantiates collaboration, in which participants can compose themselves as working groups, and where the identity of a working group *as* a group takes hold. To reintroduce an example from earlier in this book, the pattern of hyperlinks within a topic area often tacitly defines a group by the ways in which Web pages link to common sources, including one another. Sometimes this is an intentional choice by the members of certain interest groups who want to link all their pages to one another ("Web rings"). These associations become powerful mechanisms for sharing and evaluating the credibility and worth of Web information and communication. Listservs and chat rooms also attract and affiliate like-minded persons in a common conversation, though they are frequent sites of "flame wars" because these sites of association, precisely because of the common concerns of their members, can become sites of high-stakes disagreement. Modern developments of "Intranets," sometimes hermetically sealed off from the rest of the Internet by "firewalls," are designed to foster collaboration and information-sharing within organizations, while keeping these resources away from "outsiders." These enforced communities are especially strict where matters of commercial interest, so-called "intellectual property," or secrecy are regarded as paramount values.

At the same time the Internet can interfere with the formation of community, in part for the very same reasons already discussed. Some communities are not interested in encountering other perspectives and groups; it is easier to stay offline entirely and seek other forms of affiliation. Some individuals and groups are put more at risk than others are by the dangers of harassment, insult, or unwanted attention. Given the multiple lines of affiliation and community that the Internet makes possible, some communities may tend to "drown out" others. Perhaps most strikingly, the formation of strong online communities can sometimes interfere with the vitality of proximate, face-to-face communities offline. Here as in so many other respects, what the Internet gives with one hand it takes away with another;

it is neither an unalloyed good nor an encroaching danger—as we have seen repeatedly in this book, it continually presents users with inseparable elements of both.

In short, the distinct media that the Internet comprises shape, and are shaped by, groups that use them for their distinctive purposes. It is not just a set of individuals connected to other individuals, but an environment, a space, in which existing groups work and interact with each other, and in which other groups, with no initial awareness of themselves as groups, come to constitute themselves as such. News groups, operating via Usenet, are an early example of this. Web rings, discussed above, are another. Online environments originally based on simulation and role playing games (MUD's, MOO's, MUVE's, and similar spaces) provide a stage upon which actors, often with fictional or imaginary personae, can explore rooms or mazes and interact with each other. More recently, service providers such as Geocities, Tripod, and now Excite and Yahoo, have begun promoting Web environments literally called "communities" (or sometimes "clubs"), for users with like-minded areas of interest. Geocities is a typical example, offering sites organized as thematic "neighborhoods," usually named for actual place names, which subscribers can join. These communities have codes of appropriate conduct, such as allowable or banned content for Web pages, and administrators who have responsibility for surveying the pages within their community and regulating who can be part of it. As noted previously, there is an obvious parallel here with "gated communities," neighborhoods who erect actual barriers to entry, who police and restrict who can enter their area, and who often have strict codes for the appropriate standards of houses, yards, and activities within them.

The astonishing growth of these sectors of the Internet belies the idea that it is just an information and communication network; it is a space in which people come together and interact. For many users, these so-called "virtual" environments are more vital, exciting, and important to them than other areas of activity for their lives, as indicated by the amount of time they spend within them. These communities are centrally and intimately tied up with areas of interest and concern (collectors, joke-tellers, sports fans, pet owners, and so on) that are often of fundamental centrality to the sense of self and enjoyment that these participants have in living.

What we are trying to highlight here is that these media are distinctive (and hence so are the communities they help foster). Some rely on explicit self-identification, others on imagined identities (often called "avatars"). Some are openly accessible to new participants, others are decidedly not. Some are highly regulated, restricting what can and cannot be shared or done within them, others more unregulated; and where regulation occurs, some involve strict top-down management, others more consensual, group-communicated norms. The media of online community not only facilitate the formation of communities, but communities of a particular type, composition, and character—and, by implication, they discourage the formation of communities of a different type, composition, and character. In these choices, fundamental educational possibilities are implicitly being opened up, or closed off.

A second set of mediating conditions is the forms of online communication: the use of language, text, voices, graphics, and so on, as the modes through which people relate. Up until recently, the Internet was almost entirely a text-based medium. Now it is becoming more routine to transmit graphics, sound, and video. Increasingly the Internet is being used for direct audio or videoconferencing. These forms, in turn, have direct effects on the kinds of verbal interaction they support and encourage (the important differences, for example, between dialogues that are synchronous and those that are asynchronous; or those that involve written text only, as distinct from those that include voice or video transmission). On the horizon are technologies that will allow some degree of tactile contact and interaction. It seems that whenever critics identify a barrier that makes online interaction "not like real interaction," new developments begin to blur that distinction. Rilke identified the five senses (sight, sound, touch, smell, and taste) as representing five levels or degrees of intimacy. Online interaction seems to be steadily moving along that scale.

Nevertheless, text remains today the primary medium of online interaction. This category comprises not only the text of individual messages sent back and forth (for example, over e-mail), but also the form of new types of publications (newsletters, articles, and the online version of underground or samizdat publication, "zines"[23]). Here as well, writing and publication become conditions of community: both through the *processes* of collaboratively writing and composing publications, and through the *networks* of distribution through which they are shared. It is not new that communities of interest (from professional or academic groups, to political groups, to informal hobbyists) may sponsor newsletters or circulars that serve their members and help attract new members. But it is a new phenomenon when these materials can be continually adapted, revised, and added to in the processes of circulation themselves. The text or publication becomes a medium of actual community-building, and not just a mode of communication within it.[24]

Finally, it is impossible to address these issues without noting the English-centric nature of most online communication. This has significant domestic as well as international ramifications. English-speaking users are privileged to have access to more resources and more avenues for interaction than any other users. Moreover, English is not just a condition of access to a great deal of online resources and interaction. Participation in online interaction means that users who are not primarily English speakers will be exposed to this language on a regular basis and have many opportunities to practice it. The Internet becomes a medium for teaching the language and promulgating its spread. Indeed, many non-native speakers of English will find it easier to use English in online contexts, where they can type their comments as deliberately as they need to, can revise what they have written, and can receive feedback on the meaningfulness and efficacy of what they have said. This is a kind of linguistic imperialism; but the irony is that the Internet would not be the Internet, and would not have the enormous potential (as well as the enormous dangers) that it has, without a common, or at least predominant, language within it.

The third set of mediating conditions of community comprises the characteristic practices of online work and interaction, of which there are many. Earlier we focused on the issue of identity practices, which are clearly a central issue in online communities. There are myriad ways of "being online" (or, for that matter, "online beings").[25] On the one hand, humans who participate online adopt a variety of strategies of self-representation. Some are fairly literal (using their birth names, informative signature files, descriptive return e-mail addresses, and so on, as descriptors to others of who they are). Others are highly imaginary (made-up names, fictitious Web pages, avatars that represent them in MUD's and MOO's, and so on). It is a mistake, however, to draw the line too sharply between the literal and the imaginary, as if there were nothing imaginary even in ordinary face-to-face interactions, or as if a person is not in some sense "really" representing who they are even when they create an imaginary persona to stand in for them.

On the other hand, once people begin to "be" online, there is an intrinsic sense in which their identity changes precisely because they are using this technology. What they do, what they like and care about, how they spend their time, who they know, and so on, are all changed from that moment on. When these activities themselves involve online interactions and experiences, there comes an inevitable fusion between the "offline" and "online" dimensions of their being. They become, in Donna Haraway's famous formulation, "cyborgs."[26]

Online communities influence and are influenced by these multiple personae (especially because persons can be part of many online communities at the same time, as they are members of other communities). In the online environment, even more so than in other environments, one chooses, or not, to disclose aspects of one's personhood, or to disclose it in particular ways. This process is not entirely open to conscious control (one always reveals more or less than one intends, even in pretending), but to an extent "being online" means the continual selection and filtering of self-information through the portals of available media. Particular communities invite or discourage certain kinds of disclosure and participation; and they utterly ban others. Hence in a very clear sense, here as elsewhere, choosing a community means in part choosing who one is; and changing communities, or exploring new communities, is a process of exploring or experimenting with new selves.

Therefore, it is an oversimplification, we believe, to draw a clear line between online and offline activities, or online and offline identities. The assumption that face-to-face interaction is more honest or direct than online interaction is belied by participants who say that they experience quite the opposite. The idea that a person is more "real" or more themselves when they are acting in one context than in another elides a number of much deeper issues about the ways in which *all* social interactions are mediated. The belief that some communities are "real" and others "virtual" ignores what is "virtual" (imagined) about all communities and what is "real" even about online communities—as real as any community can be. So, when Howard Rheingold writes about "virtual communities,"

> People in virtual communities use words on screens to exchange pleasantries and argue, engage in intellectual discourse, conduct commerce, exchange knowledge, share emotional support, make plans, brainstorm, gossip, feud, fall in love, find friends and lose them, play games, flirt, create a little high art and a lot of idle talk. People in virtual communities do just about everything people do in real life, but we leave our bodies behind.[27]

we take this as an unintended argument for dropping easy distinctions like "real" versus "virtual" community in the first place. The term *actual* might be helpful here, precisely because it blurs the real/virtual distinction. *Actual communities* have specific characteristics that reflect the conditions, here the mediating conditions, under which they are formed and develop. A great deal can be said about these specific characteristics: but distinctions like real/virtual do not carry that analysis very far, and they obscure deeper processes at work.

We hope it is clear now what the idea of "conditions of community" does for analysis. In online environments, communities of a remarkable range and vitality are being formed, growing, and developing new ways of using the Internet (and its constantly changing capabilities) to give their own identity *as* communities new form and significance. At the same time, however, this is not happening on neutral ground or with a blank slate. The conditions of online community tend to drive communities into particular forms or patterns; and though they adapt resources to their own purposes, they are still using resources not of their own design and control. Moreover, the very conditions that have the benefits of facilitating communities also, and inevitably, have the effect of ignoring, or even excluding, other actual or prospective communities that never come into existence because they do not have the privileges taken for granted by others. And, finally, there are online communities that are quite consciously exclusive of others, in part defined *by* their desire to exclude others: as in the "safe" neighborhoods where members are reassured that they will not have to encounter dangerous or distasteful "intruders" into their gated community. Later, we will return to these issues in exploring how these conditions shape and constrain the possibilities of *educational* online communities.

Political Conditions of Online Communities

There is a dangerous misconception that because the Internet is a relatively unregulated and decentralized medium it is politically neutral. It should be clear from the analysis up until now that there are political and moral dimensions throughout the activities of people working and interacting online. For example, as we just discussed, many communities are self-policing, identifying and enforcing explicit and implicit standards about what is and is not permitted among their members. The Internet, because it links together participants from many political, value, or religious systems, is being imagined as just another liberal pluralist space. A recent television advertisement proclaimed the Internet as a place where age, gender, race, and so on, do not matter. This appears to be true, if you can only tell these things about a person on the Internet if they choose to disclose them. But this appearance obscures important issues: that whether or not people choose to represent their identities, these remain present in the ways that they think, act, and express themselves online (sometimes these qualities may be more apparent to others than the actors think). Moreover, these factors are always present in influencing the question of who is and is not even present in online environments. Fundamental questions of access are strongly influenced by location and identity. Pretending that nationality, class, gender, or disability do not matter online, when in fact they do, is one more imaginary about the type of "community" that the Internet represents itself to be.

On the contrary, says David Shenk, "Cyberspace is Republican. . . . Cyberspace is not politically neutral. It favors the political ideals of libertarian, free-market Republicans: a highly decentralized, deregulated society with little common discourse and minimal public infrastructure."[28] Indeed, one might say, it is the very posture of imagining itself to be apolitical that reveals the Internet's deepest political tendencies.

As noted in previous examples, the same things that make the Internet most appealing and useful also make it dangerous and difficult to cope with. Because the Internet is a broadly inclusive space, it continually brings one up against content, and perspectives, that are silly and pointless at best, repugnant and deeply hurtful at worst. Many families worry about this, especially where their children are concerned. Hence we see more and more attempts to carve out within this untamed frontier safe spaces that reestablish the traditional grounds of community: proximity, homogeneity, and familiarity. It is, to use Arendt's terms, an effort to make them *social*, not *public* spaces. We compared this earlier with the rise of gated communities in some neighborhoods. Similarly, as we have seen, many communities insist upon filtering software for computers in schools and libraries, or in homes. Many Web rings and "portals" involve creating archives of resources that have been screened and approved for general access, including children—participants run the risk of encountering "inappropriate" material if they venture outside of that protected space.

And so here we encounter (again) a paradox: because the Internet is a global network, it provides an opportunity to jump outside of familiar communities, to explore new communities, and perhaps to become part of them. It contains the virtue of what Arendt called "plurality," taking one outside the realm of the proximate, the homogeneous, the familiar. But one consequence of plurality is the encounter with what is not only incompatible with one's proximate, homogeneous, and familiar communities, but is actually antithetical to them (sometimes it is what the community itself was formed to avoid). So it becomes like the person who moves to a large city because of the variety of ethnic restaurants, but who never leaves the house to sample them because he or she is afraid of "those people" on the streets.

Finally, there is one important way in which the Internet is becoming configured, and that is as a commercial environment (the topic of the preceding chapter). Because the Internet has the capabilities of near-instantaneous communication and transfer of information, it has become enormously important to worldwide business and financial transactions, and it is increasingly dominated by commercial Web sites, "junk" e-mail, and ubiquitous advertisements. This commercialization, in turn, becomes a condition of community as well.

So we see, for example, growing calls for "smart communities," a term used to refer to wiring entire cities together, and into the broader Internet. There are countless uses and benefits that might come from such developments (including educational benefits), but it is clear that the primary purpose behind undertaking such investments is to promote more local and online commerce. To take a parallel, when cities first began creating Web pages to attract visitors and to provide information for their citizens, 80% of them featured business-related resources, far more than any other category (fewer than half featured any education-related resources).[29] In fact, the question today is no longer, Will the Internet become a commercialized entity? but, What sorts of economy will it support: profit-making only, or gift economies that promote the open sharing of resources, ideas, and information without regard for commercial gain? These conditions will, in turn, change the sorts of communities that come to exist online and which people will be part of them—including, one might predict, online communities that members will have to pay to join. (This is already true for subscribers to some online publications and services, which are communities of sorts.)

Increasingly, the avenues of access to the Internet, and the communities within it, require traveling through pathways that are commercialized: service providers that are linked with large telecommunications or cable corporations, or—within the Web—through portals that are controlled by private services (such as Excite) and packed with advertisements. These conditions not only shape the possibilities of community, but in significant ways limit it:

> The creators' vision was that the Web would encourage connections among diverse sites and collaboration among distributed communities, not draw a growing mass audience into ever-fewer high-traffic site . . . . The real conflict is not between commerce and community. It is between the traditional architecture of commerce (hierarchical systems of well-capitalized sources, distributors, and customers) and the traditional architecture of community (networks of one-to-one and few-to-few connections that create a sense of belonging and shared values.[30]

Finally, as we have seen, the commercialization of the Internet also means a blurring between legitimate and illegitimate commercial ventures. Already the lack of regulation on the Internet has given impetus to child pornography, betting, bank fraud, counterfeiting, drug trafficking, and black marketeering by mafias all over the world. One of the chief problems in coming to grips with these activities is that, while they are illegal in some places, they are not illegal in others (or, if illegal, unprosecutable). But when all places are linked together via this medium, the problem of one can become the problem of all. This returns us again to the conditions of online community: some of these will be labeled "criminal communities" by certain authorities, which have little or no jurisdiction over them. Yet by the same token, entirely legitimate and legal communities in other contexts (certain religious communities who use the online medium, for example), will be banned from others. We are not arguing for the equivalence of all these different sorts of communities. (Though in some cases a "mafia" from one standpoint will be someone else's "business network"; a "devout religious community" will be someone else's "fanatics"; gambling activities that are utterly banned by certain communities will be state-sponsored sources of revenue for others.) What this shows is that the Internet is a medium in which few if any overarching moral standards exist. Furthermore, the composition of the Internet as an unregulated amalgam of communities may be an ineffective environment for these moral differences to be adjudicated. This makes it all the more ironic that the primary overarching ethos of the Internet seems to be a commercial sensibility which, if it takes hold, will have an even more difficult time in delimiting legitimate from illegitimate business activity. The entire Internet will need to be labeled "*caveat emptor*"!

Space and Place as Conditions of Online Communities

Where are you when you are online? What does it mean to be with others who are also online? Is it possible to have a community "at a distance," and what sort of *place* can support such a community? In this section, as in the previous two, we return to the general ways that space and place are conditions of community, and then reexamine what these mean in understanding the online environment and experience.

The term "cyberspace," which started with William Gibson's book *Neuromancer*, has become part of our standard vocabulary for talking about the Internet. But what makes cyberspace a cyber*place*? Part of this process is users' becoming familiar with this environment, learning to recognize some of its features. The standardization of user interfaces, the similar design of Web browsers, the common basic elements of the pages they download, and other features of the online environment allow users with some degree of experience to adapt fairly quickly to new spaces they encounter there. They know their way around. However, these spaces are less amenable to the other main dimension of the space/place relation, namely, being able to customize and adapt spaces to one's own preferences and habits. The structure and contents of Web sites, the links between resources, and so on, are determined by the authors/designers of these spaces, and are not subject to modification by the casual user (as things stand now). This gives much of the Internet the feeling of wandering through paths and spaces of others' making, in search of useful and interesting things, but only by assimilating to patterns, connections, and search strategies that fit the existing design and software demands. This makes cyberspace more space-like and less place-like, as it is experienced by many users. There are few ways to leave permanent "trails" that mark the pathways one prefers to follow one's self. In this book, we have argued for the educational importance of teaching readers to be active reinterpreters and reshapers of what they find online, to become "hyperreaders."

The architecture of online space, like the architecture of buildings and other spaces, anticipates and directs personal activity along several dimensions, which we introduced earlier: these include movement/stasis; interaction/isolation; publicity/privacy; visibility/hiddeness; and enclosure/exclusion. These should not be viewed as "metaphorical" notions within cyberspace. Movement, visibility, privacy, exclusion, and so on have perfectly literal and direct application to activities and situations online. What is important to see here is the extent to which one's experiences along these various dimensions is only partly a matter of choice. It is also determined by elements of the design itself, which one does not choose (one can, for example, refuse to accept "cookies" from Web sites visited, but one cannot refuse to have one's computer recorded by a site as having visited there). The degree to which one can make choices within these dimensions is a central factor in the extent to which this environment takes on the character of a place where one can live, act, and interact with some measure of confidence and security. And, in this respect, as in others, different people will experience these features in drastically different ways.

Here is what is different about being online: In other spaces, or places, the characteristics of the environment are to some extent independent of the means used to represent them; but with the Internet these two levels are utterly intertwined.[31] Paths of movement (for example, hypertext links) are also connections of meaning making. "Being online" is both a place and a process: Samira Kawash offers an ingenious analysis of this condition in the

uses of the "@" sign, for example in e-mail addresses. Although people col-
loquially now use "@" to abbreviate locations or time ("meet Jo @ café" or
"meet Phil @ 2:00"), Kawash argues that the @ of being online (of being @
a particular e-mail address, for example), is a different sort of positioning,
one that is not analogical to being "at" other locations; rather, it is distinc-
tively a state of being online and only makes sense in that context:

> "Online" is a metaphor denoting a complex network of electrical sig-
> nals that translate inputs to my keyboard into computer operations in
> some remote elsewhere. "Online" is thus less a place than it is a mecha-
> nism of translation or transportation. [32]

Thus, the sort of place that "online" denotes is not a container, like a room
or building or square that people occupy (or can leave), separate from the
thing contained. Being online, when one is online, is itself a way of being
defined by the place where one is. *That* being can't be in any other place. So
when one is "@" a particular place (or time[33]) online, this is not the same as
being "at" a place (or time) in ordinary life.

And lest one assume that it is different only because, as Howard
Rheingold said, earlier, when we go online "we leave our bodies behind,"
there are good reasons to think that a kinesthetic sense of movement and
location persists even when users are moving through online spaces.[34]

Paul Virilio has even gone so far as to challenge the idea that online
activity and interaction involve action "at a distance."[35] Something begins
to happen to the very ideas of action, perception, and communication
when a user can, with his or her hand in a data glove or prosthetic manipu-
lator, "reach" or "touch" or "pick up" an object through a robotic arm or
sensor. Or when users can observe remote locations through video cameras
that bring their perception into spaces they could never reach otherwise.
Or when almost instantaneous communication, including voice and video,
can be achieved between persons regardless of their location on the planet.
In one way it makes sense to call these action, perception, and communication *at a distance*, but aren't they *always* "at a distance" (some distance)? In
one way it makes sense to say that these examples involve action, perception, and communication that is *mediated* by something (here, technology),
but aren't they *always* "mediated" by some processes, filters of interpretation, and social conventions? What does "at a distance" mean as a crucial,
ontological difference? Virilio suggests, not very much.

If one accepts this line of argument, then it is only a step further to suggest that the very ideas of identity, materiality, spatiality, and temporality
are becoming increasingly interdependent. If a person, wearing a data glove,

can pick up an object in a far-off location and detect its weight and temperature, *where* do those sensations occur, *when* did they occur, *to whom* did they occur? Is the person having the experience, or the glove, or the computer that is tabulating the data and converting it into electrical impulses that the hand interprets as heat, for example? Being online is always a state of being in-between, of being neither (simply) here nor there. Mediation is not something that stands between the user and something else to which one is relating (an object, a Web page, or another user)—it *is* the relation, without which the parties to an online event strictly speaking do not exist.[36]

In fact, Virilio suggests the term "virtualization" to describe this process. The media of action, perception, and communication collapse the distance/time equation into a point of instantaneity. The danger of the term "virtual" here, however, remains troubling. If the virtual environment is an art museum, have you "really" seen the paintings or not? One of the authors visited the Louvre several years ago and had to stand in a crowd to see the *Mona Lisa*. The painting was sheltered in a protective glass case with a surface that reflected back the faces of the people crowded together to see it (and in some cases, to videotape it). Did he see the *real* painting? Would he have seen it just as well, or better, through a high-quality graphic that he could have downloaded online? Similarly, is a virtual conversation with someone, mediated by a two-way video link, less "real" than a face-to-face conversation? What if people happen to be more honest in video links than face-to-face—which interaction is more "real" then?

DOES THE INTERNET CONSTITUTE AN EDUCATIONAL COMMUNITY?

There are two sets of answers to this question. First, the Internet as a whole cannot be a community; it is too disparate, too diffuse, and too inclusive. To call it a "community" would be to stretch the word beyond any useful sense or meaning. It might be better to call the Internet a "*meta-community*," in both senses in which that prefix is often used: as an overarching congregation of communities, but also as a set of conditions that make communities possible, as a space in which communities happen. This chapter has presented an exploration of some of these conditions, and the kinds of communities they make possible; conditions that also shape and constrain the possibilities of online educational communities.

One of the most important of these conditions is the way in which the Internet continually brings different communities in contact with one another. The scope of who can become part of a community is opened up;

but the threat of "intruders" who do not share the community's values is opened up also. Communities can be formed around the values of diversity and inclusivity; but when they do this they struggle with maintaining the fabric of cohesion that gives them their sense of themselves as *communities*. Disparate communities can co-exist side-by-side, as in Young's vision of the modern cityscape. But because the barriers between online groups are always provisional and semi-permeable, incursions across these boundaries (whether intentional or not) will always occur. The Internet is a prime example of what Arendt called the condition of plurality in public spaces. This is a condition whose possibilities and problems can never be entirely settled or "solved," but that need to be struggled with almost continuously, and in continually new and imaginative ways. For Arendt, it is the necessity of learning to deal with plurality, and to forge meaningful and effective social goods under such conditions, that gives the political endeavor its capacity to educate and re-educate us as citizens.

Yet, as we have discussed in this book, many communities seek ways to mitigate against the condition of plurality, in the Internet as in the other public and private spaces they inhabit (gated communities, government-imposed censorship, and so on). In this, they are resisting the possibilities of educational challenges to their belief and value systems, for themselves (which may or may not be considered up to them) but also for their children and for others who are not their children. This tension between the desire for diversity and openness to new possibilities, on the one hand, and the desire for a particular vision of familiarity and safety, on the other, constitutes one of the central debates that will shape the educational possibilities of new information and communication technologies. Decisions concerning educational access, credibility, censorship and free speech, privacy, surveillance commercialization, and the values of a critical orientation toward these new technologies are the terrain over which fundamental choices about the diversity, scope of tolerance, and inclusiveness of the Internet are being made. How these choices are made, in turn, will shape, or limit, the kinds of educational activities the Internet can support. We cannot say that there is a simple "right" way to make these choices; but we have tried to present a way of thinking through the complex and contradictory consequences of making them.

As Dewey notes the affinity of common, community, and communication, one might also note the affinity of the *polis*, politics, and the police. The Internet is a kind of *polis*, a city-state or cluster of city-states that must continually struggle with their plurality, their frictions in contact with one another, and the limits of their own capacities at self-governability. The politics of the Internet revolve fundamentally around these same elements: struggles over centralizing and decentralizing tendencies (how and whether the Internet can police itself) and struggles over the desire to maintain zones of proximity, homogeneity, and familiarity. Additionally, struggles exist over the kinds of economy that this *polis* will maintain—gift economies based on sharing non-scarce resources, or economies based on restricting access and charging for services.

These shifting determinations and self-understandings about the Internet and the types of communities that constitute it are already being constrained by how certain structural decisions concerning the Internet are negotiated today. For example, whether one will only be able to access the Internet through one company's Web applications; by how much of the Internet will be commercialized and accessible by fee only; by explicit moves of government censorship (or the more tacit form of censorship established by making certain resources scarce and expensive); by decisions about where Internet services will be accessible, and by whom, and at what cost; by technical standards that affect the design, operation, and language requirements of Internet resources; by decisions about what areas and activities on the Internet will be subject to publicity and surveillance; and so on. By and large, it must be noted, most of these decisions are being made with almost no public input. We suspect that even most users of the Internet do not know about them, who are making them, or the consequences at stake. Most important, for our purposes here, is to see these not simply as technological decisions, but as choices with significant *educational* ramifications.

Educational institutions, at all levels from primary to higher education, are trying to establish themselves as communities in and of the Internet. Choices that have implications for the kinds of communities the Internet will comprise, and how it will privilege some and disadvantage others are being made continually in those educational institutions and outside them. Such activities are neither new nor unique to the online environment itself. But the ways in which imaginaries become real, and the ways in which online communities become as or more important to users than any other sorts of communities that they have access to need to be understood as having increased importance as more learning opportunities will *require* access to and participation within the online environment.

Our second set of comments pertains to the multiple *kinds* of community the Internet can support. A chief feature of the Internet, as a meta-community, is that many communities can co-exist within it. While the conditions of community explored throughout this chapter do constrain some of these options (the Internet is not a neutral medium, by any means), they remain to a large extent flexible enough to allow alternative communities, alternative *places*, to be formed within it. We have suggested the importance of analyzing the specific features of educational communities in architectural terms, considering the ways in which these spaces shape and are shaped by participants' activities along the dimensions of movement/stasis; interaction/isolation; publicity/privacy; visibility/hiddeness; and enclosure/exclusion.

We are moving rapidly toward an educational system in which all K–12 public schools are connected online, and in which a good deal of educational content will be accessed through the Internet, whether in schools, in libraries, or in homes. We are also seeing an increased use of online information and communication technologies for the delivery of postsecondary education (what used to be called "distance education," but where distance is no longer the primary factor in access to vocational, college, or professional education opportunities). Private corporations are increasingly offering courses and training programs themselves, often outside the traditional accreditation and degree procedures. More casually, a whole host of news groups, discussion lists, Web rings, chat rooms, multi-user domains, online publications and the editorial collectives that produce them, and so on, serve important educational purposes that are outside formal institutional structures. The Internet comprises all of these forms of educational community, and will certainly give rise to new forms as well. Each of these communities has its own architectures, its own spaces for interaction, its own conceptions of publicity and privacy, its own costs and fee structures (or none at all). And there is no reason to assume that formal educational institutions will always have the greatest advantages in responding to different constituencies' educational purposes. Indeed, if some of the policy decisions we have sketched out are not decided prudently, prospective learners will seek out available alternatives. Resistance is one of the forms protest can take. Withdrawing one's self, or one's children, from certain educational communities, in favor of others, will be an option available to more and more citizens. For example, the Internet has given a tremendous boost to trends toward more homeschooling.

Alternatively, in this context as in others, people might belong to multiple communities at the same time. The Internet is not unique in this regard, but it does make these possibilities in many respects easier because of the variety of communities that are formed within it, or connected to it from the outside. These multiple communities will have varying degrees of intensity and centrality to the lives of people who join them online. It is especially important to add here that these different communities will be to varying degrees comfortable or acceptable to prospective participants. If categories like "learning community" are understood in too homogeneous a manner, then participants with different learning styles or different appetites for affiliation will be left out of them. Here, once again, the traditional associations of community with proximity, homogeneity, and familiarity can be an impediment to forming *actual* educational communities— including online educational communities, which we believe will become of even greater importance to the opportunities of learners of all ages, as we open the next millennium.

In this book we have tried to present a way of thinking about these educational policy choices that makes clear their complexity and their multiple and sometimes conflicted consequences. While specific value judgments and priorities need to be established where matters of access, privacy, commercialization, and so on, are concerned, these choices also need to be made in full awareness that their likely effects will be different—and more ambivalent—than we might expect or hope for. This is what the "post-technocratic" outlook means: trying to "fix" some problems usually gives rise to new ones. When we think that a problem has been "solved," we may only have put off the consequences we wanted to avoid, or even made them worse in the long run. And some problems may not be "solvable" at all. This way of thinking is not a formula for inaction, but of greater modesty in our aspirations for social reform or transformation, and greater suspicion toward the technologies we are relying on to "fix" the problems created by other technologies (*et cetera*). At one level, this entire book has been a sustained argument against the tendency to frame educational policies and decisions in technocratic terms, a temptation especially powerful when the subject of these policies and decisions are new information and communication technologies themselves. But at a deeper level, this book puts forth the idea that a post-technocratic way of thinking should occupy a more central place in the methods and content of education itself. As we inevitably become more involved with these new information and communication technologies, we should interact with them in the two-sided, reflective way that maintains a critical distance from our tools even when—*especially* when—we find them most "useful."

NOTES

1. The term "keyword" comes from Raymond Williams, *Keywords: A Vocabulary of Culture and Society* (New York: Oxford University Press, 1983). Here is what Williams says about "community": "Community can be the warmly persuasive

word to describe an existing set of relationships, or the warmly persuasive word to describe an alternative set of relationships. What is most important, perhaps, is that unlike all other terms of social organization (state, nation, society, etc.) it seems never to be used unfavourably, and never to be given any positive opposing or distinguishing term" (p. 76).

2. Jeannie Oakes, "Technical and Political Dimensions of Creating New Educational Communities," in Jeannie Oakes and Karen Hunter Quartz, eds., *Creating New Educational Communities: The Ninety-fourth Yearbook of the National Society for the Study of Education* (Chicago, University of Chicago Press, 1993), p. 8. For en excellent review of the literature on "learning communities," see also Katherine Bielaczyc and Allan Collins, "Learning Communities in Classrooms: A Reconceptualization of Educational Practice," in C. M. Reigeluth, ed., *Instructional Design Theories and Models, Vol. 2* (Mahwah, NJ: Erlbaum, forthcoming).

3. Nor is this nostalgia for community unique to America. The so-called "Third Way" of politics, a strategy associated not only with Bill Clinton in the U.S., but also Tony Blair of Britain and Gerhard Schroeder of Germany, is an attempt to create an alternative to the Left/Right polarity. "Its core value," say Al From of the Democratic Leadership Council, "is community." Quoted in John B. Judis, "Saving the World," *The New Republic* (May 24, 1999): 6.

4. Peter Magolda and Kathleen Knight Abowitz call this the idea of community as a "tribe." See "Communities and Tribes in Residential Living," *Teachers College Record* Vol. 99 No. 2 (1997): 266–310.

5. See John Dewey, *The Public and Its Problems* (New York: Henry Holt, 1972) and *Democracy and Education* (New York: Macmillan, 1916).

6. John Dewey, *Democracy and Education*, 5–7, 95–96.

7. John Dewey, *The Public and Its Problems*, 148–152.

8. Hannah Arendt, *The Human Condition* (Chicago: University of Chicago Press, 1958).

9. Iris Marion Young, *Justice and the Politics of Difference* (Princeton, NJ: Princeton University Press, 1990): 227.

10. Benedict Anderson, *Imagined Communities: Reflections on the Origin and Spread of Nationalism* (New York: Verso, 1991).

11. Williams, op. cit.

12. For a revealing critical analysis of the power of the "community" discourse within education, see Kathleen Knight Abowitz, "Reclaiming Community," *Educational Theory* Vol. 49 No. 2 (1999): 143–159.

13. Elizabeth Ellsworth, *Teaching Positions: Difference, Pedagogy, and the Power of Address* (New York: Teachers College Press, 1997).

14. See Arendt, *The Human Condition*; see also Natasha Levinson, "Teaching in the Midst of Belatedness: The Paradox of Natality in Hannah Arendt's Educational Thought," *Educational Theory*, Vol. 47 No. 1 (1997): 435–451.

15. For a helpful analysis of these concepts in the context of new technologies, see Michael R. Curry, "New Technologies and the Ontology of Places," available online at: www.baja.sscnet.ucla.edu/~curry.

16. Christian Norberg-Schulz, *Genius Loci: Toward a Phenomenology of Architecture* (New York: Rizzoli, 1980).

17. Rolland G. Paulston, *Social Cartography: Mapping Ways of Seeing Social and Educational Change* (New York: Garland, 1996).

18. For these examples we are grateful to Chip Bruce and Adrian Cussins.

19. Comfort is not a trivial or superficial dimension of how a space becomes a place. See, for example, Witold Rybczynski, who has written a series of popular mediations on architectural history, personal experiences of building, and the evolution of the idea of "home" in *Home: A Short History of an Idea* (New York: Penguin, 1987) and *The Most Beautiful House in the World* (New York: Penguin, 1989).

20. Henri Lefebvre, *The Production of Space* (New York: Blackwell, 1991).

21. Michel Foucault, "Space, Knowledge, and Power," in Paul Rabinow, ed, *The Foucault Reader* (New York: Pantheon, 1984): 239–256.

22. See also Marc Smith and Peter Kollock, *Communities in Cyberspace* (New York: Routledge, 1998) and the Web site for the Center for the Study of Online Community at UCLA: www.sscnet.ucla.edu/soc/csoc. Other bibliographic resources can be found online at www.socio.demon.co.uk/topicVC.html, www.otal.umd.edu/~rccs/biblio.html, www.amherst.edu/~erreich/vircom.html, and www.home.navisoft.com/edg/communities.html.

23. Barbara Duncan, a doctoral student at the University of Illinois, Urbana/Champaign, is completing her dissertation work on this subject, studying specifically how "zines" constitute focal points around which online communities are formed and identities established: *Feminist Grrl Zine Communities of Difference* (Doctoral dissertation, University of Illinois, Urbana/Champaign).

24. For a discussion of some of the implications of these changes in academic publishing, see Nicholas C. Burbules, "Digital Texts and the Future of Scholarly Writing and Publication," *Journal of Curriculum Studies*, Vol. 30 No. 1 (1997): 105–124.

25. See the exchange between Timothy Luke, "Digital Beings and Virtual Times: The Politics of Intersubjectivity," *Theory and Event* 1 no. 1 (1997), available online www.muse.jhu.edu/journals/theory_&_event/v001/1.1r_luke.html and Samira Kawash, "@, or Being on Line: A Reply to Timothy Luke," *Theory and Event* Vol. 1 No. 2 (1997), also online www.muse.jhu.edu/journals/theory_&_event/ v001/1.2kawash.html.

26. Donna Haraway, "A Cyborg Manifesto," in *Simians, Cyborgs, and Women* (New York: Routledge, 1991).

27. Howard Rheingold. *The Virtual Community* (1993). Available online: www.rheingold.com/vc/book.

28. David Shenk, *Data Smog: Surviving the Information Glut* (New York: HarperEdge, 1997): 174.

29. Alaina Kanfer and Christopher Kolar, "What Are Communities Doing On-Line?" (1995): Available online at: www.ncsa.uiuc.edu/edu/trg/com_online.

30. David Johnson, "Community vs. Commerce," *Brill's Content* Vol. 2 No. 3 (1999): 86.

31. See Michael R. Curry, "New Technologies and the Ontology of Places."

32. See Samira Kawash, "@, or Being on Line." Kawash's analysis suggests a way of exploring the prepositions through which the *on*line environment is discussed, as an important part of the "spatial practices" by which it is imagined and constituted.

33. The Swatch Corporation has just announced a new effort to define a standard, global "Internet Time," dividing the day up into 1000 units ("beats") that do not correspond to seconds, minutes, or hours, and are not subject to time zones or other artifacts of physical location on the planet. The zero point of 12:00 midnight is, not surprisingly, set by the time at Biel, Switzerland, the home of the Swatch corporation. Internet Time is the same anywhere on the Internet, at any moment. The symbol for this temporal dimension of being online is also @, as in, "I will send this to you @ 472 Swatch beats." (See www.swatch.com/internettime/beatnik_fs_time.html.) The commercial interests in bringing a standard measure of time for the transfer of banking and financial resources, information, or services should be clear, as is the benefit of having your corporation's name associated with that global standard!

34. Carmen Luke, ekstasis@cyberia, *Discourse* Vol. 17 No. 2 (1996): 187–207.

35. Paul Virilio, *Open Sky*, trans. Julie Rose (New York: Verso, 1997).

36. This situation is akin to Dewey's idea of the *transactional* character of experience, in some respects.

ᢒ INDEX ᢙ

abortion, 108
academic groups, 166
    access to computers
    attitudes of, 23–24
    conditions of, 20–21
    dispositions and accessing text versus
        production of, 51
    practical computer access, 24–25
    technical, 22–23
    types of, 3
active reading, 54–55
actual communities versus virtual, 168–69
actual educational communities, 179
AdKnowledge Inc., 48–49, 143, 148–49
adult illiteracy, 22
advertisements, 142–47, 171
agora community of ancient Greeks, 4, 127,
    161
alternative identities, 159
Amazon Books, 145
America OnLine (AOL), 73
analogical similarity, 53
ancient Greeks, 126–27, 161
anecdotal evidence, 16
anonymity online, 28
antibiotics, 12
antistasis, 87–88
Apple, 13
architecture, 127, 162–63
archives, 110–12
archiving, as an activity subset, 4
Arendt, Hannah, 155, 160–61, 170, 176
arguments, 59
assessing, as an activity subset, 4
asynchronous communication, 28
ATM machines, 122
authenticity, 98
authorship and design, 52–54
autonomous readers, 57
avatars or online personas, 74, 165, 167

bacterial strains, 12
balancing and tradeoffs, 7

Balzac, Honoré de, 51
banking online, 132
banner ads, 142, 149
Barnes & Noble, 145
Barthes, Roland, 51, 53
"Battle of the Centaurs, The," sculpture, 49
Beauvoir, Simone de, 45
Bentham, Jeremy, 115, 125
biochemical tests, 6
Blair, Tony, 180
blocking targeted information, 107–10
Bogard, William, 129–30
Bogart, Humphrey, 49
bomb-building sites, 95, 98, 151
boosterism, 3, 15
Borges, Jorge Luis, 45, 51–52
bricolage, 49, 67
browsers or users, 64
    versus hyperreaders, 55
Burbules, Nicholas C., 20, 39, 93
bureaucracy, 133, 154
Bush, Vannevar, 48

Calvino, Italo, 45
carpal tunnel syndrome, 6
Carroll, Lewis, 49
Casablanca, 49
catechresis, 89
Catholic Church, 85–86
cause-and-effect, 88–89
CDA. *See* Communications Decency Act of
    1997 (CDA).
censorship, 95–119
censorship response, 103–07
Channel One, 142
chat rooms, 29, 164, 178
child pornography, 107
code sharing, 13
coded content. *See* Labeling.
collaborative space versus delivery system, 5
collaborative writing online, 166
Columbus, Christopher, 4, 49
comfort levels in computer use, 23, 26